D1593714

THE

JAMES SPRUNT STUDIES

IN HISTORY

AND POLITICAL SCIENCE

*Published under the Direction of
the Departments of History and Political Science
of The University of North Carolina at Chapel Hill*

VOLUME 52

———————— * ————————

Editors

PARSON PETTIGREW OF THE "OLD CHURCH": 1744-1807

By

Sarah McCulloh Lemmon

CHAPEL HILL

———— * ————

THE UNIVERSITY OF NORTH CAROLINA PRESS

1970

Printed by the Seeman Printery, Durham, N. C.

FORWORD

The Reverend Charles Pettigrew was an excellent example of upward social mobility in early America, about which there have been many generalizations but few accounts as well documented as that revealed by the records of this clergyman. Perhaps a failure as a churchman, since the Episcopal, or "Old", Church all but died under his titular leadership, he was a success in achieving the status of a planter in Eastern North Carolina. Beginning life on the Pennsylvania frontier, he utilized education, profession, and marriage through the exercise of ambition and prudent care, to acquire two plantations and over thirty slaves by the time of his death at the age of sixty-three. This was the Southern success story before 1860, and as such, the account of Pettigrew's life acquires more than local significance.

Initially, my interest in Pettigrew stemmed from research in the history of the Episcopal Church in North Carolina, during which I became acquainted with Bennett Wall's thesis on Charles Pettigrew. This interest and research eventuated in the major project of editing the Pettigrew family papers, which opportunity and challenge led me so deeply into the career and family life of this man that a biography was obviously called for.

I am grateful to Professor Hugh Talmage Lefler, for whom I wrote the first essay on Church history; to Professor Cornelius O. Cathey who arranged the typing of many of the Pettigrew manuscripts; to Mrs. Memory F. Mitchell who invited me to edit the Pettigrew papers; and to my mother without whose aid I would still be reading the 18th century manuscripts. I am also indebted to the staffs of the State Department of Archives and History in Raleigh, and of the North Carolina Collection and the Southern Historical Collection in the Library of the University of North Carolina at Chapel Hill, for their untiring assistance and interest in this project.

Finally, I should like to express my appreciation to the James Sprunt Studies for the financial assistance which made possible the publication of this volume.

Sarah McCulloh Lemmon

Meredith College
May 1, 1970

TABLE OF CONTENTS

PARSON PETTIGREW OF THE "OLD CHURCH": 1744-1807

CHAPTER I

THE EARLY YEARS

Charles Pettigrew, Episcopal clergyman and planter of eastern North Carolina, was the son of French-Scottish-Irish immigrants who came to America in 1740. Educated both formally and by his own efforts, he taught, was ordained in England, and returned to live in or near Edenton for the remainder of his life. Twice married, he acquired connections and some means through both Mary Blount, his first wife, and Mary Lockhart, his second. During his life-time he was a clerical leader, being elected bishop of the Diocese of North Carolina (although never consecrated), a man of intellect, a planter who helped drain the swamps of Tyrrell County and establish plantations there, and the founder of a family of some significance in 19th century North Carolina.

The traditions of the Pettigrew family were strong and have been repeated in every branch of the family. According to their accounts, the first Petigru, spelled thus, was a French Huguenot who left France to fight in Cromwell's army, afterwards settling in Scotland. His son fought gallantly in the army of William of Orange at the Battle of the Boyne, for which service he received lands about three miles from the town of Aughnacton [Aughnacloy?], County Tyrone, Ireland. He thereupon moved to this estate to live, giving it the name of Crilly House, which remained in the senior branch of the family for many generations.[1] During the residence in Scotland the spelling of the surname was altered to Pettigrew; but it may be noted that one of the South Carolina descendants, who resided in Charleston, returned to the French Petigru.[2]

James Pettigrew, a younger son of the Irish gentleman, married Mary Cochrane about the year 1731. Although one account states that he had a classical education, but never attended college, another account claims that he studied medicine at the University of Dublin, but emigrated to America before finishing his education. His father-in-law, Captain George Cochrane, was a man of some means, and James did not come to America penniless. The belief of James Louis

[1] Genealogy Section of the Pettigrew Papers, Southern Historical Collection, University of North Carolina Library, Chapel Hill, North Carolina. Hereinafter cited as Pettigrew Papers, UNC.
[2] James Petigru Carson, *Life, Letters and Speeches of James Louis Petigru, the Union Man of South Carolina* (Washington: W. H. Lowdermilk and Co., 1920), *passim*. Hereinafter cited as Carson, *James Louis Petigru.*

Petigru that his grandfather "was wild and married Mary Cochran—a misalliance—for her beauty" would not seem to be correct.[3] Certainly Captain George Cochrane must have had adequate social standing in those days.

Upon arriving in Pennsylvania, around 1740, James Pettigrew purchased some 300 acres of land at what is now Chambersburg. Charles was born here on March 20, 1744. At some point during the years in Pennsylvania, the elder Pettigrew is reputed to have known Benjamin Franklin, who advised him to continue his medical education, although he never did so. Converted by the preaching of George Whitefield, he became "an exceedingly strict Presbyterian."[4] One family account states that on the Sabbath, his doors were always religiously closed; James Louis Petigru's biographer, in recounting the same story, says he allowed no cooking on the Sabbath. At one time, this saved the lives of his family from an Indian raid, since the Indians assumed that the house was uninhabited.[5]

The French and Indian War, erupting in 1754 after Braddock's defeat, disrupted James Pettigrew's situation in Pennsylvania, so that he moved to Lunenburg Court House in southern Virginia, where he rented land for several years.[6] At this juncture, Charles was sent to the classical academy of John Todd in Louisa, Virginia, where James Waddel was one of his teachers, probably from 1757 to 1762.[7] This son was the only one to receive a formal education, for, according to his brother William, "the rest of us staid at home."[8] Family tradition made much, in later years, of the fact that the Reverend Mr. Waddel, the famous "blind preacher," was an early educator of Charles Pettigrew. In a letter written in 1804, Waddel recalled Charles's "pious father and mother," and expressed himself as

[3] Genealogy Section of the Pettigrew Papers, UNC.

[4] *Ibid.*

[5] Carson, *James Louis Petigru*, p. 2; Griffith J. McRee, *Life and Correspondence of James Iredell* (New York: D. Appleton and Co., 1857, 2 vols.), II, 591. Hereinafter cited as McRee, *Iredell*.

[6] Genealogy Section of the Pettigrew Papers, UNC. A check of the Lunenberg County deed records at the Virginia State Archives reveals no Pettigrew name; the family tradition of rental is probably therefore correct.

[7] The reconstruction of Charles's education, which differs from the family tradition, is deduced from the life of James Waddel as given in William Henry Foote, *Sketches of Virginia, Historical and Biographical* (Philadelphia: William S. Martien, 1850), pp. 349-388. Waddel taught in Louisa, Virginia, in John Todd's school, until 1762, when he was ordained by the Presbyterian Church and accepted a call to the Northern Neck of Virginia. He was never in Lunenburg County, as Pettigrew family tradition asserts, nor did he have his own academy until 1785, much too late for Charles Pettigrew to have attended it. The family account, claiming that Charles attended Waddel's academy in Lunenburg County circa 1757-1762 has telescoped some 25 years.

[8] Genealogy Section of the Pettigrew Papers, UNC.

pleased with the account of the family's general circumstances and "especially with the prosperity which you have happily enjoyed." His signature of "your sincere friend" does not bear out the traditional claim to kinship noted in the family records, although Waddel was born in Ireland and there may have been some connection; nor is any special closeness indicated by his remark that in spite of much forgetfulness, he was "at no loss to recover your family name."[9] Unfortunately, he does not refer to the education with which he trained the young Charles.

Once again James Pettigrew moved on, although the exact year is difficult to pinpoint. The family traditions say that he moved to Granville County, North Carolina, around 1760; however, it was not until 1767 that he purchased for £60 from Howell Lewis and his wife 369 acres of land lying on both sides of the Lower Fork of Grassy Creek, "together with all houses Orchards Aples Woods underwoods timber & Timber Trees Waters & Water Courses Profites Commodities and all appurtenances whatsoever. . . ."[10] Such a move was not unusual, as a large proportion of the early settlers of this county, lying directly south of Lunenburg, were either Virginia Baptists or Presbyterians.[11] In fact, when the first Presbyterian presbytery (Hanover) was erected in the region, it included both Virginia and North Carolina.[12] A Baptist church was at Grassy Creek as early as 1755;[13] the elder Pettigrew wasted no time in deeding an acre of land to the trustees of the Presbyterian Congregation at Grassy Creek for worship "and no other use whatever," because of "the ardent desire he has to promote the Worship of God."[14] The tax list for 1767 indicates that James and his two sons Charles and George were living at home and paid the poll tax; he owned no slaves.[15] In the meantime, Charles had continued his education under the Presbyterian clergyman Henry Pattillo. The only school taught by Pattillo that Pettigrew could have attended was conducted in the home of the former in Orange County,

[9] James Waddel to Charles Pettigrew, Feb. 10, 1804. Pettigrew Papers, UNC.

[10] Granville County (North Carolina) Records, Deed Book H, p. 361. State Department of Archives and History, Raleigh, North Carolina. Hereinafter cited as N C Archives.

[11] Robert I. Devin, *A History of Grassy Creek Baptist Church, from its Foundations to 1880, with Biographical Sketches of its Pastors and Ministers* (Raleigh: Edwards and Broughton, 1880), p. 25. Hereinafter cited as Devin, *History of Grassy Creek Baptist Church.*

[12] Durward T. Stokes, "Henry Pattillo in North Carolina," *North Carolina Historical Review*, XLIV (Autumn, 1967), 376. Hereinafter cited as Stokes, "Henry Pattillo."

[13] Devin, *History of Grassy Creek Baptist Church*, p. 50.

[14] Granville County Records, Deed Book H, pp. 335-336, N C Archives. This land was deeded only one month after Pettigrew's purchase of his farm.

[15] Granville County Tax List for 1767, N C Archives.

North Carolina, between 1765 and 1774. Pattillo had preached in Lunenburg County in 1757 and 1758, and was thus certainly well known to the Pettigrews. Charles could have studied under him only one year, 1765;[16] for he was himself teaching the very next year.

Pattillo was a dedicated teacher, feeling that he and his pupils were "so like Father & sons, I love to be among them when I can."[17] Grammar, stressed heavily in his school in 1788,[18] was certainly also stressed with the young Charles. The latter always admired and respected his mentor, regarding teaching as an occupation which "requires not only uncommon strength of Constitution, but a great deal of christian [sic] philosophy, & the truest regard for the interest & welfare of Society. And I beg leave, Sir, to say, that in this favorable light I view my friend, & hope that *after generations* will derive advantages from his unwearied endeavors to diffuse useful knowledge."[19] On the back of one letter from his friend, Charles penned this poem:

> Henry! thou good!—thou great Divine!
> Thy Gifts with Heavenly lustre shine!
> And as the Sun his genial Rays
> Shoots forth in full meridian Blaze,
> Just so, the labours of thy hand
> Have reached us in this distant Land
> And shed their cheering Lustre bright
> The gladning beams of gospel light
>   Our Darkness to dispell
>   And save our Souls from Hell
> The Regions of eternal night.
>
> Thou bright acfulgents eastern star
> Jesus, the God, thou dost declare
> The saviour of our ruin'd Race
> The perfect man the God of Grace,
> and to his Cross there dost allure
> The high, the low, the rich, the poor,
>   and O that all
>   Would hear thy call
> And make their calling sure[.][20]

[16] Henry Pattillo's career is well discussed in Stokes, "Henry Pattillo." Stokes believed that Pettigrew attended Pattillo's Granville County school, which was conducted 1774-1780; however, Pettigrew moved to Edenton in 1773 and thus must have attended the earlier Orange County school.

[17] Henry Pattillo to Charles Pettigrew, Dec. 13, 1788. Pettigrew Papers, UNC.

[18] *Ibid.*

[19] Charles Pettigrew to Henry Pattillo, May 12, 1792. Pettigrew Papers, UNC.

[20] Reverse side of Henry Pattillo to Charles Pettigrew, June 21, 1780. Pettigrew Papers, UNC.

The young Pettigrew was engaged in 1766 by Mrs. Gideon Macon and Philemon Hawkins, of Bute County, to instruct their children John and Nathaniel Macon, and Benjamin and Joseph Hawkins, which Charles did until 1773. In fact, Benjamin Hawkins and "Negro Tabb" lived with their teacher in 1771.[21] In recalling these years, he wrote to Benjamin Hawkins, then recently appointed Indian Agent by Thomas Jefferson:

My brother, . . . Having mentioned your name, as standing high in the esteem of the Georgians, I confess I heard it with singular pleasure & could not but recognize my early acquaintance with you, which I believe was mutually happy, & at the same time I could not help recollecting the sentiments I then was induced [to] entertain of you, from that openness of mind & freedom of thoughts which appeared so natural to you, & which I expected would influence your future conduct through Life. In this I am happy to think from the result, that I was not mistaken in my conjectures. Believe me Sir, the prosperity and respectability of any of my old pupils gives me the sincerest pleasure, & I am peculiarly happy to find that your old school-mate Macon makes so respectable a figure in Congress.[22]

Only a year after he had purchased the Lewis farm, James Petti-grew sold it to James Johnston of Cumberland County, Virginia, for £220 and moved on to South Carolina.[23] Charles stayed behind and spent the remainder of his life in association with his adopted state. Charles's grandson, James Johnston Pettigrew, wrote of these forma-tive years that his two teachers, Waddel and Pattillo, "seem to have taken a great fancy to him in his youth, as appears from their cor-respondence, wherein allusion is made to presents of Greek books, re-ceived while at the Grammar School."[24] Such a letter or letters, how-ever, has not been found.

As a resident of a frontier county, Charles Pettigrew had to pur-chase his books and supplies from the coastal towns. A survey of his accounts with William Park & Co. of Bertie County shows that, for example, in 1770 he purchased one blank book, one ink pot, two quires of paper, one "Juvinal," one "Terance," a Cicero and an

[21] Tax Lists for 1771, Bute County Records, N C Archives. Charles Pettygrew [sic] returned three taxables. The tax list of Philemon Hawkins gave the names of the three; photocopy at NC Archives, original in the private collection of Thomas M. Pittman. See also William E. Dodd, *The Life of Nathaniel Macon* (Raleigh: Edwards and Broughton, 1903), pp. 3-4. Bute County, heavily settled by Virginians, had been formed in 1764 out of Granville; in 1778 it was divided into Warren and Franklin counties.

[22] Charles Pettigrew to Benjamin Hawkins, Dec. 16, 1802. Pettigrew Papers, State Department of Archives and History, Raleigh, North Carolina. Hereinafter cited as Pettigrew Papers, N C Archives.

[23] Granville County Records, Deed Book H, pp. 463-464, N C Archives.

[24] McRee, *Iredell*, II, 591.

Ovid, a copy of Watson's Sermons, as well as gloves, a hat, and other items of apparel. He apparently drank coffee, using sugar, ate butter from a butter pot, and liked to have handkerchiefs on hand. The following year he bought a sermon book; teaspoons, teacups and a nutmeg grater; shoe buckles, powder and shot, a gallon of rum, and a copy of Watts's Hymns. Since he ordered a razor and razor strop, one assumes that he was smooth shaven at that time.[25] A picture emerges of a young man who was seriously engaged in studying, yet who liked the niceties of life and appeared to be something of a tidy bachelor housekeeper as well as neat in grooming and appearance. That this young man had a better than average education is apparent in his nomination by Governor Josiah Martin to the post of schoolmaster in Edenton, then one of the chief centers of culture in the colony. The official document declares that "out of the confidence I have in your Loyalty, skill and Ability, . . . I do hereby Licence and Appoint You the . . . Master of the Publick school in Edenton During my Pleasure, you having been recommended to me according to Law."[26] When Charles moved to Edenton in 1773, so far as is known he never returned to Granville County again.

Edenton was noted at this time for being a Court town and for having a large number of businessmen "eminent for ability, virtue, and erudition. . . ."[27] Josiah Quincy, Jr., called it "a pleasant town" and in 1773 spent a day "dining and conversing in company with the most celebrated lawyers of Edenton."[28] Its population was around four or five hundred.[29] Lying on the north shore of Albemarle Sound, east of the Chowan River, Edenton was a busy little seaport of white frame houses and outlying plantations.

Facing a mall which leads to the inner harbor, the Georgian style brick Chowan County Court House still stands today, regarded as one of the finest in the South. Lining King Street, east and west of the courthouse, are gracious houses such as that occupied by Edmund Hoskins, the Joseph Hewes house, and the residence of Colonel Thomas Nash. Famous is the Cupola House, built about 1725 and considered a fine example of Jacobean style; at one time it was owned by Dr. Samuel Dickinson, who became a friend of Pettigrew. Situated on West Blount Street, the West Custom House was probably built around

[25] Accounts of Mr. Charles Pittagrew [sic] with William Park and Co. Pettigrew Papers, UNC.

[26] Charles Pettigrew Appointed Schoolmaster, June 23, 1773. Pettigrew Papers, UNC.

[27] McRee, Iredell, I, 33.

[28] Josiah Quincy, Jr., Memoir of the Life of Josiah Quincy, Junior, of Massachusetts, 1744-1775 (Boston: John Wilson and Son, 1874, 2nd edition), 93. Hereinafter cited as Josiah Quincy Memoir.

[29] McRee, Iredell, I, 32.

1772 by Wilson Blount, Pettigrew's brother-in-law. The house near the mall in which dwelt Josiah Collins, a business associate of Dickinson and friend of Pettigrew, was built just before the Revolution by Robert Smith. Most of these houses are of two-storied white frame construction, with large windows and double porches across the front. About five miles from Edenton lies Mulberry Hill plantation, established in 1684 by Captain James Blount, ancestor of the first wife of Charles Pettigrew. The present house, built by Pettigrew's brother-in-law, is a distinguished four-story brick one, whose extensive grounds sweep down to the waters of Albemarle Sound. Nearer Edenton is situated Hayes Plantation, where lived Samuel Johnston, Revolutionary patriot, governor, and United States Senator, and his sister Hannah, who married James Iredell. The house in which they dwelt is now called The Gate House, and is of white frame with a two-storied porch supported by four columns.[30] Those who lived in the outlying plantations, as Mulberry Hill and Hayes, found it easier to jaunt to Edenton by boat than by road, thus providing a bustling harbor scene in good weather.

This little town lay on a north-south route through the State, running from Petersburg to Edenton, Bath, New Bern, Wilmington, and Brunswick. Ferries across the Sound as well as the Chowan and Roanoke Rivers had been established as early as 1750.[31] Some of the residences of Edenton were quite pretentious, indicating the wealth which flowed from trade and commerce with Jamaica, England, and New York, in spite of the difficulties of crossing the bars of the outer Banks. James Iredell, the customs officer for the Crown at Edenton in 1774, noted the principal exports of that year as tobacco, tar, green tar, pitch, turpentine, staves and heading, pine and oak plank, cedar posts, scantling, oars, shingles, deer skins, corn, herrings, wax, flaxseed, hoops, rosin, and snake-root. In 1771, 85 vessels cleared from Edenton; in 1772, 95 vessels; and in 1773, 99 vessels.[32] Commerce was clearly the chief source of wealth. Josiah Quincy, Jr., of Massachusetts, on his southern tour, noted that "It is made a question which carries on the most trade,—whether Edenton, Newbern [sic], Wilmington, or Brunswick; it seems to be one of the first two."[33] Across the blue waters of the Sound and the inflowing rivers skimmed boats of all sorts and sizes, except when ugly squalls threatened

[30] *Historic Edenton and Countryside* (Edenton: Woman's Club, no date), illustrations, *passim*. The author has visited this area and made photographs.
[31] Charles Christopher Crittenden, "Overland Travel and Transportation in North Carolina, 1763-1789," *North Carolina Historical Review*, VIII (July, 1931), 243-245.
[32] McRee, *Iredell*, I, 565.
[33] *Josiah Quincy Memoir*, p. 95.

danger. Iredell mentioned that it took him an hour and a quarter to make a good passage across the sound.[34] In the case of a "fresh," however, a long detour had to be made via the ferry at Halifax in order to proceed southward.[35] Eventually the main highways bypassed Edenton; President George Washington, for instance, rode from Petersburg, Virginia directly to Halifax in 1791, and then on to Tarboro and New Bern.[36] The residents of the town included the Blounts, the Harveys, the Johnsons and the Johnstons, the Collinses, the Dickinsons, the Allens, the Vails, the Hardys, and others noted in the history of North Carolina. Henry E. McCulloh wrote from London to a friend that "You will find the gentlemen of Edenton very agreeable."[37] William Hooper praised "generous, hospitable Edenton."[38] Adam Tredwell, visiting from New York, thought the people "the most agreeable he had ever seen."[39]

Yet the climate left much to be desired. Malaria and other fevers were all too common. William Hooper wrote, in 1778:

We literally die daily. . . .[A] few of you from the Edenton Quarter must quit your penchant to that everlasting lake of standing water which surrounds you, & find some Country which Providence intended for the habitation of man; & if we do not fly from this very soon we shall find a habitation too permanent to be changed in this world, especially if this fever persists in his ravages.[40]

Pierce Butler of South Carolina continually worried over the health of his friends in Edenton.

Your Billious attack, for the Jaundice is nothing more or less than a redundance of Bile from relaxed habit, the consequence of impure air & great heat, confirms my opinion of Edenton being a most extreme unhealthy spott; trying beyond measure to the best constitution. The number of

[34] James Iredell to Hannah Iredell, Jan. 15, 1779. Charles E. Johnson Papers, N C Archives.
[35] James Iredell to Hannah Iredell, May 13, 1780. Charles E. Johnson Papers, N C Archives. Iredell was unable to cross the Roanoke River at any point below Halifax because "The Fresh has been very high. . . ."
[36] The Diaries of George Washington, 1748-1799, 4 vols. Edited by John C. Fitzpatrick (Boston: Houghton Mifflin, 1925), IV, 162 ff.
[37] Henry E. McCulloh to James Iredell, Sept. 5, 1768, quoted in McRee, Iredell, I, 22. The original of this, as well as certain other letters quoted by McRee, has not been located.
[38] William Hooper to James Iredell, March 22, 1781, quoted in McRee, Iredell, I, 495.
[39] McRee, Iredell, II, 495.
[40] William Hooper to James Iredell, July 15, 1778. James Iredell Papers, Perkins Library, Duke University, Durham, North Carolina. Hereinafter cited as Iredell Papers, Duke University.

THE EARLY YEARS 11

putrid ponds interspersed in the town, added [to] the stagnate state of Your Bay, is enough to breed the most pestilential disorders.[41] Smallpox broke out in 1773,[42] and malaria was a constant companion. Hannah Iredell had such a bad attack of the ague that her whole body "flew out with a violent heat and swelling" so that the doctor was unable to bleed her. The next day, however, she was much improved and was taking "the bark."[43] To William Blair, Mrs. Blair wrote, "We are all thank God very well here, which is almost a wonder the Town is so sickly."[44] To Hannah Iredell Mrs. Blair lamented that "I am very sorry the flux is in town."[45] Dr. Samuel Cutler, after moving from Edenton to Connecticut, attributed his improved health to the better climate in the north.[46] Pettigrew, too, suffered from ill health for the last twenty years of his life in the region.

Society was gay, however, in spite of the climate. Young James Iredell has left a picture of the lighter side of life in Edenton in the brief pages of a diary which he kept sporadically. Iredell was acting as the customs officer for the port and reading law with Samuel Johnston on the side. In 1773 his journal indicated that on January 1 he "drank a glass of Rasberry with the Doctor & some other gentlemen at the Doctor's apartment" before breakfast. He saw "a little race" between "a horse of Buchanan's, and a Mare of Webb's—the latter beat." He escorted several young ladies to the boat for the Johnston plantation, and attended a ball in the evening—all this on January 1. On Christmas morning, 1772, he was "serenaded before I got up with a Band of Musick, the sound of which soon raised me." He attended church after which he was Horniblow's guest for dinner. There was much tea-drinking, visiting, and seeing people to and from their boats; there was cardplaying, billiards, and backgammon too. Iredell noted at one point, "As I was walking home, called in at Horniblow's [tavern] to see *who & who were together*. Mr. Hewes & Jackson playing Backgammon, Mr. Worth & Mr. Littlejohn looking on,—just saw the Hit over and came away."[47] Robert Hunter, a visitor, "played

[41] Pierce Butler to James Iredell, May 5, 1783. Iredell Papers, Duke University.
[42] Diary of James Iredell, Jan. 18, Jan. 30, Feb. 1, and Feb. 6, 1773. James Iredell Papers, N C Archives.
[43] Jane Johnston Blair to James Iredell, Oct. 22, 1780. Charles E. Johnson Papers, N C Archives.
[44] Jane Johnston Blair to William Blair, Aug. 28, 1784. Charles E. Johnson Papers, N C Archives.
[45] Jane Johnston Blair to Hannah Iredell, June 29, 1785. Charles E. Johnson Papers, N C Archives.
[46] Samuel Cutler to James Iredell, Aug. 7, 1785, cited in McRee, *Iredell*, II, 130-131. McRee has read something into this letter, however; the original, in the Iredell Papers, Duke University, is not explicit on the subject.
[47] Diary of James Iredell, *passim*. James Iredell Papers, N C Archives.

a game at shuffleboard" and also "a game at whist." He watched "the young ladies dance this warm weather."[48] Iredell mentioned dances for the "children" at the Courthouse, a dance given by Mrs. Jones, a "little dance at Mr. Pollock's," and dancing at "Hayes" plantation. Reading material was imported as well as local. Iredell recorded his reading a London magazine and newspaper, *Clarissa Harlowe*, Fielding's *Journey from this World to the Next*, and the novel *Sir Charles Grandison*.[49] Following his marriage to Hannah Johnston, he bought a home in Edenton and moved in, "after the usual time spent in receiving and returning the congratulatory visits of friends and relatives, and the wonted interchange of those elegant hospitalities that marked that era and locality. . . ."[50] On November 12, 1772, Iredell "Heard in the Course of the Evening many discharges of Guns on acct. of Horniblow's being married to Nancy Rombough." Later he "drank two congratulatory Glasses of Wine & Bitters with Horniblow" and also "drank a glass of Mr. Jones's Rasberry which gave me rather too much spirits—Quite sober now."[51]

Such a population certainly required and could support a schoolmaster. In addition to his instructional duties, each teacher was required to serve as lay reader in the Anglican Church. General opinion of the religious disposition of the town was lower than that of its social and financial standing. Many of the leading men were Deists. The clergy generally had the reputation of belonging to the "jovial, fox-hunting race of English parsons"; they indulged in dancing and playing cards as well as drinking.[52] St. Paul's church building was much out of repair. The Reverend Daniel Earl, priest in charge, to whom Pettigrew would be responsible, wrote to the Society for the Propagation of the Gospel in 1771:

Our Church at Edenton is so much out of repair that neither minister nor congregation can stand the inclemency of the weather in it without greatly risking their health, but I am in great hopes it will be repaired before next winter.[53]

Earl himself was something of a personality. In addition to his clerical duties, he maintained a school aided by his daughter Nancy at his plantation on the Chowan River; he "taught the people the

---

[48] Robert Hunter, Jr., *Quebec to Carolina in 1785-1786* (San Marino, Calif: The Huntington Library, 1943), p. 268. Hereinafter cited as Hunter, *Quebec to Carolina*.

[49] Diary of James Iredell, *passim*. James Iredell Papers, N C Archives.

[50] McRee, *Iredell*, I, 174-175.

[51] Diary of James Iredell, Nov. 12, 1772. James Iredell Papers, N C Archives.

[52] McRee, *Iredell*, I, 149.

[53] *Colonial Records of North Carolina*, VIII, 542.

proper way to cultivate flax, and how to cure and prepare it for the looms. . . [H]e also taught how to prepare *seines* with which to take the large quantities of fish which went up the Chowan River and the Albemarle waters.'' His second wife was a widow, whom he married in order to have some one ''to take care of him and *his long silk stockings*.'' A famous verse, variously attributed and varying slightly in phraseology, is said to have been carved on a window pane [or door] at St. Paul's, to wit:

> An English brick church—
> A tumble-down steeple—
> With a herring-catching parson—
> And a God-forsaken people.[54]

James Iredell attended church irregularly, and did not note if services were held in St. Paul's or in the Courthouse. In 1770 a Mr. Bruce, evidently a lay reader, read the sermon. As Iredell said, ''nobody to make the Responses but Mr. H[ewes] & myself, & neither of us had a Prayer Book. . . . the rest of the singers were too bashful to give out a Psalm . . . I had a great mind to give out the Psalm myself.'' On another occasion he attended services with all the pall-bearers of Tommy Blount, whose funeral had occurred the preceding week.[55] This, then, was the world into which Charles Pettigrew moved.

Nothing more is known of his life for the next year; it is to be presumed that he performed his educational and clerical duties as lay-reader at St. Paul's to the satisfaction of his superiors. In the winter of 1774, he sailed for England to be ordained into the Anglican clergy; Edenton had at least converted him from a Presbyterian to a member of the ''Old Church.'' He carried with him letters to Arthur, brother of James Iredell, who was studying at the Inns of Temple, which he delivered. This brother wrote to Edenton that he had missed the opportunity to extend courtesies to Pettigrew, ''which I was very sorry for, as I should have been happy in having it in my Power to serve him.'' Arthur Iredell then went to Bath, from which he returned only to find that Pettigrew had paid a final call. Although he ''im-

[54] Mrs. N. J. Baker to Rev. William Shepard Pettigrew, March 21, 1890. Genealogy Section of Pettigrew Papers, UNC. Mrs. Baker was a direct descendant of Daniel Earl (also spelled Earle and Earll). Mrs. Baker's may have been a modified one; in 1786 Robert Hunter, Jr. reported this version:

> A broken-windowed church,
> An unfinished steeple,
> A herring-catching parson
> And a damned set of people.

Hunter was told that the parson was fond of the ''sport'' of catching herring, which ''so ridiculed him and his church that I'm told they have never preached in it since.'' Hunter, *Quebec to Carolina*, pp. 271-272.
[55] Diary of James Iredell. James Iredell Papers, N C Archives.

mediately went to Mr. Pettigrew's Lodgings, there I was told he had set off for America, a fortnight before. . . . I am afraid Mr. P. conceives but an ill idea of my Manners.''[56]

Although Pettigrew himself left no records of his journey to England and his ordination, the description of this process written by his contemporary Devereux Jarratt, of Virginia, is typical. Jarratt obtained letters of recommendation from the governor of the colony and from the commissary of the Bishop of London who resided in Virginia. Armed with these, he voyaged to England and proceeded to London to present himself to the bishop. The bishop's chaplain administered the examination and Jarratt ''passed my trials before him with approbation, and he promised to present me to the bishop. He did so, and I was ordained deacon, in the King's chapel, at Christmas, in the year 1762, after I had staid in London about four weeks.'' The next step was ordination into the priesthood, after examination by the chaplain of the bishop of Chester. This step was taken the following week, after which he returned to Virginia with ''all my letters of ordination. . . .''[57]

Pettigrew received his two ordinations from the bishop of London and the bishop of Rochester.[58] After being appointed a missionary by the Society for the Propagation of the Gospel in Foreign Parts, he returned to Edenton, arriving there on May 20, 1775, on the brink of the Revolution.[59]

[56] Arthur Iredell to James Iredell, April 27, 1775. Charles E. Johnson Papers, N C Archives.

[57] Devereux Jarratt, *The Life of the Reverend Devereux Jarratt, Rector of Bath Parish, Dinwiddie County, Virginia, Written by Himself, in a series of Letters Addressed to the Rev. John Coleman, one of the Ministers of the Protestant Episcopal Church, in Maryland* (Baltimore: Warner and Hanna, 1806), pp. 55, 71-72.

[58] George Woodward Lamb, ''Clergymen Licensed to the American Colonies by the Bishops of London: 1745-1781,'' *Historical Magazine of the Protestant Episcopal Church*, XIII (June, 1944), 128-143; Walter H. Stowe, *et al.*, ''The Clergy of the Episcopal Church in 1785,'' *Historical Magazine of the Protestant Episcopal Church*, XX (September, 1951), 273-274; Genealogy Section of the Pettigrew Papers, UNC.

[59] Charles Pettigrew to the Secretary of the Society for the Propagation of the Gospel in Foreign Parts, April 13, 1776, *Colonial Records of North Carolina*, X, 496.

CHAPTER II

THE YOUNG MAN

When Charles Pettigrew arrived in Edenton on May 20, 1775, he engaged to spend one-third of his time preaching at St. Paul's Church in that town. Although the parish was served by the Reverend Daniel Earl, he could be there only once every three weeks because of the size of his parish and the obligation to preach at other chapels within it. Pettigrew was also to hold services in Barkley Parish in Perquimans County during 1776, where there were five chapels. As he told the Society for the Propagation of the Gospel in describing his obligations, he would "make up the vacant Sundays to [the chapels] by preaching on week days—". Many Quakers lived in Perquimans; he would not accept a salary paid by a tax, but would only take the contributions of his hearers. During his first year in North Carolina as a clergyman, he baptized 120 children, six adults, and "administered the Sacrament of the Lord's Supper to Eighteen Communicants."[1] The latter sentence is indicative of one of the basic causes of the weakness of the established church in the colonies: there could be no communicants except those who had been confirmed; and since there was no American bishop, there could be no confirmation on the western side of the Atlantic.

In addition to his small salary from the S. P. G.,[2] Pettigrew received a subscription from members of the church in Edenton. The 1775 lists sets forth the contract thus:

We the Subscribers do promise to pay to the Rev.d M.r Charles Pettigrew the Several Sums Annex'd to our Names, as a Consideration for his attendance in Edenton every third Sunday, in the absence of the Rev.d M.r Earl, when Health shall permit, the same to Commence from this date, and continue for the span of one year. Edenton July 22.d 1775[3]

The sums pledged ranged from five pounds to ten shillings. One

[1] Charles Pettigrew to Secretary of the Society for the Propagation of the Gospel in Foreign Parts, April 13, 1776, in *Colonial Records of North Carolina*, X, 496.

[2] The salary ordinarily allowed was £50 per year, plus a library worth £10 and an allowance of £5 for books to be distributed to parishioners. Charles Frederick Pascoe, *Two Hundred Years of the S. P. G.* (London: 1901), 837. Pettigrew drew a bill on the Society for £20 in March, 1776, since he was beginning a new fiscal year. Charles Pettigrew to the S. P. G., April 13, 1776, in *Colonial Records of North Carolina*, X, 496.

[3] Salary Subscription for 1775. Pettigrew Papers, UNC.

item states: "Ja. Iredell, four pounds (if he is living & can conveniently pay it)." Since this entry is further marked, "Paid," one supposes that it was therefore convenient for James Iredell to give up that particular sum. This method of payment was carried on each year. An undated subscription list totals £216 "from M.ʳ Price who collected it"; in that year the sum was over-subscribed by £3.[4]

Since a permanent contract was made with Pettigrew in 1778, it appears that the Reverend Daniel Earl went into retirement. The terms of this contract required Pettigrew to conduct services on alternate Sundays in Edenton, and to perform other "sundry important duties of his function as a Clergyman." The salary was to "increase or Diminish at the commencement of every year according to the Rise or fall of the money, so as to keep it equal in Value to one hundred pounds in the year one thousand seven hundred and seventy four."[5] A list of collections, dated May 1778, shows that some had paid for one year, some not at all, some were crossed off the list, etc. In all, a total of £270.10.6 had been collected.[6] This sum, plus the list mentioned in the preceding paragraph, represents the salary collected for three years, which indicates that the contractual agreement, at least up to this point, was being kept. Thus the situation remained until the close of the Revolutionary War.

Less than three weeks after Charles Pettigrew had returned from his ordination in England, the last royal assembly was dissolved by Governor Josiah Martin, only to be followed in July by the Governor's flight to a British ship off Cape Fear. When the torch of colonial leadership passed from the hands of John Harvey, who died at this critical time, to Samuel Johnston, of Edenton, the town of Edenton became the center of Whig and Patriot activities.

The clergy was in a difficult situation. Daniel Earl wrote in August, 1775:

I should have gone to some of the Northern colonies before this time had it not been for the war-like and unquiet situation of this whole continent, where there are not, by the lowest calculation, less than 150,000 men under arms, which they are daily augmenting, and which would render traveling extremely disagreeable, especially to an unhealthy person, and therefore [I] chose rather to rely on the Almighty Author of Life and Health for sanitary means than undertake a journey under these circumstances.

He continued:

The situation of the clergy in this part of the world is at present truly critical, on account of the difficulty of comporting themselves in such a

---

[4] Undated Salary Subscription. Pettigrew Papers, UNC.
[5] Salary Subscription for 1778. Pettigrew Papers, UNC.
[6] Salary Collections, May, 1778. Pettigrew Papers, UNC.

manner as to give no umbrage to the Inhabitants. Some of them have been suspended, deprived of their Salaries, and, in the American manner proscribed by the Committees [of Safety], and thereby rendered incapable of getting any settlement in any part of the united Colonies, and all this on account of charges against them of opposing the general cause of America, and how far they are to blame I am not able to determine, but verily believe that if the most learned and eloquent Divine in England was to endeavor to dissuade the Americans from their present Resolutions he could make no impression upon them, but contrarywise rather inflame them, so tenacious are they of the measures they have adopted.

He concluded by saying:

As for my own part I have as yet kept clear of any censure among my parishioners, and I never introduce any Topic into the Pulpit except exhortations and prayers for peace, good order and a speedy reconciliation with Great Britain.[7]

Pettigrew wrote to the S.P.G. in April, 1776: "Can mention nothing with regard to public affairs for such Letters are not allowed to pass."[8] Many of the clergy tried to steer a middle course although it became increasingly difficult to do so. On the one hand, their salaries were substantially aided by the S.P.G., the majority of the clergy had been born overseas, the church was tied to the crown, and the liturgy was filled with prayers for those in authority. Yet their parishioners were putting more and more pressure on them to avow themselves for the American cause. Eventually the decision had to be made. Of the eleven members of the Anglican clergy who were residents of North Carolina in 1776, three were loyalists: James Reed, John Wills, and Francis Johnston. One, George Micklejohn, changed sides from loyalist at the time of the Regulator troubles to patriot. Daniel Earl, possibly because of his increasing age, seems to have been permitted to retire quietly in 1778 in favor of Charles Pettigrew. However, since Earl's daughter Nancy married the patriot Charles Johnson, he certainly could not have been strongly committed to the loyalist point of view. Four of the clergymen were strong patriots: Charles Edward Taylor, Charles Cupples, Nathaniel Blount, and Hezekiah Ford. The latter was the only one of the group to serve in the army; he was chaplain to the Fifth Regiment of the North Carolina Continental Line. There is no evidence concerning the political views of Thomas Burgess, who died in 1779.[9]

[7] Daniel Earl to S. P. G., August 30, 1775, in *Colonial Records of North Carolina*, X, 237-238.
[8] Charles Pettigrew to S. P. G., April 13, 1776, in *Colonial Records of North Carolina*, X, 496.
[9] Sarah McCulloh Lemmon, "The Genesis of the Protestant Episcopal Diocese of North Carolina, 1701-1823," *North Carolina Historical Review*, XXIX (1952), 445-449.

One test of patriotism was to conduct services for the Assembly. Charles Pettigrew was requested to deliver a sermon for the Assembly in November, 1777, at the church in New Bern, which he did. However, the two houses of the Assembly fell into disagreement as to whether he should receive remuneration for this service, the upshot being that he did not.[10] This little bit of by-play seems to indicate that Pettigrew was not the most enthusiastic of the patriots or perhaps his sermon, which is not extant, was insufficiently fiery. This conclusion is reinforced by the fact that he secured a substitute when he was drafted to serve with the militia in 1780. One of his friends, Richard Templeman, indicated that in his opinion, at least, the draft was plotted by Colonel James Blount, the brother-in-law of the clergyman. Templeman wrote to his friend:

I did not imagine Col Blount would carry his Vindictive disposition so far—but be it with him—I hope, as you are determined to march with the militia, youl meet every indulgence thats in the power of Gen¹ [Isaac] Gregory or the commanding officer to afford you, and that youl act the philosopher in parting with your family and going thro. the fatigues of a Summers Campaign in a Southern Climate, but poor M.ʳˢ Pettigrew I pity her much her tender nature will illy brook the parting and her anxiety will be great for your welfare and safty could you not prevail on her to spend some of the time in Pasquotank it might relieve her a little [Y]ou have the prayers & wishes of my family for your Safe return—[11]

During Pettigrew's brief stay in camp he preached a sermon to the troops on the text, "A Time of War," and composed the following battle hymn:

"A time of war!"
Heard from afar
The martial Trumpet sounds,
And Heroes brave,
Their rights to save,
Risk scars & bleeding wounds.

They take the field,
They scorn to yield;
In such a righteous cause
Rather than flie
They chuse to die
Defenders of their Laws.

God is their shield,
When in the field,

[10] State Records of North Carolina, XII, 149, 155, 159, 321, 322.
[11] Richard Templeman to Charles Pettigrew, January 10, 1780. Pettigrew Papers, N C Archives.

As in the Tents of ease;
Nor can they fall,
By sword or ball,
Unless his goodness please.

While every man,
Does what he can,
Relying on *his* power,
They cannot fail,
Tho' foes assail,
Like Lyons to devour.

For dearest rights
The patriot fights
And when he sheathes the blade
A deathless fame
His deeds proclaim
And Laurels deck his shade.[12]

He did not serve in a campaign after all, however, having finally decided to obtain a substitute, one Zachariah Carter. John Sitgreaves, aide-de-camp to General Richard Caswell, wrote the notice of discharge at Cross Creek [Fayetteville]:

Camp near X Creek 27 June 1780
These may Certify that the Reverend Charles Pettigrew a Draft from the County of Chowan is hereby discharged from his Tour of Duty he having produced Zachariah Carter an able bodied man in his Room—[13]

He paid Carter $7500 to take his place, noting: "The price of a Clergiman's exemption from Military Service in North Carolina[.]"[14] He was discharged in time to avoid the disastrous rout of American troops at the battle of Camden, South Carolina, in which half the North Carolina troops were killed or captured while the others fled with Caswell and Gates through Charlotte to Hillsborough. The South Carolina Pettigrews were active Whigs. Charles's father, James Pettigrew, served as a private in South Carolina;[15] his brother William served with General Pickens; his nephew "Big Jim" also served in South Carolina.[16] The elder Pettigrew, as his son William wrote,

had I believe as few enemies as any man, for he was somewhat skilled in Medicine & there were very few practitioners in the country, both Whig and

[12] Poems. Pettigrew Papers, N C Archives.
[13] Charles Pettigrew Discharged from Military Service, June 27, 1780. Pettigrew Papers, UNC.
[14] Notation on reverse of discharge.
[15] National Society of the Daughters of the American Revolution, *Patriot Index* (Washington: 1966), p. 530.
[16] Genealogy Section of Pettigrew Papers, UNC.

Tory would make application and were never disappointed in getting assistance, by which he was very little disturbed. He continued to live very quiet till after the restoration of peace which to him was a joyful event for he was a great Whig.[17]

Edenton was one of the three North Carolina ports to which supplies from all over the colony were sent, in the summer of 1774, for the relief of the port of Boston. It was also the seat of the famed "Edenton Tea Party" in which ladies of the vicinity signed resolutions supporting the protests of the Provincial Congress to the British government. Following the outbreak of war, the town suffered somewhat in the falling off of commerce, although privateers used its port and some French military forces came, adding excitement and a foreign flavor to social affairs. In May, 1778, there flared a brief fear of British invasion from Virginia. Mrs. Jane Blair of Edenton reported that the popping of reeds in a swamp fire caused an alarmed resident to report "large fires kindled & many guns fired out there but I do not think it was any thing but his own fears."[18] Not, however, until Cornwallis invaded the state did the citizens begin to feel the breath of war. After the British victory at the battle of Guilford Court House, in March 1781, Edenton became nervous and in May a panic broke out. Citizens fled, believing that British occupation was imminent. Samuel Johnston, who was in Philadelphia when he heard the news, wrote to James Iredell:

I am much concerned for them on this occasion, as they must have sustained great loss and inconvenience in their flight, though I flatter myself their apprehensions were greater than their danger. I by no means blame them for taking early precautions for the security of their property, but I don't think any force could at that time have been employed against them which they might not have found means to repulse. . . .[19]

A few British raids by boat on outlying plantations did occur, however. Robert Smith reported:

They have given me a pretty little Switching, but it might have been worse; they have ruined poor Littlejohn and would have left me nothing had they not have taken fright.[20]

Some ladies refugeed to Windsor. Mrs. Jane Blair sent two boatloads of household goods, followed by loaded carts; she did not return to

[17] *Ibid.*

[18] Jane Johnston Blair to James Iredell, May 17, 1778. Charles E. Johnson Papers, N C Archives.

[19] Samuel Johnston to James Iredell, May 8, 1781, quoted in McRee, *Iredell,* I, 510.

[20] Robert Smith to James Iredell, [May, 1781]. Charles E. Johnson Papers, N C Archives.

Edenton until November. Many slaves fled to seek freedom with Cornwallis's army, one report saying 20 in two nights and others at various times.[21] By August, the panic had passed, and Samuel Johnston thought Edenton sufficiently secure to return to his plantation. Cornwallis surrendered in October; John Williams wrote to James Iredell that "we were all so Elated, that the time Elapsed in frolicking, etc." and therefore he did not hold court as scheduled.[22]

There are no Pettigrew papers indicating any of the above excitement of evacuation or of victory. Other than his being drafted, the only report on Charles Pettigrew's activities came from James Iredell, who heard him preach in Camden, Currituck County, in 1779. As he wrote to his wife:

Pettigrew has been down here for near a fortnight, preaching to the People at many different places, and acquiring the character of an Apostle. The Women admire him so much that if he was not married, he might preach on the subject of *divine love* (with a glance at the *human*) to much more purpose than he did at Edenton.[23]

Following the conclusion of hostilities, life began to return to a more normal pattern; yet it could never be the same as that before 1776, especially for the former Anglican clergy. Independence had brought a revolution to the church as an institution. The constitution of North Carolina drawn up in 1776 contained two articles which related to separation of church and state. Article 31 provided that no active clergyman might be a member of the Assembly or the council. Article 34 provided that no one church should ever be established, nor any person be compelled to attend church or pay for a glebe, church, or minister unless he voluntarily agreed to do so.[24] Several ordinances affecting the church were passed at the same time. Ministers of all denominations were granted the right to solemnize marriages. Protection in property rights, however, was provided by granting that all glebes, churches, lands, etc. "heretofore purchased . . . shall be and remain forever to the Use and Occupancy of that religious Society, Church, Sect, Denomination . . ." to which they had been assigned. All arrears in salaries or other claims due the clergy up to December 18, 1776, were validated and were to be paid.[25] These provisions, plus the withdrawal of support by the S.P.G., and

---

[21] Jane Johnston Blair to Hannah Iredell, April 20, May 10, Nov. 1, Nov. 19, 1781. Charles E. Johnson Papers, N C Archives.

[22] John Williams to James Iredell, Dec. 16, 1781. Charles E. Johnson Papers, N C Archives.

[23] James Iredell to Hannah Iredell, June 14, 1779. Charles E. Johnson Papers, N C Archives.

[24] *Colonial Records of North Carolina*, X, 1011.

[25] *State Records of North Carolina*, XX, 726; XXIII, 986, 997; XXIV, 91.

the physical destruction occasioned by war itself, removed the props from under the Anglican or "Old" Church and made possible the rapid growth of evangelical sects such as the Baptists and the Methodists. Unoccupied Anglican chapels were taken over by new congregations;[26] glebe lands, in spite of the protection offered in 1776, were permitted by special acts of the Assembly to be sold.[27] The itinerant Methodist preacher, later bishop, Francis Asbury, bears witness to the destruction of churches and the dispersal of their congregations in the journal which he kept. At Nut Bush Creek he found a "broken society." Two years later, at Boisseau's Chapel, "the glory is strangely departed here." Of a visit to Hillsborough, he recounted: "I walked to the church; it was once an elegant building, and still makes a good appearance at a distance, but within it is in ruins." At Wicocon, as well, "the glory is departed."[28] Ten years after the end of the war, it appears that in all of Edgecombe County there were only two or three communicants, one of these, William Clements, a convert from the Presbyterian Church who was closely associated with Charles Pettigrew.[29] Jeremiah Norman, another itinerant Methodist, recorded in his diary a visit to Brunswick:

[26] By law, the Episcopal Church in Hillsborough was to be open to all Christians every Sunday, with the Commission deciding whose turn it was; *State Records of North Carolina*, XXIV, 606. Science Hall, an academy, met in 1785 in the Episcopal Church; Ruth Blackwelder, *The Age of Orange* (Charlotte: William Loftin, 1961), pp. 119-120. Conoconara Chapel on the Tar River in Edgecomb Parish fell into ruins after the war; Stuart Hall Smith and Claiborne T. Smith, Jr., *The History of Trinity Parish Scotland Neck—Edgecombe Parish Halifax County* (Scotland Neck, N. C.: 1955), pp. 17-18. Quankey Chapel, eight miles northwest of Halifax, was taken over by Baptists; Smith and Smith, *op. cit.,* p. 19. The church at Beaufort was used by preachers of any denomination and also as a school; W. L. Grissom, *A History of Methodism in North Carolina from 1772 to the Present Time* (Nashville: Methodist Publishing House, 1902, 2 vols.), I, 91; hereinafter cited as Grissom, *Methodism in North Carolina*. Baptists took over Trinity Church in Scotland Neck; *The Church Messenger,* Aug. 25, 1881. Baptists attempted unsuccessfully to occupy St. John's Chapel in Hertford County; John E. Tyler, "The Church of England in Colonial Bertie County" (typescript in N C Archives). They were successful in the acquisition of Outlaw's Chapel, near Powellsville, which they renamed Holly Grove; Holly Grove Baptist Church Minutes, 1822-1878, Manuscript Division, William R. Perkins Library, Duke University, Durham, North Carolina.

[27] *State Records of North Carolina*, XXIV, 825, 863, 872.

[28] Francis Asbury, *The Journal of the Rev. Francis Asbury, Bishop of the Methodist Episcopal Church, from August 7, 1771 to December 7, 1815* (New York: Bangs and Mason, 1821, 3 vols.), I, 292, 345, 354, 392. Hereinafter cited as Asbury, *Journal*.

[29] J. Kelly Turner and John L. Bridgers, Jr., *History of Edgecombe County, North Carolina* (Raleigh: Edwards and Broughton, 1920), p. 444. Clements' association with Charles Pettigrew came from his service as secretary to the Episcopal conventions held at Tarboro, discussed below.

I drew near & viewed the walls of the old church, burnt some years past. It seemed to be the remains of an elegant building, but the lofty edifice is now ruined. God neglected, as well as his House burnt. Lord have mercy on the people in this place. Turn their hearts & save their souls.[30]

In his last will and testament, John Alexander of Bertie lamented:

The manly, mas[c]uline voice of Orthodoxy is no longer heard in our land. Far, therefore, from my grave be the senseless Rant of whining Fanaticism, her hated and successful Rival. Cant and Grimace dishonor the dead, as well as disgrace the living.—Let the Monitor within, who never deceives, alone pronounce my Funeral Oration; while some friendly hand deposits my poor remains close by the ashes of beloved Daughter Elizabeth, with whom I trust to share a happy Eternity.[31]

It became necessary for the Episcopal clergy to farm, to practice medicine, or to teach school in order to earn a living.[32]

Charles Pettigrew, still young and enthusiastic, must indeed have been discouraged. The congregation in Edenton was "gay, inattentive" according to Asbury, although the latter was much pleased with Mr. Pettigrew: "I heard him preach, and received the Lord's supper at his hands."[33] Dr. Thomas Coke was also unimpressed with Edenton, but thought less of Pettigrew than did Asbury. He wrote:

I went to Edenton, a most wicked place. Here Mr. Pettigrew preaches: The people in general seemed to prefer the courthouse, which is an elegant place, so I went there accordingly, and preached to a large congregation. . . there seemed nothing but wickedness and dissipation in the tavern at which I put up . . . I suppose Mr. Pettigrew does as much good in Edenton as a little chicken.[34]

A sermon on the subject of why men despise Christianity preached by Pettigrew in 1783 may be indicative of the general attitude of the times.[35] Even his Thanksgiving Day sermon was along the same line, being on the theme: Fear the Lord and depart from evil.[36] Members

[30] Diary of Jeremiah Norman, 1793-1801, p. 938. Stephen B. Weeks Collection, UNC.

[31] Will of John Alexander, April 4, 1795. Robert B. Drane Collection, UNC.

[32] Jarvis Buxton, *Early History of the Church in America, Particularly in North Carolina* (reprinted from *The American Church Review*, July, 1876), p. 5; F. L. Hawks, "Early Church in North Carolina," *The American Church Review*, III (1850-1851), 307.

[33] Asbury, *Journal*, I, 363.

[34] "The Journal of Thomas Coke, Bishop of the Methodist-Episcopal Church," in *The Arminian Magazine*, Vol. I, quoted in Grissom, *Methodism in North Carolina*, I, 163-164.

[35] Sermon preached on April 27, 1783. Drane Collection, UNC. Pettigrew noted on the back, "Somewhat incorrect but preaches better y^n it reads."

[36] Sermon preached in December, 1783. Sermons. Pettigrew Papers, N C Archives.

of the congregation evidenced their lack of interest. Mrs. Jane Blair was more interested in writing her daughter Nelly about "a new fashion that appeared in church last Sunday"[37] than in the service itself. She also reported to her sister:

I went yesterday to church it was very much crouded [sic] we had a very good discourse but the Parson came rather too late it was two oclock [sic] before we got out.[38]

Pettigrew therefore began to become interested in the Methodist movement. In 1782 the Reverend Devereaux Jarratt of Virginia, an Anglican much in sympathy with the Methodists, approached Pettigrew with an appeal for support. Having heard, he said, that Pettigrew had attended a quarterly meeting of the Methodists, he congratulated him on "the Friendship you shew & the Assistance you give. . . ." He continued:

They are the only People, that I know of, whose Labours are considerably blest to the Salvation of Souls; & they have given the most striking & indubitable Testimonies of their Love & Adherence to that Church of which you & I have the Honour to be Ministers. They therefore claim a Right to our Patronage, Countenance & Assistance.[39]

Pettigrew accepted the challenge and lent strong support to the itinerant preachers who labored in his vicinity, corresponding with them and encouraging them, sometimes attending their quarterly sessions, and apparently shepherding them much as a bishop would. At this time, of course, these men were still members of the Anglican communion.

Caleb B. Peddicord, of Bertie County, was one such man. He appreciated Pettigrew's interest, and felt

thankful that I have those who administer suitable instruction, and naturally care for my soul welfare & usefullness. How good a thing it is to have union and fellowship tho only by Letter, it is but a little while & we shall meet I trust to superior advantage, to rest together in the Paradice [sic] of God above in glory.

He pleaded with Pettigrew to join the circuit and visit as many congregations as possible.

[37] Jane Johnston Blair to Nelly Blair, May 19, 1784. Charles E. Johnson Papers, N C Archives.
[38] Jane Johnston Blair to Hannah Iredell, May 30, 1785. Charles E. Johnson Papers, N C Archives.
[39] Devereux Jarratt to Charles Pettigrew, August 13, 1782. Pettigrew Papers, UNC. Jarratt began a great revival near Petersburg, Virginia, which lasted for two years; Grissom, *Methodism in North Carolina*, I, 8, 41, 44. He is also spoken of in Asbury, *Journal*, I, 338, 344-345. Jarratt and Asbury were friends until the Methodists left the Anglican communion.

I do believe Dear Sir that it would be pleasing to God, & a great benefit to the people, if you are enabled to visit a few of the many vacancies, in any State. It is a great pity that your usefulness in general should be confined to the small Circle of a Neighborhood, when there are so many sheep without a Shepherd "wandring upon the dark mountains"![40]

After staying at the home of Pettigrew, probably in March of 1783, Peddicord wrote to thank him and inform him of continuing efforts. He wrote:

O Sir help me by your prayers. . . . I feel great tenderness for you & family. Whilst I write it moves upon my heart. There are also a few Names in Edonton [sic] who I hope will never quit their confidence, or slacken their diligence. I felt great union with them as Christians. O that the Lord may not cut Israel Short in their Teachers, but spare you Sir to be useful to them.[41]

Another laborer in the vineyard who looked to Pettigrew for comfort and leadership was Henry Metcalf, who travelled the area of Currituck and Roanoke Island. Pettigrew thought him "a Man of very great piety & zeal. He did not last long, but died in Bartie [sic], in the full assurance of faith, as I was inform'd—"[42] Anthony Walke was another worker in Currituck. He recorded of two quarterly meetings:

[A]t both places we had a great good time of it several very powerful alarming sermons & at the Love feasts many bold & bright testimonies for God, especially at Nixonton, for all which I humbly beseech the blessed lord to make me truly thankful—

He especially hoped that Pettigrew would

see it more & more your duty to warn every man & teach every man, so that you may be the means of keeping many souls from dropping into eternal misery, the blessed Jesus grant that you may have the great comfort of seeing much fruit of your labour, may the unworthiest of Christ's despised followers say to you go in the name of the Lord, and oh! that you may be endued w.th wisdom & righteousness from above, that your tongue may be as the pen of a ready writer at all times, & may you have a double portion of the spirit of the Blessed Lord poured out powerfully on you, & may you be abundantly comforted by seeing the good pleasure of the Lord to prosper

[40] Caleb Peddicord to Charles Pettigrew, Dec. 29, 1782. Pettigrew Papers, UNC. Peddicord was a leading Methodist in the area and in 1782 was the presiding elder; Grissom, *Methodism in North Carolina*, I, 99.
[41] Caleb Peddicord to Charles Pettigrew, April 2, 1783. Pettigrew Papers, UNC.
[42] Notation by Charles Pettigrew on back of letter from Henry Metcalf to Charles Pettigrew, Aug. 8, 1783. Pettigrew Papers, UNC. Metcalf began preaching in 1783 and died in 1784; Grissom, *Methodism in North Carolina*, I, 147. Asbury called him a "man of sorrowful spirit and under constant heaviness." *Journal*, I, 364.

in your hands in all your undertakings, is the hearty prayers of the meanest of the despised *Methodists*—[43]

Edward Dromgoole was sincerely appreciative of Pettigrew's correspondence, and found excuses for the latter's failure to attend the quarterly meeting. "Now I could alledge several things to prevent your coming, and know this world we live in so well, that I am convinced, we are often crossed in those things we most desire." In reference to the "Lower Circuit" he expressed his thankfulness that Pettigrew had "made a Tour thro' those parts in the Spring. I have no doubt but the good Effects of it will be seen 'after many days.'" Dromgoole's conclusion shed a little light on the situation at Edenton and the esteem in which Pettigrew was held.

I often think of the few at Edenton, who loved the Gospel, and should be glad to hear from them, and whether they still continue in Town, and love the Word of Life. I must conclude, after begging an interest in your Prayers. I am with real love and much respect—[44]

Even Philip Bruce, who had only a "small acquaintance" with Pettigrew, corresponded with him.[45] Beverly Allen also requested the support and prayers of the clergyman. He too, however, indicated that their contacts had been entirely by letter, for he wrote: "I have long comforted myself with the hopes of seeing you face to face—And have been so often disappointed, that I am afraid to engage—"[46] In 1785 Allen went to Charleston, South Carolina, where he was ordained into the Methodist clergy, but later "fell from grace," was expelled from the Society, killed a marshall, and fled to Kentucky.[47] On the back of his last letter, Pettigrew wrote, "Alas! Poor Allen!"[48]

[43] Anthony Walke to Charles Pettigrew, Aug. 12, 1784. Pettigrew Papers, UNC. He later moved to Virginia and was reported to have gone to Philadelphia for ordination into the Episcopal clergy. Peter Singleton to Charles Pettigrew, June 10, 1788. Pettigrew Papers, N C Archives.

[44] Edward Dromgoole to Charles Pettigrew, Sept. 6, 1784. Pettigrew Papers, UNC. Dromgoole [Dromgolde] began preaching in North Carolina in 1776, moving to Virginia after 1786. In 1782 General Isaac Gregory entertained him in his home. Grissom, *Methodism in North Carolina*, I, 49-52, 102; Asbury, *Journal*, I, 340 and scattered references. He is frequently mentioned by William Ormond, Jr., in his diary; Manuscript Division, William R. Perkins Library, Duke University.

[45] Philip Bruce to Charles Pettigrew, Nov. 8, 1784. Pettigrew Papers, N C Archives. Bruce was born in 1755 near King's Mountain and served in the Revolutionary War. He was even then a Methodist preacher. Grissom, *Methodism in North Carolina*, I, 79-82, 321; mentioned in Asbury, *Journal*, I, 343.

[46] Beverly Allen to Charles Pettigrew, Nov. 17, 1784. Pettigrew Papers, UNC.

[47] Grissom, *Methodism in North Carolina*, I, 94, 98, 104, 123, 216.

[48] Beverly Allen to Charles Pettigrew, June 11, 1785. Pettigrew Papers, UNC.

Pettigrew himself desired the prayers of Francis Asbury, disappointed as he was with his lack of effectiveness in Edenton. ''I am shocked,'' he wrote, ''when I think of the command given with regard to such a Barren Tree—Pray for me that thro' the powers of divine grace I may be made to bring forth much fruit—& the happy instrument of turning many to righteousness.'' He mentioned the possibility of a trip to England for his health, when he ''would certainly wait on the good Mr Westley [Charles Wesley].'' The chief reason at this time which held Pettigrew back from taking ''a small circuit some farther to the northward,''[49] yet at the same time urged him to do so, seems to have been his health, for there are references scattered through all these letters commenting on his ailments, although except for colds or fever and ague no name is given to them. Bruce wrote of a certain mountain spring which had ''cured several of your disorder, & was Never known to fail in one case[.]''[50] Peddicord ''can rejoice that you enjoy again a measure of that distinguishing blessing health. I expect an healthy body & an holy Soul are rare.''[51] Allen called him ''one of Gods dear afflicted children'' and wished for him ''great bodily strength. . . .''[52] Pettigrew informed Asbury that he wished to go farther north ''in quest of a more healthy situation, as I am determined to leave [Edenton].''[53]

Of Pettigrew's association with the Methodists, Jarratt wrote that he had befriended them ''next to myself . . . more than any other clergyman in America. . . .'' He strongly resented Coke's comparison of the North Carolinian's effectiveness to that of a little chicken. ''Are not such things too trifling for a D.D. or L.D. or even for a B.A.'' he queried.[54]

The end of his enthusiasm for Methodism came, as it did with his correspondent Devereaux Jarratt, when in 1784 the Methodists separated from the Anglican communion and ordained clergy and chose bishops without apostolic succession. Jarratt, who had protested in 1776 against the self-ordination of some of the *''lay-preachers,''* and was indeed glad when Francis Asbury came to Virginia to reclaim ''several of the delinquents'' and retract the step, was horrified by the ultimate decision. ''And who would suppose, that, before the close of this same year [1784], *he* [Asbury] and the whole *body of*

[49] Charles Pettigrew to Francis Asbury, May 1, 1784. Pettigrew Papers, UNC. A notation on the back reads, ''A letter wrote but never sent to Mr. Asbury[.]''
[50] Philip Bruce to Charles Pettigrew, Nov. 8, 1784. Pettigrew Papers, N C Archives.
[51] Caleb Peddicord to Charles Pettigrew, April 2, 1783. Pettigrew Papers, UNC.
[52] Beverly Allen to Charles Pettigrew, Nov. 17, 1784. Pettigrew Papers, UNC.
[53] Charles Pettigrew to Francis Asbury, May 1, 1784. Pettigrew Papers, UNC.
[54] Jarratt, *Life of the Reverend Devereux Jarratt*, Appendix, p. 83.

Methodists broke off from the church, at a single stroke!"[55] Pettigrew too found himself unable to approve of this step. His Methodist friends attempted to persuade him to no avail. Beverly Allen besought him not to be angry with him for accepting ordination under the new conditions, and urged him to read "Mr. Wesleys Letter, wrote on that occation [*sic*]. [A]nd also, read Docter [*sic*] Coke's Sermon, published on the same—"[56] James H. Thomson, a schoolmaster of Charleston, defended the action by attacking the conservative Anglicans as "panting for the Lawn" and differing so much in the Liturgy of the Last Supper that "scarce a semblance of the original institution is preserved. . . ." He concluded the discussion by saying:

Let your Book of common prayer remain as it is; recommend it as an excellent formulary to be used entirely or in part at the discretion of the minister, expunge all human articles of belief, the bible is enough, for if God has not revealed himself clearly & intelligibly, I cannot conceive how man who is a worm, can give precision clearness & force to the expression; when you shall have done this, I persuade myself you will have laid a foundation broad as Christ himself has marked out; & all of his solid well informed followers would have shouted a blessing to its corner stones.[57]

Pettigrew could not accept this advice, however, in good conscience; he therefore dropped completely every connection with Methodism except toleration and remained for the duration of his life a conformist to the Anglican faith.

A combination of discouragement in his lack of success in Edenton, poor health, and financial problems led Pettigrew to consider moving to another parish. By this time he was supporting a wife and two sons, and was having a hard time making ends meet. He was informed by the S.P.G. that it would not honor his past due salary which had been unpaid during the War.[58] St. Paul's church members pledged an annual sum of £214 for "Mr. Cha.ˢ Pettigrew to perform public religious Worship & to preach on every Sunday in the Church in this Town—"[59] To judge from the notations of payments received, collecting was more difficult than pledging, so that Pettigrew was forced to add the duties of Clerk of the County in 1785-1786 for an unknown sum.[60] His friend Thomson from Charleston expressed

[55] *Ibid.*, pp. 111-119.
[56] Beverly Allen to Charles Pettigrew, June 11, 1785. Pettigrew Papers, UNC.
[57] James H. Thomson to Charles Pettigrew, Feb. 19, 1786. Pettigrew Papers, N C Archives.
[58] Reuben Harvey to Charles Pettigrew, April 4, 1784. Pettigrew Papers, UNC.
[59] Salary Subscriptions, Jan. 1, 1783. Pettigrew Papers, UNC.
[60] "Charles Pettigrew, clerk of the county of Chowan" appears in Tyrrell County Deed Book 6, p. 164, Nov. 4, 1784; and in Tyrrell County Deed Book 10, p. 59, Jan. 9, 1786. Tyrrell County Records, N C Archives. A survey of county

astonishment that he had not long since moved away. ''I beg you will remove & remove soon,'' he wrote. ''I consider your talents as not employed for the general interests so well in Edenton as the[y] probably would be elsewhere; were the people to support you decently & liberally.''[61] When, therefore he was informed by the vestry of Lynnhaven Parish at Kemps Landing [or Kempsville], Princess Anne County, Virginia that there was a vacancy, Pettigrew was anxious to secure it.

At first all seemed favorable to his appointment. Peter Singleton, one of the vestrymen, informed him on August 16, 1784, that he hoped to raise a subscription of £150. A desirable plantation was for sale. He added that ''most of the People of this County (Baptists excepted) earnestly wish to get you settled in this County.''[62] The vestry issued the official call and promised ''our late Incumbents Donation as well as the Glebe Land, both of w.ch have for some years past been Rented out, and I sincerely hope we shall have you ere long an Inhabitant of this County.''[63]

Pettigrew accepted the call. In the meantime, however, he embarked on a voyage to the West Indies to improve his health before moving to Virginia. Although he informed the Virginians that he intended such a trip, he seems to have neglected to write them precise details, so that they became uneasy about his intentions, and listened with some interest to the inquiries of other clergymen about the vacancy.[64]

Pettigrew had a satisfactory voyage and stay in Haiti. Sailing in January, 1785, he carried two slaves with him, both as attendants and as a means of raising money by selling them at the conclusion of his voyage. Phillis he found ''useful in waiting & tending'' while he was sick with a cold. The ship had to await an opportunity to cross the bar at Ocracoke, which Pettigrew improved by baptizing the children of the ''Occacockers.'' To his wife he said, ''Dont look for me till you hear We are arrived, for you need not doubt I shall be home again as soon as possible—I find myself respectfully treated on

records indicates that the clerk of the county, as distinct from the clerk of court, kept such records as tax lists, marriage license lists, lists of persons paying fines, etc.

[61] James H. Thomson to Charles Pettigrew, Feb. 19, 1786. Pettigrew Papers, N C Archives.

[62] Peter Singleton to Charles Pettigrew, Aug. 16, 1784; William White to Charles Pettigrew, Oct. 18, 1784. Pettigrew Papers, N C Archives.

[63] Peter Singleton to Charles Pettigrew, Dec. 30, 1784. Pettigrew Papers, N C Archives.

[64] John Smith to Charles Pettigrew, Jan. 10, 1785; Peter Singleton to Charles Pettigrew, March 21, 1785. Pettigrew Papers, N C Archives.

Board, by Cap. Schermerhorn & his Officers, & have a good State-Room to lodge in."[65]

After a two months' voyage he finally arrived in Haiti, where he enjoyed himself.

I am to preach in Town During my stay at the Request of the Governor & the principal gentn. by whom I find myself very politely treated. No Doubt they will make me a complimt. equal to my expences. I am invited to Dine out among them almost every Day—I find great Cause to bless God that strangers are my friends, go where I will—Living is high but I am favoured—I have taken a private lodgings upon a hill above the town which lyes on the Bay w.ch I found too sultry.[66]

Anxious though he was to recover his health, he was nevertheless concerned about the move to Princess Anne. He suggested that his wife ask one Joe Wilkins "to take George & Fortune & go to Mr. White at Kemp's Landing & I am persuaded he will set them to work planting Corn & find them till such times as I shall return & move down—"[67]

Pettigrew's letters to the vestry of Princess Anne, mailed from the West Indies, were evidently delayed in passage and left the vestry so unhappy over the situation that they decided to withdraw their call and to extend it to the Reverend James Simpson.[68] Pettigrew's adherents were extremely upset by what they regarded as a breach of faith, and so expressed themselves.[69] In his reply to the church wardens, Pettigrew was as wroth as he ever allowed himself to become.

Your Letter of y.e 6th inst.t tells me the disagreeable consequences of my not being able to comply with your Limitation respecting the Time of my removal to your parish. It found me destitute of either House or home, or ground in the County for a Crop the Cur.t Year, & using all the industry I could to get away, agreeable to my engagemt with you, which engagemt was mutual, & without Limitation as to Time, & made with this reserve on my

[65] Charles Pettigrew to Mary Blount Pettigrew, Jan. 24, 1785. Pettigrew Papers, UNC.
[66] Charles Pettigrew to Mary Blount Pettigrew, March 11, 1785. Pettigrew Papers, UNC.
[67] Ibid.
[68] Charles Williams and John Cornick to Charles Pettigrew, May 6, 1785. Pettigrew Papers, N C Archives.
[69] Singleton's letter of March 21 addressed to Edenton contained a deadline of May 1. As Pettigrew was still in Haiti as late as March 11, he must have returned to Edenton too late to move to Virginia by May 1. White wrote Pettigrew on May 7 that he had received the latter's letter of March 23 [probably from Haiti] "only last night, which was too late to be of any Service. . . ." He thoughtfully sent "Negroes George & Fortune with a Horse" back to North Carolina. Pettigrew Papers, N C Archives.

part, "that I should not remove to y.ᵉ Charge 'till I had returned from a Voyage to sea, for the Benefit of my health."—And I beg leave to observe, that I am not conscious of *such guilt*, incured by my unavoidable *noncomplyance*, as deserved *final Rejection*, after two orders of Vestry in my favour, & without anything having been alledged, whereon you could rationally found a Doubt of my integrity,—& more especially, as your Determination must necessarily subject me to many inconveniences at this season of the Year.[70]

Yet the deed was done; George and Fortune were sent home with the horse; and if it was any consolation to Pettigrew, Mr Simpson turned out to be

an improper Man to be continued in the Parish as the incumbent thereof & as he has but few hearers and have lost ground with those Friends of his that unfairly got him inducted, shou'd not be surprised if his stay shou'd be short with us, his School I conceive the only thing worth his Staying for, as his Subscription is hardly worth mentioning.[71]

By 1788 he had "resign'd his Office as Minister of this Parish and the Vestry have agreed to Induct M.ʳ Anthony Walke into the same, as soon as he obtains Letters of Ordination, which I suppose he has obtained ere this as he went some time ago to Philadelphia for that Purpose."[72]

Like it or not, Pettigrew was now committed to spending the remainder of his life in North Carolina.

[70] Charles Pettigrew to Charles Williams and John Cornick, May 9, 1785. Pettigrew Papers, N C Archives.
[71] Peter Singleton to Charles Pettigrew, April 26, 1787. Pettigrew Papers, N C Archives.
[72] Peter Singleton to Charles Pettigrew, June 10, 1788. Pettigrew Papers, N C Archives.

CHAPTER III

THE FAMILY MAN

Among the young ladies of Edenton in 1773 was Mary Blount, more familiarly known as Polly. The young James Iredell, on November 12, 1772, "met Mrs. Littlejohn & Miss Mary Blount going from Mr. Jones's." On December 9, he "Drank tea at Mr. Jones's, walked home with Mrs. Wilson Blount & Polly Blount."[1] Mary was the daughter of John and Sarah E. Vail Blount; by 1773 both of her parents were dead and she lived at Mulberry Hill with her oldest brother, James. She had two other brothers, Frederick and Wilson, and a sister, Elizabeth, who married John Beasley. Her sister-in-law, Mrs. James Blount, was formerly Ann Hall, daughter of the Reverend Clement Hall, a colonial Anglican clergyman.[2]

The Blount family was a large one in eastern North Carolina. Besides the branch in Chowan County, which was settled there as early as 1685,[3] another branch was centered around New Bern, consisting of the descendants of Jacob Blount; the best known of these in North Carolina history were William, John Gray, and Thomas, who were merchants and land speculators during the lifetime of Charles Pettigrew.[4] Members of this extensive clan held political office, both high and low, owned huge tracts of land, shipped to the West Indies and Europe, and were in general among the financial and social leaders of the day.

In 1773, when Charles Pettigrew moved to Edenton, Mary (or Polly) was twenty-five years old and unmarried. She was under the titular guardianship of her oldest brother James. Mulberry Hill, where they lived, is located about five miles from Edenton to the east. It can be reached by road, but it would have been quicker in 1773 to cross by water. A charming four story brick house, it was built by James and was a symbol of the prosperity and position of this family. The west gable of the house is noted for its fan window with a five foot radius made from one piece of wood.[5] A lawn sweeps down to Albemarle Sound; on the right a small creek permits access by boat.

[1] Diary of James Iredell. James Iredell Papers, N C Archives.
[2] Genealogy Section of Pettigrew Papers, UNC.
[3] Will of James Blount. Pettigrew Papers, UNC.
[4] *The John Gray Blount Papers*, Vol. 1, 1764-1789. Edited by Alice Barnwell Keith (Raleigh: State Department of Archives and History, 1952), pp. xiii-xxxi.
[5] *Historic Edenton and Countryside*, No. 37. The house and environs have been visited by the author.

There is a family cemetery between the house and the little creek, somewhat overgrown now but with inscriptions still legible on the stones. During the Revolution, the Blounts were great patriots; Ann Hall Blount was a signer of the Edenton Tea Party resolutions,[6] and James was named a colonel in the militia in 1775.[7] From her father, Mary inherited "one Negro wench Called Sarah and her increase," in addition to an equal share of all the profits of his estate when the oldest son reached twenty-one.[8] Mary's mother, who died in 1770, left to her eight slaves, named Venus, Sol, Fillis, Fortin [Fortune], Jim, George, Ben, and Rose;[9] a mare and saddle for her, miscellaneous silver and furniture, and all the residue of her personal estate after other bequests had been met; plus all her black cattle.[10] Mary Blount was thus something of an heiress; while the labor of her slaves and her black cattle were undoubtedly of value to her brother James, who kept a watch-dog attitude over her.

Pettigrew met Mary Blount some time between 1773 when he went to Edenton to teach school, and 1778. He must have seen her walking through town, as did James Iredell, and probably also at church, when she attended, and eventually fell in love with her. In the fashion of the 18th century, he addressed to "Miss P. B." a poem of his composition—"Fair Delia."[11]

> Fair Delia is an object sweet
> Wherein the Lovely Graces meet
> In such a group of shining charms
> As every youthful bosom warms.
> >   With melting glow
> >   Tho' cold and snow
> >   Nor can they rest
> >   While Love's warm guest!

[6] List of signers in *Historic Edenton and Countryside,* no page.

[7] *Colonial Records of North Carolina,* X, 205.

[8] Will of John Blount, Dec. 8, 1753. Chowan County Wills, p. 46. N C Archives.

[9] Fortune, George, and Ben remained for years in the possession of Mary and later of Charles Pettigrew. It was George and Fortune who were sent to Princess Anne, Virginia, to plant a crop in 1785.

[10] Will of Sarah Blount, June 6, 1769. Chowan County Wills, p. 51, N C Archives. On p. 50 is a petition by Sarah Blount dated 1756 in which she requested the sole guardianship of her children, alleging that the executors of her husband's estate were not doing their duty and that one, Charles Blount, was "pretending" that the estate actually belonged to him. The court ordered an accounting by Charles. This is an interesting example of women's legal position in the colonial period.

[11] All of the following poems are in Poetry Notebooks. Pettigrew Papers, N C Archives.

Opposition was extended by the family, as indicated by these lines of
Pettigrew's:

> What can the wretched victims do
> For tho' alas their Love is true
> She can make no return
> Tho' to ashes they burn
> Till Cupid takes their Cause in Hand. . . .

The chief objection seemed to be his lack of any financial means except
for those of a parson recently separated by the state constitution of
1776 from a permanent salary.

> These sons of folley
> Are gay & jolley
> And all their aim's my little Polley
> Both old & young
> Employ the tongue
> Nor do they fail
> With tooth & nail
> To urge what malice can invent
> To torture her with Discontent.
> Poverty with hidious Looks
> Is made to grin
> With narrow Chin
> Out from among the Parsons Books
> Now stands the frighted fair agast
> To see the Monster shew his head
> Beg[g]ing for crumbs of mouldy bread
> To break his pinching fast.

Pettigrew did not blame Polly for being afraid of poverty, but resigned himself and tried to abolish from his mind all thoughts of
marriage.

> Away ye thoughts of wed[d]ed Love
> I'm to the will of fate resign'd
> What tho' a mate I ne'er should find
> Nor e'er possess a female kind
> Yet I'll not blame th'inconstant Dove
> But still content with single life
> I'll live in Ease
> Not plagued to please
> A cross capricious wife
> Nor shall I know the thousand cares
> That ev'ry tender husband bears
> About Children & wife
> Till weary of Life
> He dies & ends the pleasing strife.

The question rose in his mind,

> O why were social passions given
> Passions so near allied to heaven
> If I must from the softer sex be driven
> If I must never share the bliss
> Sweetly to hug & toy & kiss
> A wife of my own
> Till old I am grown
> And as dead as a stone
> To every pleasure that Hymen can own.

James and Ann Hall Blount, Mary's brother and sister-in-law, sent the penurious young parson about his business. At least, some woman member of the family ordered him to seek a wife elsewhere, for Pettigrew's description of her is vitriolic.

> Her narrow pout strikes all with wonder
> But from her eyes
> The flash that flies
> Would pierce the skies
> Her Voice it imitates dire Thunder
> So her passion seems to swell
> See how her nose cocks for ye Smell
> And flush'd at the end
> Quite up to the bend
> Gives warning yourself to defend.
> Dart & run
> You son of a gun
> Good luck! how rapidly she comes
> Shewing with rage both Teeth & gums
> The Storm she outflies
> The panther outcries. . . .

The scene must indeed have been a frightening one. The Blounts had planned for Polly to marry one of her cousins, not the impecunious parson. This Pettigrew recognized, for in another poem, one line read, "O happy Blount! Is she thy bride?" while another line stated, "Yielding to B.—she must become his Wife."

He tried to turn his heart to another young lady, whose name he gave in an acrostic.

> Now let my artless pen attempt to draw
> From an Original I lately saw
> And let her *name* direct my honest Muse
> To truth—not fiction—which some Poets use.
>
> Majestic in an easy graceful mien—
> About the blooming age of seventeen.
> Refin'd her Taste—To censure not aware,

> The wise must love,—The worthless need not fear
> Her native *Ease* declares an honest Breast
> Admitting none but *Virtue* as a guest.
>
> Blest in herself—& to a parent dear
> A Mind so innocent has nought to fear.
> Kept still by guardian Angels from all harm;
> Envy, tho' cruel, never can alarm,
> Resplendent *Virtue* dress'd in ev'ry Charm.
>
> Now if to know this fair you should incline
> Spell the initial letters of each line.

It was not Martha Baker, however, but Polly Blount who became Mrs. Charles Pettigrew in 1778, in spite of her family's objections. After all, she was over twenty-one and had property of her own.

On October 29, 1778, Charles Pettigrew and Mary Blount were married.[12] She was thirty, he thirty-four. No mention is made of the living arrangements of the young couple, but from the addresses of letters to Charles Pettigrew it appears that they lived "near Edenton." John Pettigrew, their first son, was born August 2, 1779. The following day, Charles expressed his rapture "in Miltonic verse":

> A *child!* an *infant!* of what importance.
> An heir of *endless Bliss,* or *endless wo!*
> A helpless "particle of *breathing dust,*"
> In which an *angel-embryo* lies conceal'd!
>   And tho' *conceiv'd in Sin,*—in *Sin brought forth*
> Into a world of dangerous *Snares,* & *woes*
> *Innumerable,* ready to *destroy*
> A hand *unseen* still *guards* the feeble Charge.
>
>   *Angels,* sent by an indulgent *god*
> Who condescends to stile himself 'Father
> *Of spirits,'* keep their constant watch, to *save,*
> And still *defend Him* thro' *this Vale of Tears,*
> Till *recall'd* by th' eternal *Father's Love,*
> To enter on a *rich inheritance,*
> Purchas'd by the *great merit* of *his Death,*
> *Who,* tho' divine, *hung on a Cross,* & *bled,*
> To *expiate the guilt* of Adam's fall.
>
>   And when conducted to the State of *Man,*
> *Their tender Care* is still employ'd to *save*
> From *youthful Vice,* & lead into the paths
> That tend to *peace,* & *endless Happiness.*

[12] Charles Pettigrew to Mary Blount, 28 October 1778. Chowan County Marriage Bonds, p. 128, N C Archives. Ironically, the witness was James Blount, deputy clerk of court. The wedding took place the next day. Genealogy Section of Pettigrew Papers, UNC.

When *lapsed Nature,* both *impure & weak,*
Would straight obey the subtile *Tempter's Voice,*
He feels a *secret power,* still *drawing back,*
And still *inspiring* with a *sacred Awe,*
Of majesty divine.—Such is their Care,
Unless, by *vile abuse, constrained* to *leave*
Th' abandon'd *charge* within the Roaring *Lyons* pow'r.

But while he to his *guardian Angel* does
Attend, & *freely follows* when *he draws*
From flatt'ring *Vice's* fatal *snares,* in
Bright Virtue's narow [sic] *path,*—or straight obey
His *wholsome Dictates,* & his *strong impulse*
To good;—The *smiles of Heaven* attend his *steps,*
And make him happier *far,* than He would *be,*
Were all the Kingdoms of the World to *own*
Him, as their *Lord,*—give *homage to his Name,*
And *strict observance* pay his awful Nod.[13]

Some five months later Charles Pettigrew was drafted into service in the North Carolina militia, to march to South Carolina where Cornwallis was endeavoring to ''roll up'' the southern colonies and defeat General Horatio Gates. Whether it was his clerical status, his personal health, or the ''tender nature'' of Mrs. Pettigrew and the new infant can only be surmised; yet for one or more of these reasons, Pettigrew obtained a substitute and did not go. Colonel James Blount and his wife must have been extremely annoyed over what they would surely have regarded as a dereliction of duty.

In 1781 a girl was born to Charles and Mary Pettigrew but she lived only eight months. A tender elegy by her father commemorates her.

''An Eligy on the Death of a Little Daughter—5th Septr. 1782''

Wing'd wth paternal Love my tho'ts arise,
Now view my infant Angel in ye skies!
Behold her there, amidst the blessed throng.
Hark! hark! she vies in ye celestial song
Of hallelujah to the God of Love,
With the incarnate Son, & mystic Dove!
To the marriage the fair bride is come;
Her Angel-guards present her now at home,
In finest Linen, white & clean array'd,
Her spotless innocence is now display'd!

[13] August 3, 1779. Pettigrew Papers, UNC. At the end, a notation dated Oct. 16, 1783, reads: ''Transcribed from a Detach'd piece of *paper,* accidentally found among some Rubbish, *which seems to have been the Original,* from the inac[c]uracy of the writing, & the want of capitals to begin many of the Lines.''

Distinguished thus, her lovely form doth shine
With heavenly lustre, & an air divine.

My tho'ts shall henceforth often wing their flight
To greet her in those Mansions of Delight,
And still my Soul shall praise the God of Grace
For such Redemption to our lapsed Race!
That now our Infants are the ninety nine
Who no repentance need,—but grace divine
Makes all their infant pow'rs in glory shine.[14]

A second son, Ebenezer, was born March 10, 1783.[15] At this time
the little family was living "on a plantation about a mile from Edenton, N. C. on the north side of the road leading down the Albamarle
[sic] sound & just across what was then called Blounts mill."[16] Some
kind of financial arrangements had been made by this time regarding
a division of John and Sarah Blount's estate; for in a letter to his
wife while on his voyage to the West Indies in January, 1785, Pettigrew spoke of the sale of twenty barrels of corn and added, "You
need not however My Dear be under the smallest uneasiness for I
believe the Estate is very Clear—" He suggested to her that she get
a friend to buy for her pork to feed the Negroes, "for I don't love
the thought of buying Bacon for the negroes, & pork I am affraid
will not be to be purchased at any Rate. Eight hundred or a thousand
weight of pork if fit for Bacon would do." Mrs. Pettigrew's nature
must not have been too "tender" for she frequently was given business
to attend to, and on this same occasion Pettigrew remarked that he
"had forgot to make an accompt of it."[17] He also asked her to
handle the sending of two hands to Virginia to start a crop preparatory to what he hoped would be their eventual removal to Kemp's
Landing.[18] His love for her and for the two little boys is apparent
in his letters. "Be assured that you & the Children have been, and are
still much on my Heart—" he wrote from Ocracoke as they sailed
toward Haiti. He signed himself "Your ever Const. & faithful Loving
& tender Husband."[19] From Haiti he planned little gifts for his wife.
"I intend to bring you a silk exactly the Colours of the one you had
dyed & sundry pretty things besides. The silk I have chose al-

[14] Poetry Notebooks. Pettigrew Papers, N C Archives.

[15] Genealogy Section of Pettigrew Papers, UNC.

[16] Fragment of memoir by Ebenezer Pettigrew, dated 1842. Pettigrew Papers, UNC.

[17] Charles Pettigrew to Mary Blount Pettigrew, Jan. 24, 1785. Pettigrew Papers, UNC.

[18] Charles Pettigrew to Mary Blount Pettigrew, March 11, 1785. Pettigrew Papers, UNC.

[19] Charles Pettigrew to Mary Blount Pettigrew, Jan. 24, 1785. Pettigrew Papers, UNC.

ready—''[20] In March he forwarded a letter from Eustatia saying, "kiss our Dear little Boys which I will repay with Compound interest at my return—'' In a postscript he added that he had a second opportunity by another ship to send a letter. ''I would not grudge my Dear Girl should opportunity offer to write you twice every Day, for be assured you employ my happyest thought—The greatest pleasure I have enjoyed since I left you, has been in presenting you & my dear little boys together with myself at the throne of grace, & figuring to my immagination [sic] the happiness of our meeting, which must be greatly increased by this anxious & painful separation—I often anticipate the pleasing moment when I shall see you, & enjoy the mutually fond embrace.''[21]

Balked of his attempt to move to Virginia, Pettigrew finally, in February 1786, moved his entire family to Harvey's Neck in Perquimans County, to a plantation named Belgrade.[22] It does not appear that he purchased it, but rented from some one, perhaps one of the Harveys. Belgrade was located on the western shores of the Perquimans River looking across the wide waters of the great estuary to the distant shore line.[23] Here were Pettigrew's Quaker friends; here he had preached during the war years when he had Daniel Earl's parishes; here he had influential friends among the sons of the patriot John Harvey. Perhaps here he could find happiness. Some glimpse of his inferior status in the eyes of the Blounts while he lived in Edenton is reflected obliquely in a parenthetical remark to a friend, "for I could not live there any longer.''[24] When the traveller Charles William Janson was in Edenton in the 1790's, he was told that the inhabitants had "driven their minister away," and that "The baptism and the burial service are dispensed with.''[25] At the time of the move to Perquimans, Mrs. Pettigrew was pregnant and the move caused the premature birth of twins, who died. Eleven days later Mary Pettigrew also died. Recorded in the family Bible is the following:

[20] Charles Pettigrew to Mary Blount Pettigrew, March 11, 1785. Pettigrew Papers, UNC.

[21] Charles Pettigrew to Mary Blount Pettigrew, from Eustatia [Eustatius Island], March 11, 1785. Pettigrew Papers, UNC.

[22] Fragment of memoir by Ebenezer Pettigrew, dated 1842. Pettigrew Papers, UNC.

[23] Price and Strother Map, 1808. William P. Cumming, North Carolina in Maps (Raleigh: State Department of Archives and History, 1966), Plate IX.

[24] Notation dated March 1786 on the back of a letter from James Thomson to Charles Pettigrew, Feb. 19, 1786. Pettigrew Papers, N C Archives.

[25] Charles William Janson, The Stranger in America, 1793-1806 (Reprinted from the London Edition of 1807 with an introduction and note by Carl S. Driver. New York: The Press of the Pioneers, 1935), p. 104. Hereinafter cited as Janson, The Stranger in America.

Mary Pettigrew, one of the most worthy of her sex, departed this life on the 16th March, 1786—and was laid in one tomb with her twins.

> With modest lustre all her goodness shone,
> The wife, the mother was excelled by none;
> Was lov'd thro life, lamented in her end.
> O Tomb! much honoured, keep thy three fold Trust!
> Till the last Trump demand their precious Dust.[26]

Pettigrew wrote two days later:

Yours of 19th Feb. I recd. 2 Days ago—It found me at the House of Mourning, & incapable of comfort from any thing of a temporal Nature. I had just accompanied the breathless remains of my dear, dear, dear companion to the House appointed for all living at an old burying ground where she now sleeps w.th her fathers—She died the 10th Day after being delivered of twins whose birth was premature. . . . The fevers so incident to the Climate had in the run of 18 months past much impaired her strength so that on taking violent cold on my removing out of Edenton to a House a good deal out of repair . . . she was taken with a kind of pluracy, & her fever was such that 7 Blisters could not break it—[27]

Wilson Blount[28] wrote to his brother-in-law from New Bern where he then lived, expressing to him:

the distress I feal on this unhappy event. I have been for this long time coming to Edenton, for a visit, for no other purpose but to see my friends there. . . . I have always understood she was happy as to her situation in life, & of y.r kindness & attention to her, which affords me great Consolation for which I shall always consider myself under every tie of friendship & respect to you.

He regretted that he had never met Pettigrew, but would be glad to take care of his "daughter" should he care to commit her to the care of her aunt and uncle.[29] Peter Singleton received a copy of the epitaph & also an "Eligy" on "The Death of a Lady." He sent his

[26] Genealogy Section of Pettigrew Papers, UNC.

[27] Notation dated March 1786 on the back of a letter from James Thomson to Charles Pettigrew, Feb. 19, 1786. Pettigrew Papers, N C Archives.

[28] According to his father's will, Wilson Blount was to be reared by his aunt, Mrs. Mary Moor. He was already married in 1772, as indicated by James Iredell's diary. Some time before 1778 he moved to New Bern, from where in 1782 James Iredell wrote an unflattering comment to his wife: that Wilson Blount went to Charleston with a group under flag of truce "upon some frivolous pretext or other, but no doubt to purchase goods. Too much of this trade, I fear, is carrying on." Quoted in McRee, *Iredell*, II, 27. Later on he seems to have helped his nephew John Beasley attend medical school in Philadelphia, but to have become involved in some sort of financial imbroglio over the Beasley estate. He had no children. Pettigrew Papers, *passim*.

[29] Wilson Blount to Charles Pettigrew, April 25, 1786. Pettigrew Papers, UNC.

condolences from Virginia "on the loss of so valuable a Partner, and doubt not your affliction must have been great." Continuing with advice, he encouraged Pettigrew to bear his loss:

... but as I am writing to a Divine & a man who's Prudence & Rectitude I have a great opinion of, it wou'd be but waste of time, to recommend resignation &c.ᵃ, for sure I am You'll say, as did good old Eli, it is the Lord, let him do what seemeth to him good, and I am really pleased that you must no doubt often have the pleasing Reflections, that each had assisted the other in the mutual duty of Husband & Wife in striving together for your Spiritual & temporal welfare, w.ᶜʰ made your love perfect & gave that Worthy Lady a right, as a good Christian, to cry out w.ᵗʰ her last breath "Lord Jesus, receive my Spirit."[30]

William White wrote to Pettigrew at the same time, to whom the latter replied with thanks and appreciation. "Yet while I mourn my loss, I bless the indulgent father of Spirits, who hath called her home, I trust, to one of those many mansions where *Peace, & Love, harmony & uninterrupted* Joy *eternally* reign." Although these Virginia friends pressed him to visit them for a change of scene, he declined, feeling "too much abash'd, on a recollection, of my being reprobated by the Vestry."[31]

Left a widower with two small boys, one aged seven and the other not quite three, Pettigrew considered moving to Georgia, "as a climate better suited to a weak & debelitated Constitution as the weather is undoubtedly less variable from its proximity to the Tropics . . . Yet tho' alas, I am not doing much good—I wish to live on acc.ᵗ of my Children—"[32] He also toyed with the idea of moving to Tennessee, then still a part of North Carolina, as many Carolinians were doing. Hardy Murfree, the Revolutionary patriot, who eventually did just that himself, gave Pettigrew letters of introduction to several of his friends in that new country: Colonel Anthony Croutcher, Colonel James Robertson, and Colonel Anthony Bledsoe.[33] He did neither of these, however, but remained for two years at Belgrade before reaching any decision.

He finally determined, in January 1789, to "settle some of my Land on Lake Phelps in Tyrrell. . . . I think of moving over the

[30] Peter Singleton to Charles Pettigrew, April 26, 1787. Pettigrew Papers, N C Archives.
[31] Charles Pettigrew to William White, July 3, 1787. Pettigrew Papers, N C Archives. The fact that two letters of such different dates as this and the preceding one of April 26 arrived at the same time comments on the informality of mail delivery.
[32] Notation dated March 1786 on back of a letter from James Thomson to Charles Pettigrew, Feb. 19, 1786. Pettigrew Papers, N C Archives.
[33] Hardy Murfree to Charles Pettigrew with enclosures, May 9, 1787. Pettigrew Papers, UNC.

ensuing summer or fall, to live at the Canal," he wrote to Henry Pattillo.[34] This he did in the fall,[35] taking Jackie and Ebenezer with him to live on his own land and supervise personally the farming. Tyrrell County lay in a different world from that of Edenton. Sparsely populated and dotted with swamps, it was the habitation of "bears, wolves, panthers, wild deer, rattlesnakes, moccasins, black snakes, horse racers, mosquitoes, bullfrogs," and lesser degrees of annoyances and dangers.[36] An English traveller in 1786 recounted a night spent in the region:

What with the noise of bullfrogs and common frogs, the cry of panthers in the woods, and the chattering of Negroes in their quarters, besides the continual scampering of large rats about the room and across Le Jeune's bed, joined to the intense heat of the weather, there was no possibility of sleeping.[37]

Richard Haughton, who surveyed and explored the area in 1787, wrote a description of it in his diary. Many fine trees grew there, such as cypress and juniper, which made excellent shingles; poplar, chestnut, oak, black gum, sweet gum, "pappa," and maple. Some of the trees were from four to seven feet in diameter. In the swamps grew "very high thick reeds."[38] In the thick darkness of the woods at night, the lightning bugs "were just like so many burning candles."[39] In the swamplands great fires would burn for weeks, eating out the decayed vegetable matter from beneath the surface and causing the unwary to break through. Ebenezer Pettigrew described an 1806 fire:

. . . burning over the whole face of the earth & in some places trees of 2 & 3 feet diameter up by the roots in others every bush reed & stick smooth leaving but few trees of any kind standing, the juniper swamps it is said are entirely ruined. In them it has burned the trees down & then burned them up, so that they are quite clean—At one time there was so much smoke in the atmosphere that it was disagreeable to the eyes even in the house.[40]

It was such fires as these which, so Edmund Ruffin believed, left

[34] Charles Pettigrew to Henry Pattillo, Jan. 9, 1789. Pettigrew Papers, UNC.
[35] In the Fragment of a Memoir, 1842, Ebenezer Pettigrew recalled the date as November, 1788. However, several letters written by Charles dated November 9, 1789, relating to church matters, are headed "Perquimans" which was the county in which Harvey's Neck was located. The 1789 date has been accepted as the correct one.
[36] Hunter, *Quebec to Carolina*, p. 270.
[37] *Ibid.*, p. 273.
[38] Lake Company Papers. Josiah Collins Papers, N C Archives.
[39] Hunter, *Quebec to Carolina*, p. 274.
[40] Ebenezer Pettigrew to James Iredell, Jr., April 18, 1806. Pettigrew Papers, N C Archives.

great hollows in the earth into which the water drained and created Lake Phelps [Scuppernong], Lake Pungo, and north of Edenton, Lake Drummond in the Great Dismal Swamp. The water of Lake Phelps was slightly colored, but that of Lake Drummond was the hue of madeira wine. Groves of "black laurel" added a wild beauty to the scene.[41] Through the swamps ran the Alligator [spelled Aligator in the 18th century] and Scuppernong Rivers, which provided the chief transportation of the region. Sailboats were the ferries from Edenton to the southern shore, where a plantation or an inn was the terminus; "canoes" were smaller, private conveyances; carts carried the unloaded passengers and goods over execrable roads to their destination. Robert Hunter required four hours to sail from Edenton to Mackay's Tavern, a distance of fifteen miles; when proceeding farther by land, he climbed on the shoulders of a slave to get through the swamps. From Mackay's Tavern the next day he rowed in a canoe for four hours to travel thirteen miles to meet the "stage waggon."[42] Among the authorized public ferries were those operated by Clement and Sarah Crooke and James Wood from Plymouth to Edenton, Lockhart's, Ryan's, and Thomlinson's [sic] landings.[43] So difficult was travel in Tyrrell County that in 1789 a number of inhabitants petitioned the North Carolina legislature for permission to vote other than at the courthouse, because of "many of them having to go by water the distance of sixty miles, and others who travel by land have very broad waters to ferry over, are often prevented by bad weather and contrary winds, by reason of which they are deprived of their suffrage." The Assembly granted three additional polling places.[44] In 1792, it was deemed necessary to require ferries to carry passengers free on court and election days.[45] An 1802 petition for a road in Tyrrell County pointed out that persons travelling by horse & carriage to Plymouth to court had to cross petitioner's farm and take down the fences to pass through. The petitioner requested a road which would "head several large swamps which are Dangerous to travil in frosty weather" instead of traversing his farm.[46] Another petition sought to lay out a "footpath" to

[41] Edmund Ruffin, *Sketches of Lower North Carolina and the Similar Adjacent Lands* (Raleigh: The Institution for the Deaf and Dumb and the Blind, 1861), pp. 194-198, 233-237.

[42] Hunter, *Quebec to Carolina*, pp. 268-270.

[43] Ferry Papers, Oct. 7, 1790. Tyrrell County Records, N C Archives. A performance bond of £500 was required.

[44] *State Records of North Carolina*, XXV (Chapter IX of Laws of North Carolina, 1789), p. 11.

[45] *Laws of North Carolina*, 1792, Chapter LXVII.

[46] Road Papers for 1802. Tyrrell County Records, N C Archives.

Gum Neck from the Grape Vine Landing.[47] Charles William Janson saw an alligator in 1798 on the Alligator River. "It was of the same species as the crocodile of Egypt, from which it differed very little."[48] Summer squalls and occasionally a hurricane further added to the dangers of crossing the Sound and of farming in the region. Janson, in describing the culture of corn, wrote:

In the middle of summer, when the stalk has attained its full height . . . a storm of wind and rain, accompanied perhaps by hailstones as large as marbles, will sometimes lay waste the fields in particular directions for many miles. The people call these unseasonable and destructive storms, summer gusts, or summer squalls; but they are generally whirlwinds, with deluges of rain. In the Carolinas . . . these are more frequent, and about once in five or seven years a dreadful hurricane, similar to those of the West-Indies, totally destroys the grain, tears up the loftiest trees, drives the ships from their anchors, and carries them often a great distance into the woods, or on the beach, destroying the unfortunate mariners.[49]

Charles Pettigrew experienced a destructive storm in the early fall of 1795, which "has destroyed I verily believe, on the most moderate calculation, one half of the corn in this lower part of the County . . . but with me, I think it has taken nearly 2/3ds."[50] A terrible storm on April 10, 1789, wrecked a number of ships off Roanoke Island.[51]

Some of Pettigrew's Edenton friends—Josiah Collins, Nathaniel Allen, and Dr. Samuel Dickinson—who had formed the Lake Company to drain and develop the swamplands, desired the minister for their neighbor and persuaded him to move to Tyrrell County, which was devoid of an Episcopal cleric. In May, 1789, they promised him equal use of the canal which they had dug to connect Lake Phelps with the Scuppernong River, "as an Inducement for him to become a neighbor."[52] The following November the Pettigrews, father and sons, moved. Little Ebenezer remembered it thus:

. . . my father took his effects in two small vessils & went over to the mouth of Scuppernong river, where his things were taken out the vessils & put in the court house which was on the plantation of Benjamin Spruill who then kept the tavern for the court house. . . . On the sunday evening after we had arrived I suppose on the latter part of the week, my father with his sons & the old lady who kept house for him, together with a few servants with his effects in carts set out for a place which he had rented from William Little-

[47] Road Papers, Jan. 27, 1808. Tyrrell County Records, N C Archives.
[48] Janson, *The Stranger in America*, p. 314.
[49] *Ibid.*, p. 412.
[50] Charles Pettigrew to John Pettigrew, Sept. 19, 1795. Pettigrew Papers, UNC.
[51] *The State Gazette of North Carolina* (Edenton, N. C.), April 23, 1789.
[52] Tyrrell County Land Deeds, Book 10, pp. 343-344; May 7, 1789. N C Archives.

john of Edenton & about five miles from the mouth of the Run to take up
our abode, but when we arrived, the house was without a window shutter
(glass it never had) and a thunder squall rising he thought best to turn
back to a house for shelter we had passed nearest where we were, the owner
called Levi Rowe, at which house we remained, that is myself & brother
about two months. Here I will remark my recollections & feeling at arriving
at the Littlejohn house. An old hip roofed house without door or window
shutter, in the midst of an old field without a fence around it, with a number
of cattle feeding in it (for there was great range near by) with their bells
ringing together with the thunder at intervals and my anxiety from fear of
the squall, produced in me a feeling that no time can obliterate. In a strange
land and knowing no human being but those who came with me. I have never
since heard a cow bell in an old field or gloomy woods that it did not bring
back to my recollections in a most vivid degree the Littlejohn old field & all
its horrors.[53]

By the next June, however, the Pettigrews were in a house overlooking
Lake Phelps. Here for a while the father found peace. Writing to
a fellow Episcopalian, he described the scene.

Where I am seated before the Door of my Cottage, three beautiful Holleys
defend me from the rays of the sun with their grateful shade, and at the
same time as Ever-greens furnish a fit Emblem of the permanency of *pure
friendship,* . . . let us wait with resignation for the call of Heaven, to join
our *dear departed friends,* no more again to feel the pang of separation
forever.

In this abstracted situation, the surrounding scene is truely romantic
& beautiful while I enjoy the gentle Breezes, which are so grateful to res-
peration [*sic*]. On my right is the Lake, which gives an extensive prospect,
& presents me with a fine southern & western Horizon over the tops of a
circular streak of woods, apparently much diminished by distance. To this a
hazyness in the atmosphere may contribute in a certain degree. —A vast
plain of water fills the intermediate space; which, in respect to the time, &
the manner of its formation into so large & beautiful a Reservoir, must ever
be a subject of conjecture only, as neither tradition nor history afford any
assistance to the curious enquirer.

On my left, the Scene is agreeabl[y] reversed. The trees are luxuriantly
tall & shady, being dressed in a foliage of the richest verdure, while the
fertile field, which lies extended along the verge of the Lake eastward, ex-
hibits the vegetative power of nature in such a degree as arrests the attentive Eye from every other terrestrial object. And shall it not thence be
elevated to the God of nature, accompanyed with an aspiration of grateful
praise?[54]

All was not perfect, however, even to Pettigrew. He confessed
that "Although the soil is uncommonly fertile, 'though the Lake

[53] Fragment of memoir by Ebenezer Pettigrew, dated 1842. Pettigrew
Papers, UNC.
[54] Charles Pettigrew to John Leigh, June 29, 1790. Pettigrew Papers, N C
Archives.

affords a beautiful prospect, & is an unfailing source to overflow our
Rice-Lands, . . . yet when warmed by the genial heat of the Sun in
summer, it is rendered so prolific of flies & insects of every species,
that it becomes intollerable to horses & horned cattle."[55]
    Still restless and unable to settle on his future, Pettigrew moved
back to Edenton some time before May, 1792. He told his friend
Henry Pattillo:

> I am returned from my Farm at the Lake, & resident in Edenton. They
> have contributed an annual provision for my Life or During my stay among
> them. I would prefer the farmer's Life, but when on the farm, I found my
> attention wholely engross'd, so that it became necessary that I should either
> quit the farm or the pulpit; For I found it impracticable to serve both God
> & Mamon [sic].[56]

    Edenton had grown to a population of some 1,200, almost double
its size of 1773 when Pettigrew went there for the first time. The
English traveller Robert Hunter thought the houses

> very indifferent and all built of wood. The streets I believe have been
> regularly laid out but are rendered irregular from the straggling of the
> houses. . . . They have a noble ropewalk here, which was built before the
> war. Their prison is very indifferent; they are going to build a new one.
> Paper money passes in North Carolina as well as hard cash. . . .[57]

    Mr. Butler's warehouse had burned in 1789; public opinion decided
that the wooden structures were too dangerous and a fire company
was needed.[58] Consequently, the year before Pettigrew returned, a
number of solid citizens such as Josiah Collins, Nathaniel Allen,
Samuel Dickinson, William Littlejohn, Thomas Iredell, to mention
some of the most familiar names, had incorporated a fire company.[59]
Society had roughened somewhat in this once elegant little sea-port;
the critical visitor Janson told of one Thomas Penrise of Edenton
who, detected cheating some sailors at cards, in the ensuing scuffle
"gouged out three eyes, bit off an ear, tore a few cheeks, and made
good his retreat." A group of three ruffians beat up a schoolmaster,
for which "a Carolina court of justice amerced them in a small fine
only."[60]
    Back in the midst of this society, only 48 years old, eligible, Petti-
grew met Mary Lockhart of Scotch Hall in Bertie County, across the
creek from Edenton, and began to court her. Mary's father, a Scots-

---

[55] Ibid.
[56] Charles Pettigrew to Henry Pattillo, May 12, 1792. Pettigrew Papers, UNC.
[57] Hunter, Quebec to Carolina, pp. 265, 267.
[58] The State Gazette of North Carolina, Dec. 10, 1789.
[59] Laws of North Carolina, 1791, Chapter LX, p. 28.
[60] Janson, The Stranger in America, p. 309.

man, had died in 1753; her mother, the sister of General Alexander Lillington of Revolutionary fame, raised the family until all the children were grown and married except Mary. The mother and daughter were living together in Bertie in 1792 on a plantation of 200 acres cared for by ten slaves. They had also taken into their household a Mrs. Pambrun, a penurious widow, who remained with Mary Lockhart for many years as a sort of pensioner.[61] Although there is no record of the initial meeting of Pettigrew and Miss Lockhart, by the fall of 1793 they were considering marriage and he was assisting her with business. In a letter written while he was returning from a trip to Tarboro, he addressed her as "My dear Girl," and described some land which he had viewed for her. He told the owner that he regarded the price as

very extravagant, considering the circumstances in which it stood, & that if I purchased, it would be for you,—that you would be obliged to rent it annually from your Mother—and that it was not improbable that she might outlive us all, at the same time, adding a prayer for the long continuation of her Life, telling him that I expected she would surpass a hundred. I also observed that if you married, the addition of a Dozen of hands [slaves] more, would soon render the purchase very dear to anyone else who might purchase it.

He had met some of her friends in Tarboro, who were very cordial toward him, but no more so "than your Bertie friends towards me." He concluded:

I cannot tell when I shall have the pleasure to see you, but as soon as I can—I am not very well today—but must preach at Col. Mackeys fun.[1] on my way to the Lake.

God almighty bless & direct both *you* & me! With every sentiment of the truest esteem and regard I am My dear Girl. . . .[62]

A few weeks later Mrs. Sally Clements of Tarboro wrote her good friend "Miss Polly" that she had heard "that you are shortly to enter into Hymens bands If that is the case I wish you all the happiness this life can afford you I hear It is to M.r Petigrew [sic] I think

[61] Genealogy Section of Pettigrew Papers, UNC; Alexander Lillington to Elizabeth Lockhart, Dec. 12, 1779, Pettigrew Papers, N C Archives; Elizabeth Lockhart Appointed Guardian, April 27, 1756, Pettigrew Papers, UNC; Bertie County List of Taxables, 1788-1793, N C Archives; Rebecca Barnes to Mary Lockhart, Aug. 6, 1792, Pettigrew Papers, N C Archives [postscript: "give my love to Mrs Pamboune Mr Turner tells me she is at scotch H"]; Deposition of Mary Lockhart Pettigrew circa 1819, Pettigrew Papers, UNC ["Elizabeth Pembrun lived many years in and about Edenton in a state of Widowhood and departed this life within a few years past—"]. The State Historical Marker for Scotch Hall in Bertie County indicates a house built in 1838, not the residence of the Lockharts.

[62] Charles Pettigrew to Mary Lockhart, Oct. 6, 1793. Pettigrew Papers, UNC.

you will be happy for he is [a] good man[.]''[63] It may be that the couple were considering a move, for Mary Lockhart's nephew, Thomas Barnes, informed her that

It has been quite out of my power to go to Franklin agreeable to my promise to see about the Land you was anxious to know of, but from the best information I can gather it would by no means answer your purpose. There is not above two hundred acres & that but of a very indifferant quality.[64]

The exact date of the marriage of Charles Pettigrew and Mary Lockhart is not known. No marriage bond has been located, and although a copy of the family Bible gives the date of June 12, 1794, there has been an erasure. However, in April 1795, Pettigrew wrote to Mrs. Mary Pettigrew in Bertie;[65] they were then married and were living at Scotch Hall together with the elderly Mrs. Lockhart, Mrs. Pambrun, and the two Pettigrew boys.

This was apparently a happy marriage. Although Pettigrew was fifty and his bride forty-eight, and although his letters to her do not express the youthful love of his earlier marriage, nevertheless there was a deep and abiding love between them. He wrote to her frequently while on journeys. In one letter he said: ''It seems late in the Day for you & me to write love-letters to one another—I must however send you one. . . .'' He then described a little boy, ''stout, ruddy & heavy,'' adding, ''I almost wish when I look at him, that I were his father, & you his Mother. But it is I hope best as it is. I am contented to have no more, as it will be Easier for you not to have any.''[66] He signed himself ''yours inalterably.''[67] To his sister Mrs. Mary Verner, he wrote in 1800: ''She is a great oconomist & an excellent wife.''[68] A clerical friend, in response to a letter from Pettigrew, replied: ''. . . it gave me the Sincerest pleasure to hear how happy you have been in your Selection of a companion for your

[63] Sally Clements to Mary Lockhart, Dec. 12, 1793. Pettigrew Papers, N C Archives. Mrs. Clements was the wife of William Clements who served as secretary to the Episcopal diocesan conventions held in Tarboro, 1790-1794; see William Clements to Charles Pettigrew, Sept. 13, 1794. Pettigrew Papers, N C Archives.

[64] Thomas Barnes to Mary Lockhart, April 13, 1794. Pettigrew Papers, UNC.

[65] June 12, 1794, is probably correct; although Samuel A'Court Ashe, ed., *Biographical History of North Carolina* (Greensboro: Charles L. Van Noppen, Pub., 1908, 8 vols.), VI, 399, gives the date as 1795, this is obviously erroneous. For 1794, see Genealogy Section and Charles Pettigrew to Mary Lockhart Pettigrew, April 8, 1795. Pettigrew Papers, UNC.

[66] Charles Pettigrew to Mary Lockhart Pettigrew, July 8, 1795. Pettigrew Papers, UNC.

[67] Charles Pettigrew to Mary Lockhart Pettigrew, Aug. 29, 1795. Pettigrew Papers, UNC.

[68] Charles Pettigrew to Mary Verner, May 26, 1800. Pettigrew Papers, UNC.

remaining days on earth. . . ."[69] He praised her highly to his two sons:

In respect to the conduct which I wish you to observe towards your mother, it is proper to observe, that it will always be no less your interest than your duty, to pay her every attention that would be proper and becoming to an own mother. To this she has a just claim, for sundry weighty reasons; as,

1st. Because she has treated *me*, your *father;* with every attention which might have a tendency to augment or increase a felicity which I have enjoyed in my union with her almost without jar or interruption; and, in a word, has in all respects been every thing that I could have wished or desired in a wife. May you have as much to say with equal truth, when you shall have been as long married, as I have been to her!

She has spirit, without which, no woman was ever good for any thing; she has also a considerable share of discernment, so that an impropriety of conduct towards her would be sure to be noticed, and perhaps excite a proper degree of resentment on her part. I must therefore, as a father who loves you, and wishes above all things else of a temporal nature, to promote your interest and happiness, request that you will observe the exactest propriety in your deportment towards her; that you will at all times, observe the strictest decorum, and that upon all occasions you will be kind and obliging. She is very capable of advising you in your affairs, no less so than myself, who have a thousand times been advised by *her,* and I now beg that you will attend to her *directions,* as to the wise counsels of a parent. To such attention from you she is, in the second place, entitled—

Because ever since she has been my wife she has been your mother also, not in *law only,* but in the exercise of an unwearied attention to what she thought would promote your interest, or rational gratification; indeed I have often been prompted by her in matters of indulgence towards you both. Then forget not to exercise the same tender care and indulgence towards her, in her disconsolate and widowed state, when I shall be no more to comfort her.[70]

When away, he remembered the homely little necessities, such as purchasing a piece of linen or some salt, and repaying Mrs. Rombough's hospitality with "a Barrel of Cyder" sent over by canoe from Scotch Hall to Edenton.[71] Playfully he remarked that "even homeliness puts on the form of comelyness, if not of beauty itself, by growing familiar to us—This I dare say you can attest from

[69] Robert Johnston Miller to Charles Pettigrew, May 6, 1795. Pettigrew Papers, N C Archives.
[70] "Last Advice of the Rev. Charles Pettigrew to His Sons, 1797" (printed pamphlet, 12 pp.), pp. 6-7. Pettigrew Papers, N C Archives. Hereinafter cited as "Last Advice to His Sons, 1797."
[71] Charles Pettigrew to Mary Lockhart Pettigrew, April 8, 1795. Pettigrew Papers, UNC.

experience, & our long acquaintance prior to our happy union—"[72] In turn, Mrs. Pettigrew was kind to the boys, giving each a filly to be trained as a riding horse,[73] and sending Anthony out to gather walnuts for a special treat upon the boys' return from college.[74] His sons, fifteen and eleven when they acquired their step-mother, were taught to call her Mother. He was still forgetful; he forgot to leave his tax lists, and he forgot his umbrella; his wife took care of the first matter, and Mrs. Horniblow of the second.[75]

The education of his sons was a matter of concern to Pettigrew. While he probably taught them himself for the first years, since he had been a schoolmaster, in 1793 they attended the school of Lemuel Lewis, presumably in Edenton.[76] By the spring of 1794, however, he had decided to send both of them to the new University of North Carolina at Chapel Hill,[77] of which he was a trustee.[78] A year later, in March of 1795, he set out on the trip to Chapel Hill with both boys. After a cold journey of over one hundred miles, he settled his sons and returned to Scotch Hall.[79]

The correspondence between John and Ebenezer, on the one hand, and their father on the other presents an excellent picture of education during the early days of the University. The college year was divided into two terms, one of which began in January and ran until mid-July, with one week's vacation at that time; and the other a fall term, from August until December 15. The boys did not usually come home for the short vacation, but were sometimes sent for without regard to the college calendar. Usually a slave went for them with a cart or a double chair in order to bring back their belongings; sometimes also, Pettigrew returned with them. In both 1795 and 1796 he went up to see them in July at the term's end, in spite of the heat

[72] Charles Pettigrew to Mary Lockhart Pettigrew, July 8, 1795. Pettigrew Papers, UNC.

[73] Charles Pettigrew to John Pettigrew, Sept. 19, 1795. Pettigrew Papers, UNC.

[74] Charles Pettigrew to John Pettigrew, Oct. 8, 1797. Pettigrew Papers, UNC.

[75] Charles Pettigrew to Mary Lockhart Pettigrew, Aug. 29, 1795. Pettigrew Papers, UNC.

[76] Receipt for tuition, Dec. 19, 1793. Pettigrew Papers, UNC. The charge was £9 for two sons for 6½ months.

[77] Charles Pettigrew to Dr. Andrew Knox, April 22, 1794. Pettigrew Papers, UNC. It should be noted that this decision was reached just prior to his second marriage.

[78] See below, Chapter VI, for a discussion of his election and tenure.

[79] Charles Pettigrew to Mary Lockhart Pettigrew, March 15, 1795. Pettigrew Papers, UNC. In describing the weather, he wrote: "We have stood the Cold to admiration hither to. . . . The flax, you may rely on it, is entirely cut off by the frost; for I never saw it freeze much harder."

and the likelihood of fever and ague from becoming overtired. Judging from the boys' requests for books, for clothes, for new shoes, and for money, a servant must have been kept busy going back and forth between Edenton and Orange County. Examinations were quarterly, with trustees invited to attend and join in the questioning, an exercise which General William R. Davie faithfully attended, while Pettigrew was present once and perhaps twice.

The first few months of their residence, John and Ebenezer lived in the home of a Mr. and Mrs. Kimbel; but the Kimbels soon decided to move to Kentucky and the boys had to move into a room at the college, supplying their own beds. In the winter of 1796 their room was given to someone else and they had to move in with four other boys, two "sober young men" and two small boys.[80] The only other room vacant accommodated eight and John and Ebenezer preferred not to be so crowded. The "Chinces or what we call Sabines" were extremely numerous, so much so that John was compelled to set the table legs in water "by which means I escape them as they are in general bad swimmers."[81] Complaints about the college food were also voiced. John did not think the bread "near as good as Fillis bakes for herself to eat; it is impossible to discribe [sic] the badness of the tea and coffee, & the meat generally stinks, & has maggots in it."[82] On another occasion, John reported that the steward had provided so poorly that "the Trustees gave him a severe overhall, and I believe threatened him severely."[83]

The course of study was classical. Both boys took Latin and grammar to begin with. They had "a great many of the notes to learn, and the rules to pars which makes it midling difficult."[84] "Cornelius nepos" was their first Latin book, followed by Sallust and Caesar. The following year, the Latin continued, but when the others studied French, the Pettigrews took Greek.[85] During their last year, arithmetic and geography were added; the geography text

[80] John Pettigrew to Charles Pettigrew, April 5, 1795; May 4, 1795; April 12, 1796. Pettigrew Papers, UNC. John's letters were very detailed and have been frequently quoted.
[81] John Pettigrew to Charles Pettigrew, June 27, 1797. Pettigrew Papers, UNC.
[82] John Pettigrew to Charles Pettigrew, Oct. 3, 1795. Pettigrew Papers, UNC. On Feb. 23, 1796 he wrote that the food was so poor that "we shall have to get in hollow trees, & do as the *bears* do. . . ."
[83] John Pettigrew to Charles Pettigrew, June 27, 1797. Pettigrew Papers, UNC.
[84] John Pettigrew to Charles Pettigrew, April 5, 1795, Pettigrew Papers, UNC.
[85] John Pettigrew to Charles Pettigrew, Feb. 23, 1796. Pettigrew Papers, UNC. Delano taught Latin, but Ker and Holmes taught Greek.

was Morse's *American Geography*.[86] John gave his father the daily schedule:

> . . . before sunrise in the morning we have to attend prayers and study untill eight, & then eat brakefast and go in again at nine, study untill twelve, we dine and go in at two, we study untill five, then we have nothing appointed for us to do untill next morning; on Sunday we have prayrs in the morning as usual at twelve we have a Sermon red, and at four we are questioned uppon religius questions.[87]

By 1797, some 100 students were enrolled. This meant an increase in pranks and other student body problems. One letter from John reported that:

> . . . one of the students was banished; it was for going to a cotten [*sic*] picking after eight at knight; he with some others, had left the Colledge before, after eight, & received private admonition by the Faculty; after that two of them went to this cotten picking.[88]

"Cursing & swearing . . . even from the smallest to the largest" increased, and Tom Paine's *Age of Reason* became the favorite book.

> They prefer it to all the books that were ever wrote since the creation of the World; they also say that he was sent into the World to set menkind to liberty; but I would not have you think that they are all of this opinion but there are a great majority of this cast.[89]

Each letter from the father to his sons contained some advice. They were urged to be good examples to their roommates.

> You certainly have had superior Opportunities to acquire the *knowledge of your duty*, both in a *civil* & a *religious* point of view. Let it be seen in your behavior,—& don't disgrace your *father*, & render abortive the pains he has taken to make you useful, *praiseworthy* & immitable characters. Above all things, as there are so many of you in the same Room, beware of differing among yourselves. This would be very disgraceful[.] Quarrels generally begin about the merest trifles. Permit me therefore to hope you will not be *triflers*, but men in respect to close application to your studies,—men—In prudence,—men in patience & christian benevolence towards one another—
> Endeavor to be at all times superior to such *little resentments*, as are generally excited in *little minds*, by the *indiscretions* of such as are not happy enough to *know any better*, & are indeed objects of *pity* rather than of *resentment*. [torn] any one can be rude & unmannerly, teach him better

---

[86] John Pettigrew to Charles Pettigrew, March 22, 1797. Pettigrew Papers, UNC.

[87] John Pettigrew to Charles Pettigrew, May 4, 1795. Pettigrew Papers, UNC.

[88] John Pettigrew to Charles Pettigrew, Oct. 3, 1795. Pettigrew Papers, UNC.

[89] John Pettigrew to Charles Pettigrew, April 12, 1796. Pettigrew Papers, UNC.

behaviour by your Example of decency & moderation, & he will be ashamed
& reform.[90]

On another occasion he urged John to set a good example for Ebenezer:

I hope you will not be behind him in any thing which may have a final
tendency to make you both useful & respectable in whatever station a wise
& unerring providence may place you—The time of Life is but short, &
youth is the season for improvement, improve therefore every moment, in
its hasty flight, to the acquision [*sic*] of useful knowledge.[91]

When Pettigrew thought John had spent money at a tavern, he
chastised him.

I think it by no means reputable, for Students to be found in public houses,
unless in Cases of *necessity*. And I hope you do not go for the sake of
Company, particularly the company of such of your fellow students as
may have contracted a fondness for such places, & the company which too
generally frequent them.

However, when the boys' step-mother kindly suggested that ''T'' in
John's accounts could stand for Travel as well as for Tavern, Pettigrew graciously accepted her interpretation.[92]

He stressed religion, especially in his ''Last Advice'' in 1797,
writing to them:

Above all things, strive to imbibe the *sacred spirit of* religion; it consists in the *love of God shed abroad in the heart.* This *love,* where it is,
regulates the *conduct* of the christian towards every one with whom he may
be conversant; it is *this principle,* and the *exercise* of it, that can make him
happy, both in life and death—and it is this principle, (namely,) the love
of God prevailing in *his soul* in *time,* that prepares the christian for the
full and *final* enjoyment of *God in eternity!* where the righteous shine as the
brightness of the firmament, and as the stars with undiminished splendor
for ever and ever. May God almighty bless you, my sons! and make you
better and more useful men than your affectionate father has had it in
his power to be.[93]

It is easier to judge the effects of college education on John than
on Ebenezer, because the former wrote all the letters to his father.
They showed a steady improvement in grammar, spelling, vocabulary, and depth of thought. Ebenezer was a good deal younger and
did not benefit as much from his stay at Chapel Hill. Nevertheless,
they thought well of their instructors and both boys apparently used

[90] Charles Pettigrew to John Pettigrew, Sept. 19, 1795. Pettigrew Papers,
UNC.
[91] Charles Pettigrew to John Pettigrew, Oct. 8, 1797. Pettigrew Papers, UNC.
[92] *Ibid.*
[93] ''Last Advice to His Sons, 1797,'' p. 12. Pettigrew Papers, N C Archives.

their time well, even if John was sufficiently frivolous on one occasion to join a singing school and on another to take dancing. The lack of discipline, however, and several serious arguments between students and faculty, plus the libertarian ideas of deism which prevailed, caused Pettigrew to withdraw his sons at the end of their third year. In a letter to Joseph Caldwell, acting president of the University in 1797, he explained that he needed John at home to assist him with farming, and that he thought Ebenezer too young to be left at Chapel Hill without his older brother. He pointedly objected to the "Oaths & imprecations" which abounded among the students.

An Education without the fear of God, may suit those who confine their views to *this world*, & to the *present life only*, but to one who expects his Children are to survive the ruins of time, in a state of immortal & endless existence, where the practice of virtue or vice *here* shall make the eternal Distinction *there*, between the happy & the miserable, such an Education must be very shocking.[94]

The assistance with farming was merely an excuse. Although John had earlier expressed a great desire to round off his education by travelling,[95] Pettigrew tried to place his son with Robert Whyte to read law; but Whyte declined to accept him as he did not think his rural situation was as conducive to a good education as a city position would be.[96] Pettigrew finally located John with Dr. Andrew Knox of Nixonton to study medicine, where a son of Henry Pattillo was also a resident student.[97] Ebenezer attended school in Edenton and formed close friendships with several young men there, such as James Iredell, Junior and Thomas B. Haughton; he also continued to correspond with some of his former classmates at the University for several more years.[98]

Charles Pettigrew had continued his farm management at the Lake in Tyrrell County even while living at Scotch Hall, and finally reached the decision in 1797 to move there. A family memoir gives the month as January, and says that at first

[94] Charles Pettigrew to Joseph Caldwell, Nov. 10, 1797. University Papers, UNC.

[95] John Pettigrew to Charles Pettigrew, March 22, 1797. Pettigrew Papers, UNC.

[96] Robert Whyte to Charles Pettigrew, Sept. 30, 1796. Pettigrew Papers, N C Archives. Pettigrew had officiated at the marriage of Robert Whyte to Pheddy Glasgow, daughter of his friend, Colonel Glasgow. Marriage License, Nov. 7, 1795. Pettigrew Papers, UNC.

[97] Ebenezer Pettigrew to Thomas G. Amis, Aug. 6, 1798. Pettigrew Papers, UNC.

[98] The exchange of letters is revealing as regards not only education at UNC but also at Princeton, which young Iredell and Haughton attended. The friendship of Pettigrew, Haughton and Iredell continued throughout life.

My Grand Father [Charles Pettigrew] moved into a house, formerly occupied by one of the old settlers of the Country named Alexander, situated on the Eastern ten feet ditch, where the brick kiln now is. . . . The frame of the present dwelling was first erected at the Lake, in the Spring of 1797, it was afterwards brought to Belgrade and completed in the ensuing Fall. It was moved to where it now stands in the Spring of 1834.[99]

The house was still standing, together with at least one of the original outbuildings, occupied and in good repair, as late as the summer of 1967. It was an unpretentious story-and-a-half frame house, with a front porch and a sloped roof at the rear, standing on level, sandy ground which was heavily wooded. All around, the swamp oozed up at the slightest pressure. Here Pettigrew made his home for the remainder of his life, overseeing Belgrade Plantation, on which he resided, and his first plantation at the Lake which he called Bonarva, where the bulk of his rice was grown. Mrs. Lockhart, Mary's mother, died in 1796;[100] Mrs. Pambrun moved to Belgrade with the Pettigrews.

Although Pettigrew did not visit his parents after 1768 when his father moved to South Carolina, he heard from his brothers and sisters occasionally, and at least once his brother William came to North Carolina to see him. All seemed affectionately interested in one another in spite of their separation. When the Methodist circuit rider Philip Bruce was in the western part of North Carolina in 1784, he saw Pettigrew's sister, Mrs. Martha Witherspoon of Wilkes County.

We preach[ed] at her house; She Expresses the Greatest desire to see you at her House, & believes it would be the greatest advantage to your health[,]

[99] ''Belgrade'' in Genealogy Section of Pettigrew Papers, UNC. Sally Clements wrote to Mary Lockhart Pettigrew, ''I heard My Dear Friend that you have removed from Scotch Hall to Terril.'' April 10, 1797, Pettigrew Papers, N C Archives. In September, 1797 Pettigrew paid a tax of $2.00 on ''a two wheel carriage called a chair . . . without a top on wooden springs, to be drawn by one horse, for the conveyance of one person. . . .'' giving his residence as Tyrrell County. Pettigrew Papers, UNC. John, in discussing transportation home from the University, supposed that friends with a cart ''would take down a chest of books to Windsor, from whence they might easily be conveyed down into Tyrrel[l].'' John Pettigrew to Charles Pettigrew, May 27, 1797. Pettigrew Papers, UNC.
[100] Will of Elizabeth Lockhart, Bertie County Wills, p. 66, N C Archives. Mary inherited the residue of her mother's estate, although it consisted only of personal property. They must have resided at Scotch Hall only as long as Mrs. Lockhart had the dower right. A careful search of Bertie County tax lists and deed books was not very informative, as several conveyances by Mary Lockhart Pettigrew listed in the indexes could not be located. Three lawsuits grew out of debts owed each other among the Lockhart siblings; see Chapter V below.

for the springs Near her house have cured several of your disorder, & was Never known to fail in one case[.][101]

Pettigrew's brother Ebenezer was in 1789 a member of the South Carolina House of Representatives. While attending a session in Charleston he wrote expressing his desire

. . . to see you & your dear little boy & I am the more concerned on account of being fully persuaded we will never meet again. . . . I experienced the bad effects of them unholsom swamps it is long since I expected to receive a line from some faithful friend full of the mornful [sic] news of your death. I can assure if I was sircumstanced so that I could take a jurney I would enjoy great pleasure in a visit to your country. . . . Bro. James lives about 40 miles from Georgetown—and requested to mention the circumstance to and request you to write him.[102]

He then gave other news of the remainder of the family. Ebenezer displayed some of the same interest in religion which his older brother Charles personified, although he was Presbyterian rather than Episcopalian. He seemed of a very pessimistic cast.

William Pettigrew visited his brother Charles in the early spring of 1795; on the return trip to Abbeville, South Carolina, he rode by Wilkes County to see Mrs. Witherspoon "but was very little the better for rideing so fare [sic] out of my way &c[.]" Back in South Carolina, he sent the message that:

. . . each professes a desire to see you which I would be very happy you would gratify & I think it in your power. . . . our best wishes to you & Sister [Mrs. Pettigrew] may your happiness and Friendship for each other increase with your years till time has wore you out & you have no further ralish for the transitory injoyments of time and fully Prepar'd for entering into that happiness that await the Just[.][103]

In 1800 Charles received a letter from his sister Mary Verner, giving all the news of her family. In his reply, he expressed the appropriate sentiments, and indicated his special interest in "my namesake *Charles.* . . . Should he be induced by the prevalence of bad counsel, or bad Example to set out wrong, he may never return to the path of Life, virtue & happiness. . . . I pray God to avert such things, as the anxious fears of Love are apt to suggest, & that he may keep you all under his holy protection." Although he wished to see his brothers, "do not expect it on this side of eternity. . . . You seem to

---

[101] Philip Bruce to Charles Pettigrew, Nov. 8, 1784. Pettigrew Papers, N C Archives.
[102] Copy of a letter from Ebenezer Pettigrew to Charles Pettigrew, Feb. 22, 1789. Pettigrew Papers, UNC.
[103] William Pettigrew to Charles Pettigrew, April 27, 1795. Pettigrew Papers, N C Archives.

have considered a jealousie that my station or circumstances in Life, have made me inattentive to my relations. So far from that, that my most anxious thoughts are about them, & these increase with my days. I sincerely wish a promising youth or two of my Nephews would come & live with me—such as are modest, Discreet, & teachable."[104] When William wanted to make a fresh start in Georgia, Charles wrote to his former pupil Benjamin Hawkins, then Indian agent in that state, soliciting his aid in finding William employment as a surveyor.[105]

Pettigrew was also interested to some extent in the family of his first wife, Mary Blount. Since he had not been welcomed by them, however, it was to the education of the next generation that he devoted his attention. His wife's nephew, Frederic Beasley, was sent to Princeton to study, thereafter becoming an Episcopal clergyman and finally provost of the University of Pennsylvania.[106] During his four years at Princeton, Frederic corresponded with his uncle and received advice and guidance from him. Pettigrew's opinion of Princeton was high; it was "a kind of Elysium to a youth of genius," yet he warned Frederic not to become intoxicated by vanity and self-conceit. He wrote, ". . . but permit me as you Ask my advice to tell you honestly that it will depend greatly on the principle by which your actions are governed. . . ." He asked him to read Addison, Locke, Grotius, Newton, Boyle, and Littleton before he read Thomas Paine.[107] Frederic was a serious young man and followed his uncle's advice. It was not his desire to become a lawyer, although his father had wished it, but instead he inclined toward the ministry. His replies to Pettigrew are detailed on the subject of what he had read and his reactions to philosophy and theology. In 1797 he recommended Paley's *Evidences of Christianity* to his uncle for reading.

The surprizing comprehension of mind, the extent of information and the habitual piety which appears in that work render him an ornament to his species to his religion, and deserve the warmest approbation of all the friends to christianity. . . . I now find that the most ignorant men are the most positive in expressing their opinions and that thousands ridicule the Scriptures who have not the smallest acquaintance with them. This you

[104] Charles Pettigrew to Mary Verner, May 26, 1800. Pettigrew Papers, UNC.
[105] Charles Pettigrew to Benjamin Hawkins, Dec. 16, 1802. Pettigrew Papers, N C Archives.
[106] John Henry Hobart, *The Correspondence of John Henry Hobart* (New York: Privately Printed, 1912, 6 vols.), III, 325-329. Hobart was the energetic Episcopal bishop of New York who assisted in reviving the Episcopal Church in North Carolina after 1810.
[107] Charles Pettigrew to Frederic Beasley, March 1, 1796. Pettigrew Papers, N C Archives. There are five letters extant, although internal evidence indicates more were exchanged.

know is too frequent in North Carolina—and even among those characters who should set examples to the rest and who are supposed to be the wisest. He concluded by asking for Pettigrew's opinion on his teaching languages at the University of North Carolina.[108] However, by 1799 he was pursuing theological studies and recommended that Ebenezer be sent to Princeton to complete his education. "It will be of the greatest advantage to him—and you could not send him at any time of the year better than at this—and perhaps not at a more proper period of his life."[109] Beasley had a distinguished career, to which it would appear that Pettigrew had contributed in no small degree.

Pettigrew was also interested in the welfare of the Lockhart family after he acquired a connection by his second marriage. Always a great correspondent, he wrote to David Lockhart, a cousin, who was a merchant on Teneriffe Island, and met with a gracious response. After congratulating the newly married couple, Lockhart remarked on their situation:

Were I and my Sister to remove our present situation here, We certainly wou'd point Out to Ourselves that Country where so many of Our nearest Relations reside; but the insanity of Your Climate throws an insurmountable Bar in Our way: Other parts of Your Continent are infinitely healthier; but even so, I cannot say that I cou'd with any satisfaction to myself make choice of any to fix myself in; as Your present political Systhem by no means meets with my Acquiescence.

He solicited an exchange of beeswax and rice from America for Teneriffe wine.[110]

David was the most remote relative with whom Pettigrew established contact; for the most part, he was quite busy keeping up with the numerous nieces and nephews of his wife, of whom 28 have been identified. Those mentioned most frequently and affectionately were Rebecca Barnes and Elizabeth Pugh. Rebecca Barnes' husband died in 1795, and Pettigrew wished to bring her and two little children to live with him and their aunt. Pettigrew wrote to his wife while spending the night at Mrs. Barnes' on a journey: "I found our Children (God bless them!) namely Miss Betsey & Mrs. Barns, also Master Tommey all well, and nothing now is wanting but your Company to make us not only well, & pleased, but quite happy. . . ."[111] However

[108] Frederic Beasley to Charles Pettigrew, Feb. 6, 1797. Pettigrew Papers N C Archives.

[109] Frederic Beasley to Charles Pettigrew, March 18, 1799. Pettigrew Papers N C Archives.

[110] David Lockhart to Charles Pettigrew, Aug. 24, 1796. Pettigrew Papers N C Archives.

[111] Charles Pettigrew to Mary Lockhart Pettigrew, July 8, 1795. Pettigrew Papers, UNC. Pettigrew was en route to Chapel Hill to see his sons and to attend the examinations.

Mrs. Barnes decided to remain where she was, to the regret of young John Pettigrew, among others. He wrote to his father:

Mrs. R. Barnes I believe has resigned the thought which she once entertained of going, & living with her Aunt which I am very sorry for; even if it was only on my own account, for I am certain that I could never be otherways than happy in the presence of so amicable a Lady, & more especially one for whom I have such a singular regard. I am affraid that she is overpowered by the petitions of her Neighbors, & Slaves, who I believe are very desirous for her continuance which certainly is an excellent proof of her good qualities.[112]

Pettigrew also teased a little about "old Cousin Pugh" who was courting a niece, "Miss Betsey."

The little widow got *her* feet wet, but was too hardy to recieve [sic] any injury; I am affraid she will be too tough for our old Cousin Pugh—Don't you think so? . . . Miss Betsey does not say she will have him yet,—but who can tell the results?—a constant drop will wear a stone. . . .[113]

Pettigrew found, in his wife's family, a closeness and an acceptance which he had never known before, as his own family had moved south when he was only 24, and as he was never fully accepted by the Blounts.

[112] John Pettigrew to Charles Pettigrew, March 22, 1797. Pettigrew Papers, UNC.
[113] Charles Pettigrew to Mary Lockhart Pettigrew, March 15, 1795. Pettigrew Papers, UNC. In this letter Pettigrew announced Barnes's death, and stated his hope of "bringing them all down with me together. . . ."

CHAPTER IV

THE CLERGYMAN

Between the time he was rejected by Lynnhaven Parish in Princess Anne, Virginia, and his final removal to Tyrrell County, Pettigrew carried on his clerical duties. During this time he lived first in Edenton, then moved to Perquimans, from thence to Tyrrell for three years, back to Edenton in 1792, over to Bertie in 1794 when he married Mary Lockhart, and finally in 1797 to Tyrrell again. Although each of these places was accessible to Edenton either by boat or by land, nevertheless there could not have been very consistent service given to St. Paul's Church or to any other group in the far-flung parish. It is little wonder that one Harmon wrote to Pettigrew in 1792 asking for the use of St. Paul's Church for the Baptist congregation. Pettigrew passed the request on to several Episcopal laymen who seem not even to have constituted an organized vestry, for their action. The reply was a firm one:

... we do in the most absolute manner reject Mr Harmons proposals ... We are in hopes that while you live amongst us, we shall be at no loss for a Clergiman of our own way of thinking, and Should we be unfortunate enough to be deprived of your Ministry, we still indulge a hope, that we shall always be able to procure an Orthodox Minister to fill the Episcopal Chair P. S. We wish these Sentiments Communicated to Mr Harmon[.]

The letter was signed by Nathaniel Allen, William Lowther, John Little, Luther Dickinson, and five other citizens of Edenton, with an appendix adding the names of William Littlejohn and Joseph Blount.[1] While the rejection was due particularly to the dislike of Episcopalians and Baptists for each other, it is nevertheless evidence of the negligence with which regular services were held.

While resident in Tyrrell County from 1789-1792, Pettigrew attempted to revive religion there by using the glebe for financial support. As far back as 1777, the House of Commons of North Carolina had considered a bill to sell the Glebe House and Land in Tyrrell but the bill had not passed.[2] The Glebe House was still being shown on the 1808 Price and Strother map, but was probably then only a

[1] Episcopal Gentlemen to Charles Pettigrew, July 15, 1792. Pettigrew Papers UNC.
[2] *Colonial Records of North Carolina*, XII, 42, 162, 178. April 26, 1777, "Mr Corrie moved for leave to present a Bill for impowering certain Commissioner therein mentioned to sell the Glebe House and Land in the County of Tyrrell.'

location rather than a building. Pettigrew wished to have the property sold and the money used to build decent chapels for the people. Samuel Chesson, representative to the House from Tyrrell, was asked by Pettigrew to introduce a petition to restore the land to the control of the church and thus permit it to be disposed of. Citing the fact that Pettigrew had to ride twenty miles to preach at the court house, and twelve miles to the one and only chapel, the suggestions to Chesson for the petition stated that: "The only Chapel we have, is more like a Deadfall than a Chapel, & is indeed dangerous for a congregation to be in." If the legislature would confirm the property to the church, it could then be sold for enough to build proper houses of worship. "As the civil authority affords no encouragement to religion, is it good policy think you to discourage it" concluded the memorandum.[3] No action was taken, however.

During his peak years, such as 1784, Pettigrew was apparently a powerful preacher. Anthony Walke, who although a Methodist at the time was later ordained into the Episcopal clergy, once wrote to his mentor:

I have very often thought of you wth great respect Love & Reverence & I think I shou'd leap for Joy were I to hear of you to preach in my reach, I have twice sat with great delight hearing the precious truths that dropt from your lips & I most humbly desire to be one that praises God for sending such Messengers to declare glad tidings to a lost world.[4]

Jeremiah Norman also testified to his abilities, saying:

I rested myself and went to the chapel to hear Mr. Petegrew. . . he used elegance & sublimity of language. The text was, God is Love.[5]

By 1789, however, Pettigrew had almost entirely ceased preaching to the large congregations which he seems to have attracted during his years of interest in the Methodist movement. He wrote to Henry Pattillo:

I preach chiefly at home to a few attentive hearers, with almost no exertion. When I used to preach to great crowds I generally incurred a fever. If I do little good, I am content to receive nothing for it. However I sometimes

---

[3] "Hints for Mr. Chesson," Pettigrew Papers, N C Archives. Pettigrew noted on the outside, "The above consists of a few hasty thoughts given to Mr. S. Chesson to open & assist his mind on the petitions with which he was entrusted For the restoration of the glebe to the parish & the redivision of the County, at the assembly." The glebe must have been taken over by the Overseers of the Poor, as no state law expropriating it was ever passed. Chesson served in the assembly in 1788, 1789, and 1790; R. D. W. Connor, ed., *North Carolina Manual, 1913* (Raleigh: Uzzell Printers, 1913), p. 820.

[4] Anthony Walke to Charles Pettigrew, Aug. 12, 1784. Pettigrew Papers, UNC.

[5] Diary of Jeremiah Norman (1793-1801), p. 520. Stephen B. Weeks Collection, UNC.

find myself very happy in a kind of unstudied paternal address, & seeing the correspondent sensations excited in my hearers. They are generally good moralists & good neighbors.[6]

His general discouragement was reflected when he wrote to his sister in South Carolina:

I have preached this 6 years past without gratuity or reward, nor shall I ever ask anything. I wish I could do some good; but I find mankind have greatly degenerated in the last 20 years. . . . But this [Anglican] being too cold a religion, the Baptists and methodists undertook to animate them. This they did by what I call the *grimmace of preaching*.

Such preachers worked them up by "fire & brimstone," he continued, by which the people were "warmed, but not instructed." When the fire cooled off, their religion had fled.[7]

Occasionally he was very occupied with clerical duties, as he indicated in 1794 to his friend Dr. Andrew Knox.

The sunday before Easter I had to preach fore & afternoon—on good friday also, & on last sunday namely Easter I preached & administered the Sacrament in Church, & then had to cross the Creek & preach at the funl of Doctor Hosmar—next friday & sunday I am to preach again—[8]

He also wrote to inform his wife that he would be leaving Edenton "to go down to Harvey & to preach there next sunday."[9] Generally, however, his activities seem to have been chiefly holding funeral services and performing marriages, although more of the former than of the latter. He received ten pounds from Mrs. Penelope Barker for "attendance at the Funeral of Mr. Barker" in 1788, riding from Perquimans to Edenton to do so;[10] in 1789 Samuel Johnston requested him "to officiate at Mrs. Blair's Funeral to-morrow afternoon. . . ."[11] While they were living at Scotch Hall in Bertie, Mrs. Pettigrew received a letter from F. P. Lennox asking her intercession in securing the services of the clergyman.

I write my Dear Madam on a very melancholy occation, it is to get you to request the favor of Mr. Pettigrew to come up here early tomorrow, to preach a funeral Sermon, for our poor unfortunate friend Mr. Hunter. . . .

[6] Charles Pettigrew to Henry Pattillo, Jan. 9, 1789. Pettigrew Papers, UNC.
[7] Charles Pettigrew to Mary Verner, May 26, 1800. Pettigrew Papers, UNC.
[8] Charles Pettigrew to Dr. Andrew Knox, April 22, 1794. Pettigrew Papers, UNC.
[9] Charles Pettigrew to Mary Lockhart Pettigrew, Oct. 8, 1795. Pettigrew Papers, UNC.
[10] Receipt, Feb. 27, 1788. Pettigrew Papers, UNC.
[11] Samuel Johnston to Charles Pettigrew, March 12, 1789. Pettigrew Papers, UNC. This was the same Jane Johnston Blair who wrote to James Iredell and Hannah Johnston Iredell, quoted above several times.

do My Dear Mrs. Pettigrew urge him to come, as we wish to have the funeral over as soon as possible.[12]

A request for his attendance at the marriage of John Roulhac to Miss Gray was made in 1794 by the groom.

Give me leave to request your Company at Mrs. Gray's, tomorrow 28th instant; My being unacquainted with the Propriety of the request Comming from me or not, on a like occasion, will I hope be a Sufficient Excuse for so late an application, when probably your attendence by appointment to Some other Place may be Expected.[13]

There is also extant the marriage license of Robert Whyte to Pheddy Sheppard Glasgow issued Nov. 7, 1795, bearing this notation by Pettigrew:

The within marriage was duely solemnized in presence of Col. Glasgow the father of the Lady, besides Col. Shepperd, & other family connexions & neighbors, agreeably to the form prescribed & used by the protestant Episcopal Church of America. . . .[14]

The scarcity of such records, among the numerous papers in the Pettigrew Collections, is worthy of comment. In 1798, after Pettigrew had moved permanently to Tyrrell County, a visitor to Edenton commented cynically on conditions there.

At Edenton, in North Carolina, the people are so far lost to the sense of religion, that they have suffered a handsome brick episcopalian church, the only place of public worship in the town, to fall into decay. . . . The church-yard at Edenton is open to the carnivorous beasts which prowl about that country; and when cattle have grazed, and hogs rooted in it, they retire to rest in the neglected church. Having driven their minister away, the ceremony of marriage is performed by a justice of the peace, who having first freely indulged at the festive board of the happy couple, and generally late in the evening, hiccups over a few lines, and this serves as a bond for life. The baptism and the burial service are dispensed with.[15]

The evidence is such as to indicate that efforts to establish a flourishing church organization in this area would be fraught with great, if not insurmountable, difficulties.

By 1787 the Episcopal Church in the United States had been established and had become self-perpetuating. Beginning with a meeting at Chestertown, Maryland, in 1780, steps were taken to draw together all the Episcopal churches in the various states and to adopt a constitution providing for their liturgy and government.

[12] F. P. Lennox to Mary Lockhart Pettigrew, Sept. 11, 1796. Pettigrew Papers, UNC.
[13] John Roulhac to Charles Pettigrew, Sept. 27, 1794. Pettigrew Papers, UNC.
[14] Marriage License, Nov. 7, 1795. Pettigrew Papers, UNC.
[15] Janson, *The Stranger in America*, p. 104.

The first General Convention was held in New York in 1784, but neither North Carolina nor New England sent delegates. At Philadelphia the following year, the revised American liturgy and the new constitution were adopted.[16]

The next problem was to secure bishops for the United States within the line of apostolic succession. Unwilling to follow the example of the Methodists, who had simply begun their own line, the American Episcopalians sought consecration in England. The English church required the oath of allegiance to the Crown, which of course Americans could not take; the first American to be consecrated bishop, Samuel Seabury of Connecticut, therefore received his orders at the hands of the non-juring bishops of Scotland. In 1786, however, Parliament passed a law permitting the English bishops to consecrate Americans without requiring the oath; William White of Pennsylvania and Samuel Provoost of New York were accordingly consecrated in Lambeth Palace the following year. In 1790 James Madison of Virginia was also consecrated in England. Meanwhile, in 1789 the New England churches ratified the constitution of the Episcopal Church in the United States and Bishop Seabury was formally included with the others.[17] As soon as there were three bishops, the episcopate was self-perpetuating, so that by 1790 the American church was clearly independent. The first bishop to be consecrated in America was Claggett, of Maryland.[18] It may be noted that the two Carolinas and Georgia had no part in these proceedings.

Bishop White soon launched an effort to locate stray congregations and to bring the southernmost states into the union. In the course of these efforts, he wrote to Governor Samuel Johnston of North Carolina requesting his assistance. The governor passed the letter on to Pettigrew, who immediately contacted those clergy known to him. To Leonard Cutting at New Bern he wrote, in the fall of 1789 and shortly before he moved from Perquimans to Tyrrell:

His Excellency Governor Johnston informs me that he has been wrote to by the *Right Rev.*[d] *D.*[r] *White* of Philadelphia, who expresses a desire that the *Clergy* of the episcopal Church in this State, should *meet,* in order to consult on such measures as may tend to promote the declining interests of their Church. I flatter myself that the striking necessity of this step will appear

[16] William Stevens Perry, *The History of the American Episcopal Church* (Boston: James R. Osgood & Co., 1885, 2 vols.), II, 26-32. Hereinafter cited as Perry, *History of the American Episcopal Church.*

[17] *Ibid.,* II, 66-125.

[18] Protestant Episcopal Church in the United States of America, *Journals of the General Conventions; from the year 1784, to the year 1814, inclusive* (Philadelphia: John Bioren, 1817), 1792 *passim.* Hereinafter cited as *Journals of the General Convention.*

to each individual of us at first view. I confess that I have long seen with most sensible regret, the *smallness* of our number, whilst the opposing *Enemies* of our Church are so numerous, & indefatigable in their Exertions to weaken our hands, & seduce her Members to their different Communions.

He thereupon invited Cutting to a meeting at Tarboro on the second Thursday in May, 1790, and urged him to pass the word along to any clergy resident to the southward.[19] A similar letter was addressed to one Parson McDougall, who seems to have been an imposter,[20] and to Nathaniel Blount, among others.

No reply was received from McDougall, but both Cutting and Blount were enthusiastic. Cutting, who was a northerner, wrote that he experienced "a peculiar Pleasure, & Satisfaction" when the letter arrived, as "it is the first Opportunity of a Correspondence With any of my Brethren that has presented since I have been in N. Carolina. . . ." He continued:

The Expediency, & Utility of a Consociation of the Episcopal Church in the United States, is universaly allowed, and eagerly desired by every Friend to Order, & Religion, & every Exertion, & every decent Means conducive to so desirable an End is truly laudable; consequently S.r I most cordialy agree to your Proposal of Meeting at Tarborough.

Cutting, however, had fallen ill with one of the many complaints of the climate, and was "afraid you will be puzzled to read" his letter.[21]

Blount also responded eagerly, suggesting that laymen should be included in the invitation, if possible one from every county in the state. He recommended circular letters, calling for an election of delegates to a convention to be held the following fall. He concluded with a comment on the Methodists, who had not followed the Episcopal method:

I think your observations upon the Methodists is very just. [I]ndeed who can hear of their Conduct, and think them unblameable, with respect to their present separation and former pretensions.[22]

[19] Charles Pettigrew to Leo[nard] Cutting, Nov. 9, 1789. Pettigrew Papers, N C Archives.

[20] The doubt is raised by the fact that his name is not on the list of those licensed by the Bishops of London prior to 1776 nor on any list of clergy ordained by American bishops. A remembrance written by Robert Johnston Miller in 1830 stated that McDougall "proved to be an imposter which had a very pernicious influence on the minds of many who were friendly to the cause of the Church. . . . He was then living in Halifax. . . ." Quoted in Smith, *Edgecombe Parish, Halifax County,* p. 26. *The State Gazette of North-Carolina* carried an ad on Oct. 29, 1789, that the Rev. Samuel MacDougall would open an academy 17 miles above Halifax at his house.

[21] Leo[nard] Cutting to Charles Pettigrew, Nov. 28, 1789. Pettigrew Papers, N C Archives.

[22] Nathaniel Blount to Charles Pettigrew, Jan. 29, 1790. Pettigrew Papers, N C Archives.

In spite of the interest they displayed, however, neither Cutting nor Blount attended the first meeting.

The Tarboro convention was duly held, with four persons present: Pettigrew and James L. Wilson of Martin County for the clergy, and Dr. John Leigh and William Clements of Tarboro, both laymen. Leigh, a physician, practiced both medicine and politics in Edgecombe County; he served in the General Assembly from 1790 to 1796, being speaker in 1795 and 1796.[23] Clements, a former Presbyterian, was especially active in the succeeding events, serving three times as secretary, and being chosen in 1794 as a lay delegate to the General Convention, although he did not attend. His wife was a friend of Mary Lockhart Pettigrew. This convention in Tarboro, in spite of its smallness, nevertheless proceeded to take action, acceding to the constitution of the Episcopal Church in the United States and appointing a committee consisting of Pettigrew, Wilson, and Leigh to reply to Bishop White. They also decided to call another meeting in Tarboro for the following November.[24]

The reply, addressed to the Committee of Correspondence of the Episcopal Church, is in Pettigrew's handwriting. He stated the facts of the meeting, and then announced that "We highly approve of the Constitution, & Cannons, and chearfully subscribe & accede to the union." He concluded:

The state of our Church in this common wealth is truely deplorable, from the paucity of its Clergy, & the multiplicity of opposing *sectaries,* who are using every possible exertion to seduce its members to their different communities. This grievance however, we hope will be redressed in time, by the encrease of its faithful Labourers. And we esteem it a most fortunate Circumstance, that providence has advanced a gentleman of so wellknown integrity & Zeal for the interest of the Church, & of Religion in general, as the *Right Reverend Doctor White* of Philadelphia, to preside in the Episcopal Chair.[25]

In a second letter, addressed to Bishop White, Pettigrew attributed the small attendance at Tarboro to the fact that he had inadvertently called it at "the most busy season of the year" for the farmers, which included the clergy,[26] and made future plans for such conventions to be held in the fall.

[23] *Manual of North Carolina, 1913,* pp. 458, 459, 600.

[24] Proceedings of the Convention of the Clergy at Tarborough, June 5, 1790. Pettigrew Papers, N C Archives. Bishop Joseph Blount Cheshire of North Carolina collected the proceedings of the Tarboro[ugh] conventions and published a limited edition pamphlet in 1882.

[25] Charles Pettigrew to the Committee of Correspondence, June 5, 1790. Pettigrew Papers, N C Archives.

[26] Charles Pettigrew to Bishop William White, June 6, 1790. Pettigrew Papers, N C Archives.

Ever a writer of letters, Pettigrew wrote to Dr. John Leigh of Tarboro immediately upon his return to his plantation Bonarva, to urge the publication of an advertisement drawn up by Leigh and Wilson "in the sundry papers printed in the State." He promised to find the necessary money somehow, by wringing it "from the hand of even the closest *Clinchfist*" among his brother clergymen, if needed, "by the cogent *pleas* of justice, good humour & honour." He concluded with a glimpse of himself: "Two heavy crosses I have are, a poor crazy constitution, & a miserable Clump of an Overseer, whom I am obliged to oversee."[27]

The November, 1790 meeting was held, with Parson Micklejohn present and presiding, while John Norwood was secretary. No list of those present has been found, but Pettigrew was not there. However, business was attended to, with a Standing Committee named for the state and an annual meeting provided for. Appointed to attend the General Convention to be held in New York in 1792 were Micklejohn, Pettigrew, and Wilson for the clergy, and Dr. John Leigh, William McKenzie of Martin County, and Joseph Leech of New Bern for the laity. Dr. Solomon Halling of New Bern was recommended for ordination, and was accordingly ordained the next year by Bishop Madison of Virginia. The convention concluded by appointing the following October, 1791, for its next meeting.[28]

In the meantime, Bishop White had received Pettigrew's letter describing the first convention, to which he replied a year later, August 1791. He expressed the hope that "as our Communion generally throughout the Country seems recovering from a condition in which the War had left us, we hope, that this is, in some measure, the case with you."[29] As it was almost time for the next state convention, Pettigrew delayed replying, hoping to have good news to report; but he was taken ill and could not attend the meeting. As he said, "But being seized with a tertian ague, two or three days before I was to have set out, I found it out of my power to give my atten-

[27] Charles Pettigrew to John Leigh, June 16, 1790. Pettigrew Papers, N C Archives.
[28] Joseph Blount Cheshire, ed., *The Early Conventions: Held at Tawborough* [*sic*] *Anno Domini 1790, 1793, and 1794* (Raleigh: Spirit of the Age Press, 1882), pp. 13-15. The only reference to this meeting in the Pettigrew Papers is a hasty and rather obscure letter from James L. Wilson to Pettigrew saying that the convention was small. "The western Members had like to carry out our next meeting to Hillsborough." This was probably because Micklejohn, of Granville County, presided. James L. Wilson to Charles Pettigrew, Dec. 30, 1790. Pettigrew Papers, N C Archives.
[29] Bishop William White to Charles Pettigrew, Aug. 8, 1791. Pettigrew Papers, N C Archives.

dance, as the distance was about a hundred miles."[30] However, he missed nothing, for the meeting was not held, due to the lack of a quorum.[31] He expressed the hope that the delegates would go to New York for the 1792 General Convention, but expressed much doubt, as "the Distance is great, & the Journey must be attended with both fatigue & expence." Money was hard to come by, and the clergy were "indigent." Although he himself was anxious to attend, there was a conflict with a meeting in Hillsborough of the Board of Trustees of the new University of North Carolina, of which he was a member. He concluded his report:

Our Church in this State, is indeed at a very low Ebb, & could I see how my attendance at Convention should be promotive of its interest in any degree, I am sure no consideration of a temporal nature should preponderate.[32]

In other words, there did not seem to be much use in going.

The actions taken by the two Tarborough conventions were laid before the 1792 General Convention, but since no one was present from North Carolina, the only action was a motion to "preserve" them. Rev. James L. Wilson had sailed for New York, but because of contrary winds he arrived after the meeting had adjourned. Upon his request, however, this fact was entered into the Journal of Proceedings. Dr. Leonard Cutting, formerly of New Bern, was also in New York, serving as secretary to the House of Bishops.[33] He did not return to North Carolina.

A confusion of dates led to the failure of the 1793 fall convention. Pettigrew rode to Tarboro the first week of October, only to find that "there was no convention." Solomon Halling, "from want of communication with the Rev.d M.r Wilson, knew not of any fixed time" and "was hurt at your disappointment," so he wrote Pettigrew. He bestirred himself, however, at Pettigrew's request, to issue calls for a November convention. He placed advertisements in the New Bern paper and also those of Fayetteville and Halifax. He talked personally with Nathaniel Blount, who promised to come "if his own and the health of his family permit." Then he sounded a note of urgency:

The situation of the Protestant episcopal church in this State is truly deplorable—and there is so little sense of religion among the people generally, who profess themselves of this communion,—that at times, I despair of our

[30] Charles Pettigrew to Bishop William White, March 12, 1792. Pettigrew Papers, UNC.

[31] Ibid.

[32] Charles Pettigrew to Bishop William White, March 12, 1792. Pettigrew Papers, UNC.

[33] Journals of the General Convention, 1792.

success. . . . If [we] had as much zeal as the separatists there would be some hope.[34]

When the meeting assembled on November 21, Pettigrew was ill again and could not attend. Only six persons were present: Wilson and Halling for the clergy, together with a new minister, Joseph Gurley, who stayed only a short time in the state; and Dr. John Leigh and William Clements of Tarboro, the old faithfuls, plus F. Green of New Bern for the laity. Their sole business was to plan one more effort for May, 1794, giving special attention to a better publicity campaign. Halling was particularly disappointed at Pettigrew's absence. He pointed out that they had deemed it inadvisable even to consider the election of a bishop because of the smallness of their number. The need of a bishop was of course great, and Halling believed that Pettigrew was the best qualified person.

I beleive [sic] it will be the general wish that You should be elected to the Episcopacy of North Carolina—My exertions shall not be spared on this occasion;—and You must not refuse;—consider it is a call from Heaven; and reflect on your former vows—Excuse me, if I speak freely,—but my whole soul is engaged in this important business.[35]

To this plea Pettigrew addressed a lengthy reply, indicating his own disappointment at not having been able to attend. He heartily wished for the success of Halling's endeavors, concerning which, however, he had grave misgivings.

But such is the coldness, & such the inattention of those in general, who profess themselves members of our Church, with respect to things of a religious nature, that I am affraid your so laudible exertions to draw together a full convention, will not be Crown'd with suitable success. As you very Justly observe, they are not even *Lukewarm*.

He agreed that a head for the church in North Carolina was indeed essential, for the sake of *"regularity, good Order, & respectability,"* which required "one vested with authority to *preside*, as *primus inter pares."* He acknowledged that there needed to be the power "to *ordain*, to *sensure*, to *suspend* or *degrade"* as well, but exercised by concurrence of the Clergy rather than by the bishop alone. This might have been an indirect reference to Parson McDougall. Continuing, he reported the good news that the church was flourishing "in some of the eastern States" with the Presbyterians and the Episcopalians happily coexisting. This he could not say, however,

[34] Charles Pettigrew to Mary Lockhart, Oct. 6, 1793. Pettigrew Papers, UNC; Solomon Halling to Charles Pettigrew, Oct. 28, 1793. Pettigrew Papers, N C Archives.
[35] Solomon Halling to Charles Pettigrew, Dec. 15, 1793. Pettigrew Papers, N C Archives.

for the Baptists, whom he regarded as "the most inimical to our Church. They divide Congregations, & seduce the most serious & thinking people, by a variety of artifice." He rejected the suggestion that he should be elected bishop.

But as my abilities are circumscribed within so narrow Limits, & my strength so far short of my inclination, I despair of it being ever in my power to make a useful minister of Jesus. What you write me in reference to myself, respecting the choice of a person for consecration to the Office of B-p, is so far from flattering, that, *to me* it is truely mortifying. It turns my thoughts inward upon myself, & awakens a painful consciousness of my being far,—very far from adequate to the due & proper discharge of the duties of that *humbler Office*, with which I have the honor to be already vested,—and much more, alas, how much more! unfit for the discharge of a more awful Trust, with the additional Duties of a *spiritual Overseer* in the Church & Household of God. . . . You must therefore never expect me to offer as a Candidate.[36]

Halling was not the only one who had thought of Pettigrew for the position of bishop. As early as 1791, Dr. John Leigh had indirectly broached the matter by saying that "I see no reason why we cannot appoint, or recommend, one of those now in the State; If the appointment of a Bishop will tend in any degree to raise once more the fallen state of our Church, I'm clearly convinced that it shou'd be done."[37]

A circular letter was drafted by Wilson and sent to as many persons as he knew to be churchmen. In it, he begged all churchmen to assemble at the church or courthouse on "an early day" to elect "Persons of good Morals and unexceptional Characters to act as a Vestry" with the duty of securing a clergyman as often as possible, and a lay reader for other occasions. Every effort should be made to have the "Blessed Sacrament of the Lord's Supper" at least three times a year. "By this means it appears probable the Members of our Church may again be collected, many of whom it is to be lamented, wander as sheep without a Shepherd."[38] Wilson showed great initiative and energy in his work toward revival of the church.

Finally, in May 1794, sixteen persons gathered in Tarboro and proceeded to organize the diocese of North Carolina. Six of the clergy were present: Pettigrew, Wilson, Blount, Halling, Gurley, and Robert Johnston Miller,[39] the latter being the only one from the

[36] Charles Pettigrew to Solomon Halling, Feb. 2, 1794. Pettigrew Papers, N C Archives.

[37] John Leigh to Charles Pettigrew, March 29, 1791. Pettigrew Papers, N C Archives.

[38] Printed Circular Letter. Pettigrew Papers, N C Archives.

[39] Miller was a Lutheran clergyman who desired ordination into the Protestant Episcopal Church. In 1821 his wishes were finally granted. Jacob L. Morgan, ed.,

western part of the state. Micklejohn had lost interest, and eventually moved to Virginia; there were no others. The faithful John Leigh and William Clements were among the laymen present, as were also Robert Whyte, at whose marriage Pettigrew later officiated, Dr. Isaac Guion of New Bern, and delegates from Beaufort, Lincoln, Edgecombe, and Pitt Counties. The convention opened on Wednesday, May 28, and adjourned the following Saturday, in contrast to all the other conventions which had been one-day affairs.

The convention opened with a sermon by Pettigrew, who was replacing the tardy Gurley, and Pettigrew remained in the chair as convention chairman. A committee was named to draw up a constitution for the diocese of North Carolina and to report the next day. Thursday was spent as a committee of the whole to consider the report of the constitutional committee, but at noon there was a brief resumption of the regular session in order to adopt a resolution that "The Convention conceived it necessary to proceed to appoint a Bishop Elect" and that the election should take place on Saturday. All day Friday was spent working on the constitution and drawing up a form for recommending a bishop to the General Convention; there are no minutes of the discussions. Dr. Guion of New Bern was in the chair during most of the deliberations of the Committee of the Whole.

On Saturday, May 31, the Rev. Mr. Gurley read prayers; the committee presented a form of recommendation for the Bishop-Elect. At noon the balloting took place, and "it appeared that the Rev.[d] M.[r] Pettigrew was duly elected." The convention then elected six laymen to the Standing Committee, who proceeded to elect six of the clergy to serve with them. There is no record in the Journal of the Convention that the constitution was adopted, but this must have been an oversight on the part of the secretary, for a constitution was appended to the Journal and was sent to the General Convention in Philadelphia. Finally, Halling, Wilson, Leigh, Guion, and Clements were chosen delegates to the next General Convention.[40]

The preamble is the most interesting part of the constitution, describing as it does the condition of the Episcopal Church in North Carolina.

Whereas there are numbers of good People in this State, who have been educated in the faith of the P. E. C., and many other Religious and well disposed persons, who appear to be desirous to Worship God according to

---

History of Lutheran Churches in North Carolina (United Evangelical Lutheran Synod of North Carolina: 1953), p. 25; *Biographical History of North Carolina,* IV, 325-328.

[40] Copy of the Journal of the Convention of the Protestant Episcopal Church Held at Tarborough in 1794. Pettigrew Papers, N C Archives.

the forms used in Said Church; We the Clergy & Lay deputies in Convention met, have thought it adviseable to form a Constitution for the future Government of said Church; And humbly pray at the throne of heavenly grace that our indeavors may prove effectual to the promotion & extension of Virtue and true Religion.

Article 7th provided for the election of vestries in order to procure clergymen for congregations not having them; Article 9th stated that clergy were to be "amenable to the Convention for any Immorality, or misbehaviour, and for Countenancing and encouraging any doctrines contrary to the holy Scriptures, Comprehended in the Articles of our Church;" and Article 11th announced that no person "professing himself to be a Clergyman of the P. E. C. shall be permitted to Preach in any of the Churches or Chapels in this State, untill he shall produce his Orders unto the Rector or Minister of said Church or Chapel, or to the Vestry."[41]

The certificate of election of the bishop was devised by the members of the committee, since they did not know Pettigrew well enough to use the prescribed form. It was addressed to Bishop White, the presiding bishop, and went thus:

We the subscribers having met in Convention at Tarborough, in North Carolina, on the 20th [should read 30th] Day of May one thousand seven-hundred & ninety-four, for the purpose of considering the declining situation of the protestant episcopal Church in this state, and having chosen the Rev.[d] Charles Pettigrew as a person fit to be our Bishop, & worthy to be recommended for consecration to that holy Office,—But being sensible that the great Distance at which the Laity as well as the Clergy of this State live from each other deprives us of sufficient personal acquaintance with one another to subscribe a Testimonial in the words prescribed by the general Convention of the protestant episcopal Church have thought it necessary & proper to make some deviation therefrom, which we presume to hope will be no obstacle to our laudable pursuits. We therefore do hereby recommend to be consecrated to the Office of a Bishop the said Reverend Charles Pettigrew; whom, from his morallity, Religious principles, piety of Life,—from the personal knowledge we have of him, & from his sufficiency in good Learning, and soundness in the faith, We are induced to believe worthy of being consecrated to that important Office,—We hereby promise & engage to recieve [sic] him as such when canonically consecrated & invested therewith, and to render that canonical Obediance which we believe to be necessary to the due & proper discharge of so important a *Trust* in The Church of Christ. And we now address the Right Reverend Bishops in the Several United-States, praying their united assistance in consecrating this our said

[41] Copy of the Constitution of the Protestant Episcopal Church in North Carolina. Pettigrew Papers, N C Archives. The articles relative to clerical behavior may have been drawn with McDougall as an example of their need. There are other instances where imposters had been accepted by congregations, thus causing trouble.

Brother & canonically investing him with the Apostolic Office & powers.—
In *Testimony* whereof we hereunto subscribe our Names the Day & year
above written.

The only signature missing from this certificate was that of James
Adams, of Edgecombe County; whether he abstained or had already
departed is not known.[42] Copies of all proceedings were made by
William Clements, at whose home Pettigrew had stayed,[43] and were
sent to him at Scotch Hall.

A year elapsed before Pettigrew forwarded the documents to
Philadelphia; he did so because the time of the General Convention,
at which he was expected to be consecrated, was drawing near. His
cover letter to White explained the delay: he was afraid that the
certificate of election might be so irregular that he would be denied
consecration, a very embarrassing situation; he therefore sought
White's advice first, in order to avoid such an unhappy event.

I am Affraid that my Right Reverend Fathers may not think fit to admit
such a deviation from the *general* Canon, & that the Convention, at Your
City, in Sept.ʳ next, may refuse to rescind or alter the form already prescribed for that purpose. Should such be the Case my feelings would be
very sensibly hurt on the Occasion. Permit me therefore, *Right Reverend
Father, to request your Opinion, and advice in this Matter.*

He was also concerned that there might be a difficult examination
which he would have to undergo.[44]

Bishop White resolved the problem of irregularity in the election
certificate by quoting two new canons adopted in New York in 1792
which the North Carolinians had not seen. Persons not having a
personal acquaintance with candidates either for holy orders or for
bishop could subscribe that "We believe yᵉ Testimony contained in
yᵉ above Certificate; & we join in yᵉ Recommendation of A. B. to yᵉ
Office of ————, on sufficient Evidence offered to us, of yᵉ Facts set
forth" provided that at least two persons on the Standing Committee were personally acquainted with the candidate. He therefore
proposed to submit the election certificate to the General Convention,
and assured Pettigrew that "we may presume on their entertaining
an Inclination to do whatever is in their Power, for the increasing

[42] Copy of enclosure with letter from Charles Pettigrew to Bishop William
White, June 9, 1795. Pettigrew Papers, N C Archives. Note the lapse of a
year before Pettigrew wrote to White.
[43] William Clements to Charles Pettigrew, Sept. 13, 1794. Pettigrew Papers,
N C Archives. The contents indicate having received a letter of thanks from
Pettigrew; Clements also mentions "Mrs. Pettigrew." Pettigrew had married
Mary Lockhart two weeks after being elected Bishop.
[44] Charles Pettigrew to Bishop William White, June 9, 1795. Pettigrew Papers,
N C Archives.

of ye Respectability & ye providing for ye further Increase of our Church." He reassured Pettigrew that no examination would be required, as it had not been required of them when they went to England; but that it was earnestly recommended that due regard should be paid to choosing persons who had some knowledge of literature.[45]

Thus encouraged, Pettigrew set out in August from Scotch Hall for the journey to Philadelphia. From Edenton he dropped a line to his wife:

We got over without any rain but it pursued us close to the wharf. . . . The yellow fever they say is not at Portsmouth & Capt Clarke says we have no business at Norfolk—Should I find it in the way any where, I will, you may depend on it, stop short; & be it as it may, I will make all possible dispatch to get home again—I forgot my umbrella but Mrs. Horniblow has lent me a very good one unasked—[46]

To his sons at the University in Chapel Hill he wrote two weeks later :

I set out a fortnight ago to meet the general Convention at Philadelphia agreeably to my appointment,—But when I had got well on in my Journey towards Norfolk, where I intended to go on board the Packet, the reports of the yellow fever, & the mortallity which attended it were such, that I concluded it the most prudent to return,—so that I have declined going at this time, if ever—[47]

He excused himself to Bishop White with a longer explanation.

Had I proceeded, it is probable I should have found the Packet stopt, —if otherwise it would been very dangerous to have gone on board with passengers flying from the Disorder, after taking the infection perhaps,— and could I have got on board of a Vessel bound for either Philad.ª or Newyork [sic], the danger would have been equal, besides being obliged to perform quarrentine after our arrival, which would have defeated my intention of being at the Convention. The Journey by land would not be much short of five hundred miles—besides it is the most sickly season of the year, so that It is probably I might not arrive before the rising of the Convention. From all these considerations I have concluded to post pone it, for a more favorable time.[48]

This was the closest Pettigrew ever came to consecration; as the years passed, his motivation weakened. He did not remain in com-

[45] Bishop William White to Charles Pettigrew, July 6, 1795. Pettigrew Papers, N C Archives.
[46] Charles Pettigrew to Mary Lockhart Pettigrew, Aug. 29, 1795. Pettigrew Papers, UNC.
[47] Charles Pettigrew to John and Ebenezer Pettigrew, Sept. 19, 1795. Pettigrew Papers, UNC.
[48] Charles Pettigrew to Bishop William White, Sept. 5, 1795. Pettigrew Papers, N C Archives.

munication with White, for the Bishop noted in his memoirs, ''Why nothing was done afterwards, for the carrying of the design into effect, is not known, unless it be the decease of the reverend person in question, which must have happened not long after.''[49]

In addition to his regular duties as a clergyman, Pettigrew did, however, make some effort to encourage the organization of the church in the state following his election. To him Robert Johnston Miller reported the baptism of 85 infants and nine adults in the year 1794-1795, and the deaths of six of his congregation. He further suggested a working agreement between the Lutherans and the Episcopalians in the state, for their mutual benefit; and he offered to go to the General Convention of 1795 in Philadelphia if Pettigrew was unable to go and would let him know in time.[50] A circular was prepared by Pettigrew recommending the election of vestries in all counties and parishes, ''whereby their Society may be brought into an Organized State & readers be employed in the Different Churches & Chapels as heretofore untill a regular Ministry may be procured—''. In the same circular he asked for election of lay deputies for the fall convention in October, 1795.[51] There is, however, no record of such a convention being held; in fact, there was no further state convention until 1817. A group of Episcopalians at Mt. Tirzah in Person County requested help from Pettigrew in obtaining a minister; they were especially interested in securing the ''Rev.ᵈ M.ʳ Bisset.'' Pettigrew replied that while he would ''always be happy to render your Parish any service that may lie in my power,'' he did not attend the General Convention and was therefore unable to contact Mr. Bisset. He promised to keep the letter and, if he attended the 1798 convention, would ''endeavour to negotiate the affair agreeable to your Directions.''[52] Charles Moore, who was postmaster at Mt. Tirzah, wrote Pettigrew again, informing him that they had elected a vestry and two wardens, and had been trying ever since to secure a clergyman. He was despondent, however.

As I was from my childhood, brought up in the Church of England and since I have arrived, to Mans Estate have had some opportunity, to examine the Tenets & practices of other Denominations, the more I know of my sisters, the closer I am at[t]ached to my Mother Church, and the flourishing of the Protestant Episcopal Church is a circumstance very near my heart, but I have to lament that the few of us that are in this and the neighbouring

[49] William White, *Memoirs of the Protestant Episcopal Church in the United States of America* (New York: Swords, Stanford, and Co., 1836, 2nd ed.), p. 172.
[50] Robert Johnston Miller to Charles Pettigrew, May 6, 1795. Pettigrew Papers, N C Archives.
[51] Draft of a Circular, Oct. 10, 1795. Pettigrew Papers, N C Archives.
[52] Charles Pettigrew to Charles Moore, Nov. 2, 1795. Pettigrew Papers, N C Archives.

Counties are almost as Sheep without a Shepherd, and many who formerly
were of that Church from a motive of piety, have been drawn aside to other
Denominations, not having an Opportunity of Worshipping God in the way
they have been brought up in. Should we be so happy as to have a worthy
pious Pastor of the Church fixed among us, I make no doubt but many
wou'd return to the Bosom of our Mother and the rising Generation wou'd
be nourished under her Wings.

Moore also sent Pettigrew the names of other Episcopalians, in
neighboring Granville and Warren Counties.[53] There is no record,
however, that the bishop-elect ever contacted them.

Solomon Halling, at New Bern, also kept in touch with Pettigrew.
He reported to him that the death of his wife, and his own illness,
had hindered him in his work. Nevertheless, he had called the Vestry
together "and consulted them upon the propriety of acting as You
had directed, and urged the extreme necessity, of adopting the
measures You had proposed, for the advancement of the interests of
our Church. . . ." He felt, as did the vestry, that election of vestrymen ought not to coincide with the fall political elections, "as Many
are then either too much interested in the issue, or intoxicated with
liquor, and the opposition that might follow, in consequence of
Numbers of other sects, being then present." The conclusion had
been reached to hold vestry elections on Easter Monday, as had been
done in the past. His comments on the growth of the Methodists and
Baptists indicated that they were at that time contending with each
other "for the victory" and not proselyting from the Episcopal
Church as much as formerly. He even thought that the rotation of
the clergy might help his own denomination,

for although, from what I have observed among them [the two sects], they
all preach, upon the same subjects, in the same language, and almost in the
same words, and that upon almost any text of scripture;—yet these same
sentiments, delivered by different people, have all the effects of novelty.[54]

Perhaps Pettigrew's inactivity was due to his poor health; it
might have been occasioned by his absorption with his new wife, the
education of his sons just at this time, or his removal to Tyrrell
County from Scotch Hall. Nevertheless, the contrast with the ac-
tivity of the itinerant Methodist clergy and also the Presbyterian is
genuinely astonishing. Francis Asbury, a man no younger than
Pettigrew and from all accounts in no better health, travelled hun-
dreds of miles every year, swimming rivers on his horse in icy
weather, reaching every state on the seaboard; while Pettigrew did not

[53] Charles Moore to Charles Pettigrew, April 21, 1796. Pettigrew Papers,
N C Archives.
[54] Solomon Halling to Charles Pettigrew, April 19, 1796. Pettigrew Papers,
N C Archives.

even travel to Bath, New Bern, or Washington, and certainly not as
far away as Wilmington. It may be that his personal humility was
too great for him to assume leadership, or possibly he recognized his
own limitations, for he wrote to Bishop White in his letter requesting
advice on his consecration that:

I most sincerely wish that some Episcopal clergyman of eminence, would
come into our State. I would very cheerfully resign my appointment in his
favor. We are but few, & the vacancies numerous. . . .[55]

He attempted to initiate correspondence with each clergyman of whom
he heard. After Halling left New Bern, Thomas Pitt Irving was
ordained deacon and served there for some years. However, although Pettigrew wrote to him, ''he made me no return, and I
troubled him no further.''[56] He encouraged his nephew, Frederic
Beasley, in his theological studies. Yet a greater effort than this was
needed to preserve the church in North Carolina, and it was not
forthcoming.

In 1798, the year of the next General Convention, yellow fever
made its appearance in Philadelphia and forced the postponement of
the meeting until 1799, at which time it was held. Although Bishop
White notified Pettigrew of the change in date,[57] it does not appear
that the latter made any plans to attend. No other convention is
mentioned in his correspondence after this date, although triennial
conventions were held regularly.

Halling was eager for Pettigrew to be consecrated.

But my D.ʳ Sir, we want a superintendent, and it is with great regret I have
heard that You was not at the last General Convention.—Can You not be
consecrated at any other period? If possible, it is my sincere wish that it
could be speedily effected, there are several here, who wish for confirmation,
—What an happy union might be cemented among the members of our
Church, by the frequent use of all it's sacred ordinances![58]

Pettigrew's most severe critic, however, was Nathaniel Blount, one
of his closest friends, even though chiefly by correspondence. Blount
chastised him in a letter of 1798.

At the time of our Convention at Tarborough, I was at first, (for particular reasons) opposed to our recommending (then) any person to be Con-

[55] Charles Pettigrew to Bishop William White, Sept. 5, 1795. Pettigrew
Papers, N C Archives.
[56] Charles Pettigrew to Nathaniel Blount, Aug. 23, 1803. Pettigrew Papers,
N C Archives.
[57] Bishops William White and William Smith to Charles Pettigrew, Aug. 8,
1798. Pettigrew Papers, N C Archives.
[58] Solomon Halling to Charles Pettigrew, April 19, 1796. Pettigrew Papers,
N C Archives.

secrated a Bishop;—but finding so great a Majority in favour of the measures,—was at last willing to join in doing it. How then am I disappointed in its stop[p]ing at that, and matters of the Church being no better conducted since than before. Nothing that we did then,—has, that I know of, been of consequence at all.

He further pointed out, "nor have I ever known why you did not apply for Consecration;—hope you did not decline without some great and good reason." Yielding to a chronic melancholy, Blount bemoaned the state of the church.

Oh! the deplorable situation of the Episcopal Church in this State! What a handle is it to those who may wish its downfall! which we have too much reason to believe are not a few. Glad would I be to see a revival from its declined & languid State; to see Order and discipline established upon the most permanent Basis. But alas! what reason have we to expect it; What further attempts could be made that wou'd probably have any desirable effect?[59]

Although Pettigrew's reply to this letter satisfied Blount as to his reasons for not having been consecrated, he was not yet through with the subject.

Perhaps it wou'd been better if you had endeavour'd to get a [state] Convention & made a formal resignation; but dont know whither it wou'd been best or not; or whither a Convention cou'd been got. Had you by some other means informed the members of the last Convention, believe that might been sufficient.[60]

This concluded the subject of consecration, and no further reference was made to it in the remaining years of Pettigrew's life.

The impossibility of electing another bishop unless Pettigrew resigned, and the fact that, unconsecrated, he could neither confirm members nor ordain clergy, contributed to the continuing decline of the church until, in 1815, there was not a single Episcopal clergyman in all of North Carolina.

[59] Nathaniel Blount to Charles Pettigrew, Sept. 15, 1798. Pettigrew Papers, N C Archives.

[60] Nathaniel Blount to Charles Pettigrew, Jan. 17, 1799. Pettigrew Papers, N C Archives. This letter sheds light on the difficulties of the postal service at that time; addressing the letter "To be lodg'd in the Post Office at Edenton," although Pettigrew lived across the Sound, Blount wrote inside, ". . . as I expect you live some distance from there, think it may be best to write to the Post-master there, either to contrive it to you, or by some means let you know of it."

CHAPTER V

THE BUSINESS MAN

Charles Pettigrew, like practically all Southerners, was caught in the syndrome of land and slaves. Not only was this due to his environment but also, psychologically and more subtly, to an inner drive to prove that he could support Mary Blount Pettigrew in the style to which she was accustomed. More and more of his attention was devoted to this aspect of his life after 1778, the year in which he was first married in spite of the gloomy Blount prognostications that he would be a poor man all his life.

Pettigrew first acquired "a negro property" by his marriage; to this he began to add "lands and improvements," as he wrote to his sons in 1797 when he thought he was dying.[1] Mary had inherited one slave from her father and eight from her mother; from this number Pettigrew sold two when he made his trip to the West Indies in 1785; yet by 1790 he was the possessor of sixteen slaves, and in 1800 owned 34; of which number his second wife probably contributed seven.[2] As he said to his two sons, "This (though alas a most troublesome property) I have carefully kept for you as a sacred deposit. I have been so far from squandering or spending it, that I have carefully improved it, by all the frugality and economy I have been master of."[3]

An owner of slaves must either "squander it" or become possessed of land. Pettigrew chose the latter course, purchasing land from time to time in Tyrrell County across the Sound from Edenton, where there was much land still open not only for purchase but also for land grants from the State of North Carolina. He acquired property through both means. Although he wrote to Henry Pattillo that he "had been a proprietor there" since 1779,[4] the earliest deed of record is 1781, and no taxes were paid in either 1782 or 1784, the two years for which there are tax lists for Tyrrell County. Since these were war years, there is probably no discrepancy; Pettigrew may well have bought land in 1779 without its being recorded until later, with the same thing being true of tax returns. At any rate, his

[1] "Last Advice to His Sons, 1797," p. 8. Pettigrew Papers, N C Archives.
[2] Heads of Families in North Carolina, 1790. Census Records, N C Archives; Tyrrell County, North Carolina, U. S. Census of 1800, microfilm in N C Archives.
[3] "Last Advice to His Sons, 1797," p. 8. Pettigrew Papers, N C Archives.
[4] Charles Pettigrew to Henry Pattillo, Jan. 9, 1789. Pettigrew Papers, UNC.

first purchase was of 50 acres, "more or less" as the old deeds state, from Josiah Phelps, from whose family came the name of Lake Phelps. He began to build up a contiguous piece of property lying between the Scuppernong River and the lake from then until 1789, purchasing from Evin Spruill, Francis Ward,[5] John Norman, and the Lake Company, plus three land grants. One piece of property which lay on the south side of the Sound he purchased but later sold; it did not lie adjacent to his other land. He also sold a tract to the Lake Company of equal size with a piece bought from them. By 1789, then, the year in which he moved to Tyrrell with his two boys for the first time, he owned some 650 acres, "more or less," in the vicinity of the lake, including 160 acres on the Sound which he later sold, as mentioned above. This was the majority of his property; it was chiefly unimproved land out of which he hoped to create a plantation. Following his second marriage, when he decided to move permanently across the Sound, he purchased in four transactions from Benjamin Alexander, Asa Phelps, Joseph Alexander, and James Dillin, some 175 acres near the present town of Creswell which became his home plantation, Belgrade.[6] The heart of this plantation was the Dillin land. As William Shepard Pettigrew wrote in 1838,

[5] Both Francis Ward and one Col. Sprewel are mentioned by the Methodist circuit rider William Ormond as having been kind to him in 1797. Friday, July 21, and October 15, 1797. Journal of William Ormond, Junior, 1791-1803. William R. Perkins Library, Duke University, Durham, North Carolina.

[6] Tyrrell County Deeds, N C Archives. A tabulation of land acquired follows:

Deed Book	Date	Acres	Grantee (Grantor)
Book 6, p. 126	July 5, 1785	192½	from Francis Ward
Book 6, p. 164	Nov. 4, 1785	192	from John Norman
Book 6, p. 173	Nov. 24, 1785	90	to John Norman
Book 7, pp. 14-15	April 3, 1781	50	from Josiah Phelps
Book 7, p. 26	June 28, 1781	90	from Evin Spruill
Book 7, p. 72	April 6, 1781	100	from Francis Ward
Book 8, pp. 281-2	Oct. 29, 1782	214	Land Grant #217
Book 8, pp. 286-7	Oct. 29, 1782	50	Land Grant #136
Book 10, pp. 59-60	Jan. 9, 1786	160	from Thomas Saint
Book 10, pp. 112-3	Jan. 7, 1785	214	to Dickinson & Allen
Book 10, p. 194	Feb. 24, 1787	100	to Collins, Allen & Dickinson
Book 10, pp. 262-3	Nov. 6, 1787	105	from Collins, Allen & Dickinson
Book 12, p. 49	May 18, 1789	100	Land Grant #474
Book 12, p. 152	July 1, 1796	56	from James Dillin
Book 12, p. 258	Oct. 25, 1797	65½	from Benjamin Alexander
Book 12, p. 284	Dec. 10, 1794	160	to Samuel Chesson
Book 12, p. 344	Jan. 29, 1799	7	from Asa Phelps
Book 12, p. 408	June 17, 1799	50	from Joseph Alexander

There is a plat of his first purchase, drawn by John Hooker, Surveyor, in the Pettigrew Papers, UNC.

Belgrade has been settled at least a hundred years. The name of the first owner was John Bateman, one of the old settlers & grandfather of Gen. Daniel Bateman, the name of the second was John Bateman, son of John Bateman, the name of the third was Dillin, from whom my Grand Father purchased the place in the Spring of 1797 [actually 1796]. The tract consisted of sixty acres [fifty-six], forty cleared for which he gave about six hundred and forty dollars [320 pounds].[7]

Some of the boundary marks are extremely interesting: the great gassing place, the Boxing Swamp, the Indian Swamp, all indicative of the kind of land he must try to drain, clear, and plant. Pettigrew believed he had made a good investment; to his sons he described the lands as "some of the most valuable in point of fertility, timber and conveniency to trade, in the county."[8] Access to and from the Bonarva or lake plantation was provided by the use of the Lake Company's canal, known as the Collins Canal. In 1789, as an inducement to Pettigrew to settle in Tyrrell County where there was no clergyman, the three members of the Lake Company, Josiah Collins, Nathaniel Allen, and Dr. Samuel Dickinson, "in consideration of their friendship and Esteem" for Pettigrew, gave him the right to drain his land into their canal or into Maul Creek, both of which were on their property. He also had the privilege of taking water from their canal if it would not injure their crops or mills, provided he consulted them before doing so. When repairs to the canal were necessary, he was to pay a share. In return, should Pettigrew build a canal, the Lake Company was to have the privilege of draining into it.[9] This deed of gift was indeed an inducement, and was a valuable privilege without which the later plantations could not have been established except at much greater expense. Belgrade, however, was not dependent on this canal, as it had access to the Scuppernong River.

The Collins Canal was authorized by Tyrrell County Court in 1785, at which time it was ordered that:

Samuel Dickinson, Josiah Collins & Nathaniel Allen Esq.re be permit[t]ed to Cut the Canal through the publick Road near South Fork Creek they Keeping a Sufficient Bridge over the same for the passage of Travellers.[10]

Robert Hunter, in 1786, saw a vessel unloading slaves who were to build the canal. He wrote:

Mr. Allen has a brig arrived today from the coast of Guinea. She has only been seven months on her passage out and home and has a hundred

[7] "Belgrade, 1838," in the Genealogy Section of the Pettigrew Papers, UNC.
[8] "Last Advice to His Sons, 1797," p. 8. Pettigrew Papers, UNC.
[9] Tyrrell County Deeds, Book 10, pp. 343-344, May 7, 1787. N C Archives.
[10] "Collins, Allen, and Dickinson" folder, Josiah Collins Papers, N C Archives.

slaves aboard in the state of nature (women and men). They talk a most curious lingo, are extremely black, with elegant white teeth. They shipped corn to Guinea, which turned out to a great profit, and the Negroes at twenty-eight pounds sterling by that means did not stand them in near the money. They are all from twenty to twenty-five years of age. Mr. Allen has bought them to drain a lake on the other side of the sound (which was discovered about thirty years ago) by digging a canal seven miles long. He expects to finish it by Christmas if it ceases raining (which I am in hopes it will do, as the weather appears now more settled), in keeping 150 slaves daily at work. The expense, he says, will be £3,000 at least, but when the work is accomplished he will have cleared 100,000 acres of the finest woodland that almost was ever known (oak, sycamore, poplars, cypress, etc.)— which is an amazing object and a very great undertaking. I wish with all my heart he may succeed.[11]

Thomas Trotter, a Scotsman, was hired to oversee the mechanical aspects of draining, irrigating, and running the mills which operated from the flow of the water down from Lake Phelps to the Scuppernong River. Nathaniel Allen wrote to Pettigrew in 1790:

I expected to have had the pleasure of dining with you to day at the Lake, but the favourable account you give me of our matters there, with the confidence I have in M.[r] Trotter have inclined me to postpone that happiness 'till this day week, when I shall be glad to see you at our lower habitation.

I am much pleased that the Ram answers so well, the purposes of its maker. . . .[12]

By 1799 the Lake Company property had been developed to the extent of having three tenants—Isaac, Charles, and John Norman; two barns, one stable, one machine house, one saw mill, one grist mill, one ware house, and two dwelling houses with out houses.[13]

A disagreement marred the relationships between Pettigrew and the three company owners. In 1796 while Pettigrew was living in Bertie County at Scotch Hall, the Lake Company demanded a re-survey of their common boundary on Maul Creek. Pettigrew was extremely upset, and wrote a fragment in which he cited all the irritants which had occurred during the past ten years.

Have you gentlemen, so soon forgot the obligation of my accommodating matters so much to your interest by so advantagious an exchange of Land [in 1787] for which I had neither the quantity nor the quallity in return? Is it not enough to deny me the priviledge of draining into the Canal, after taking away a natural benefit, by shutting up Maul Creek, while but little water is vented thro' the Canal more than for the use of your mills whereby

[11] Hunter, *Quebec to Carolina*, p. 267.
[12] Nathaniel Allen to Charles Pettigrew, July 25, 1790. Pettigrew Papers, N C Archives.
[13] List of Property, June 1799, Pettigrew Papers, UNC.

the Lake is now got so full as to overflow its Banks to the great injury of my Land & the entire deluging of my plantation while I am denied a Ditch to carry it off? What [torn] have I been employing my hands near, or quite a fortnight in the sickliest parts of the season now five or six years for, on the Canal to clear the sides & deepen it by taking out the sawdust from your Mills, whereby it is rendered shallow? And what are my advantages to counterbalance all the Disadvantages, to which I have tamely submitted for the sake of peace & quietness. Have I ever been allowed so much as a clear path along the Lake to the Canal? It is true, I sometimes ride along the Road & have a small quantity of rice carried once a year thro' the Canal. But is this an Equivalent? In the name of everything that ought to be dear to a gentleman—Where is your gratitude? Where your Justice & Equity? Have I rendered myself deserving of such treatment? By what? I know not unless it is by happening to possess a small quantity of Land there, long prior to your knowledge of the place.[14]

The court records of the case, if such there were, have been lost; some degree of friendship appears to have been lost also, for the exchange of letters between Pettigrew and Allen fell off sharply. Yet the storm may have cleared the air; no other disagreements arose; eventually, after his father's death, Ebenezer Pettigrew built a canal of his own and shared vicissitudes with the next generation of Collinses who were his neighbors on the lake.

Further to provide for his sons, Pettigrew bought land in Tennessee. He told them his reasons:

Should it please God to prolong your lives, you may think it best to sell your possessions in this low country, and to move westwardly. If you should, be sure to procure a good and convenient spot, and well situated for health; that is, *high,* and not having any low or marshy ground to the southward of the house. Such low lands, if brought into cultivation, are extremely unwholesome, from the copious exhalations which are thrown in upon a family by the southwardly winds, which prevail naturally in the summer season. The lands which I have procured for you in Cumberland are, I hope, good; and should you think of going to that country, they will be valuable —and although you might not approve their local situation, you will be able to sell them and buy where you would choose to live.[15]

Since he himself was not entitled to a Revolutionary land warrant, not having served, he bought 800 acres of land from Henry Fleury, merchant, heir of Sergeant Henry Fleury of the Continental Line who was entitled to a thousand-acre grant. The land lay ''in the County of Sumner in the ceded Territory south of the River Ohio late a part of the state of North Carolina situated on both sides of

[14] Fragment of a Letter by Charles Pettigrew, March 27, 1796. Pettigrew Papers, UNC.

[15] ''Last Advice to His Sons, 1797,'' pp. 11-12. Pettigrew Papers, N C Archives.

the East fork of Roaring River.''[16] Probably upon the recommendation of Hardy Murfree, who had gone to Tennessee, Howell Tatum[17]
was chosen by Pettigrew to serve as his attorney in Tennessee and
a power of attorney was sent. Problems plagued both Pettigrew and
his son Ebenezer concerning this Tennessee land. For one thing,
no survey had been run and the exact location of the land was uncertain. If it were within the Indian boundary, it would have to be
relocated; that line had not been surveyed either. Then there were
taxes to be paid; with the uncertainty of the mail, it was difficult
to send hard money from Tyrrell County, North Carolina to Sumner
County, Tennessee, with any assurance that it would arrive safely.
For instance, Tatum wrote to Pettigrew in 1797:

I have seen M.[r] Gatling and also the person who located H Flureys land,
but am still at a loss to know whether it is in the Indian boundary or not,
tho I have, from their information, seen it. [T]he reason why I cannot be
certain is that the land has not been run and there are various opinions on
the course it will take, I mean as to the locality of the line. I have therefore
thought it most advisable to pay the Taxes, as they are low. . . . The taxes
for the present year cannot exceed two dollars. . . . That sum you will
please remit by the month of August or September next.

The Lands are, in my opinion, very good if they lie where the locator
informs me they do, but they are not Lands of what is called the first quality,
tho conceive them to be good second rate.[18]

A few months later the boundary was run, and Tatum recorded the
grant and the deed.[19] Two years later Tatum sent the grant, deed,
and statement of expenditures to Pettigrew by "a Mr. William
Merideth, who is known to Mr. Jonathan Jacocks. . . . These I flatter
myself you have received before now. If not, Mr. Jacocks will direct
you, where Merideth is to be found.''[20] By 1800 the fact that the
owner was not a Tennessee resident had almost lost Pettigrew the
land. As Tatum informed him:

. . . the assistant assessors have in many instances exceeded the powers vested
in them by law, and erroneously returned lands of no residenters, with which

[16] Bertie County Deeds, Book R, pp. 98-99, April 9, 1796. N C Archives. The
Fleury patent was granted May 20, 1793, No. 2131. See also ''A List of Warrants Issued to the Officers and Soldiers in the Continental Line Raised In &
Belonging To the State of North Carolina,'' p. 46, N C Archives.
[17] Tatum, a resident of North Carolina, had gone to Nashville by 1790 and
perhaps as early as 1785. *Major Howell Tatum's Journal While Acting Topographical Engineer to General Jackson* (Smith College Studies in History, Vol.
VII, Nos. 1, 2, and 3 [Northampton, Mass: October, 1921 to April, 1922]), p. 5.
[18] Howell Tatum to Charles Pettigrew, Feb. 7, 1797. Pettigrew Papers, N C
Archives.
[19] Howell Tatum to Charles Pettigrew, July 11, 1797. Pettigrew Papers, UNC.
[20] Howell Tatum to Charles Pettigrew, March 30, 1799. Pettigrew Papers,
UNC.

they had nothing to do—This has happened in your case, where, altho the land was not subject to the tax, they have officiously given it in for Henry Fleury, by which it would have been sold, had I not have discovered it and to prevent the evil of contention, paid $1.98.7 which I conceived would be more agreeable to you than creating a (probably) lawsuit.[21]

Pettigrew's nephew Major John Witherspoon, who went to Tennessee in 1800, offered to assist his uncle in any way that he could. He reported in 1802 that money Pettigrew had sent for taxes had not been received by Howell Tatum, but Witherspoon had paid him out of his own pocket.[22] Pettigrew suspected that the bearer of his last letter, one Smith, had kept the money for himself and forged a new letter which did not mention the enclosure of some five or six dollars. Having anticipated difficulties of this kind, he

had determined to send no more money without taking a Receipt, & wrote my Letters & set out with the Money & them for M.[rs] Smiths But met them on the Road having set out on their Journey so that I had not an opportunity to take a Receipt, but If I recollect right gave the money & Letters to M.[rs] Smith herself amongst a number of her neighbours who were walking the road with her. . . .[23]

Witherspoon replied that not only had the money not come, but that the sheriff had sold the land for non-payment of taxes. "I shall proceed to Redeem the Land[.] If you have any Receipts for the money you have sent which has not come to hand you can Send them on—to enable Major Tatum or myself to recover it from those sent by[.]"[24] Since Pettigrew had no receipts, he forwarded a deposition by Ebenezer that

some time in the fall of 1799 he Saw his father, the Revd. Charles Pettigrew Deliver several Dollars to Mr. John Davis of the State of Tenessee telling him these was four which Said Davis promised to deliver to the Honourable Howell Tatum of said State together with Two letters further this Deponent Sayeth Not.[25]

No depositions were sent for the delivery of the money to Mrs. Smith. Not until the year of his death, in a letter which Pettigrew probably never saw, was the location of the land ascertained as to its taxability;

21 Howell Tatum to Charles Pettigrew, Sept. 11, 1800. Pettigrew Papers, UNC.
22 John Witherspoon to Charles Pettigrew, Aug. 5, 1802. Pettigrew Papers, N C Archives.
23 Charles Pettigrew to John Witherspoon, Sept. 22, 1802. Pettigrew Papers, N C Archives.
24 John Witherspoon to Charles Pettigrew, March 4, 1803. Pettigrew Papers, N C Archives.
25 Deposition of Ebenezer Pettigrew, Sept. 28, 1803, in letter from Charles Pettigrew to Howell Tatum, Sept. 12, 1803. Pettigrew Papers, UNC.

as Tatum said, "the numerous divisions of counties often perplexes agents in this business."[26] The money was not mentioned, but the problem remained for Ebenezer to worry over for the next ten years. As a sidelight on the movement of farmers to the west, Tatum told Pettigrew:

> I am sorry to hear of the general failure in Crops within your State last Season, but hope enough will be made, or has been raized to support those who do not emigrate—Our crops were abundant, and has of course procured us a considerable increase of citizens[.][27]

Although Pettigrew acquired slaves from his first wife, to which he added real estate of some 700 acres of land in North Carolina and 800 in Tennessee, his second marriage produced chiefly lawsuits. Mary Lockhart's mother lived at Scotch Hall, apparently with dower rights; although she left a few special bequests to her children and grandchildren in her will, with the residue going to Mary, her death in 1796 left to Mary largely debts to collect from her brothers and their heirs. There was no land, although there were probably a few slaves, for Mary to inherit as the residual legatee, yet she had all the problems of being executor.[28]

George Ryan, brother-in-law of Mary Lockhart Pettigrew, owed her a debt of £449, for the "Duckinfield lands." In turn, he was owed some six or seven hundred pounds by George Lockhart, Mary's brother.[29] Ryan died; before the suit was over Lockhart also died; so that the cases became extremely confused, with Charles Pettigrew *et ux.* suing George Ryan's administrator, and George Ryan's administrator suing George Lockhart's executor.[30] Pettigrew spent a great deal of time at court in Edenton at each term, as the case dragged on. At the April term, 1795, he sent a note to his wife: "My

[26] Howell Tatum to Charles Pettigrew, Feb. 26, 1807. Pettigrew Papers, N C Archives.

[27] *Ibid.*

[28] Taxables List, 1784-1787 and 1788-1793, Bertie County, N C Archives, show that Mrs. Elizabeth Lockhart owned 200 acres of land and that the number of her slaves increased from 8 to 10. However, her land, including Scotch Hall, must have been hers by dower right only, because she did not dispose of it in her will nor is there any recorded deed transfer. Charles Pettigrew helped his wife to settle the estate; on Nov. 16, 1796, he delivered "a Negro Boy Abel which was Divised to M.rs Evins by the last Will & Testament of Elizabeth Lockhart Dec.d" and received a receipt for the same. Pettigrew Papers, N C Archives.

[29] Edenton District Court Records, April 5, 1795. N C Archives. Charles Pettigrew served notice of the suit on Cornelius Ryan, son of George, on July 6, 1795.

[30] Edenton District Court, Execution Docket, April Term, 1799 and October Term, 1799. George Lockhart's executors paid George Ryan's administrator £44, while Ryan's administrator paid Lockhart's executor £1.15.0. The case had been appealed from Bertie County Court to Edenton District Court.

suit has not yet come on, nor am I certain whether it will this term."[31] The defendant argued that he had not defaulted on the debt ["The Defendant pleads no asumpsit"] and was given additional time in which to settle.[32] The debt was still not paid, so that the case came up again in the October term. Pettigrew advised his wife, "Baker [clerk of the court] tells me, we must suffer a *non-suit*, and be obliged to commence a *new one*, in another form as an action of Debt, in order to recover. This will throw the costs upon us again—so that we shall be obliged to take the *3d. heat*, or loose [*sic*] the stake, agreeably to the rules [of] raceing."[33] In April term, 1796, by consent of both parties, the defendant withdrew his plea of the act of limitations. The jury decided that the defendant had not fully administered the estate and had sufficient assets to satisfy the Pettigrews' demand. Pettigrew was awarded damages of £255 in addition to the debt,[34] for payment of which the court probably placed Ryan's executor under a performance bond. In October, 1796, nothing had been paid; at court that session a Fi-Fa action was brought. The minutes are missing for this year, but the execution docket bears the notation that the tax fee was paid, nothing else.[35] Once again, in April term of 1797, Pettigrew went to court; there is no notation of the disposition of the case.[36] In all probability, it was settled out of court by the payment of some amount of money by Ryan's estate, even if not all. Perhaps there is a connection between such an agreement and the fact that in the fall of 1797 Pettigrew paid cash for a parcel of land in Tyrrell County. Finally, another nephew of Mary Lockhart Pettigrew, James Bryan, paid some $200 which he owed to his aunt, in 1798.[37]

Pettigrew was involved in three other lawsuits during his lifetime. In 1785 he sued one Francis Allen for an unknown sum, but the sheriff could not find Allen. In 1787 he sued one Thomas Price for a debt of £20, which he collected.[38] These were both minor cases. In 1799-1800, however, he was involved in another lengthy suit in Tyrrell

[31] Charles Pettigrew to Mary Lockhart Pettigrew, April 8, 1795. Pettigrew Papers, UNC.

[32] Edenton District Court, Minute Docket, April 9, 1795. N C Archives.

[33] Charles Pettigrew to Mary Lockhart Pettigrew, Oct. 9, 1795. N C Archives.

[34] Edenton District Court, Minute Docket, April 9, 1796. N C Archives.

[35] Edenton District Court, Execution Docket for October Term, 1796. N C Archives. The total amounts were: Debt, £449; Damage, £255.2.5-3/4; Tax, £3.4.8; Clerk, £5; Sheriff of Bertie County, £0.11.8; Cryer, £0.1.8. Blake Baker was Clerk of Court.

[36] Edenton District Court, Execution Docket for April Term, 1797. N C Archives.

[37] James Bryan to Charles Pettigrew, March 17, 1798. Pettigrew Papers, UNC.

[38] Chowan County Court of Pleas and Quarter Sessions, Execution Docket, June 1785 and September 1787. N C Archives.

County against Joseph Oliver for trespass. Many suits for trespass were brought during this period of history; it was easy for a neighbor to move across a boundary to benefit himself for a road or a fence; it was also easy to squat on another's land without being detected sometimes for years. Since Oliver was appointed a constable and gave bond of £250,[39] he was assuredly not a squatter. He must, therefore, have erected a fence or claimed a boundary which did not accord with Pettigrew's ideas, so that the latter brought suit. Although in July term of County Court, 1799, Oliver was found not guilty, in September he signed bond to abide by an arbitration decision. He evidently did not so abide, because in April, 1800, a new awards jury was named consisting of Nathan Hoskins, Samuel Spruill, and John Bateman, whose decision was to become a rule of Court.[40] The decision was:

Arbitrators being Chosen by Sd Court to Settle a Certain Dispute of Controversy between the Revnd Charles Pettigrew plaintiff & Joseph olive [sic] Defendt after haveing Examined & hear the evidence on both parties Do award & Determind that the Sd Joseph Olive[r] be acquited of the Suit in trespass brought against him by the Sd Charles Pettigrew we Devise & Determine that Each partie pay his own Costs on said Suit as witness our hands this first Day of May 1800[.][41]

The judge, Charles Spruill, then handed down the decision. Pettigrew was infuriated, and wrote across the bottom of the award:

Charles Spruill's miserable Copy of a no less miserable award, through the influence of an equally miserable & wicked Testimony given by himself, in the Decision.

Costs were 4/6, beneath which Pettigrew scrawled, "Enough too, unless he could have done it better." Pettigrew made new motions at the next two terms of court, to force Oliver to pay £5, but without result; his suit was ended unsatisfactorily for him.[42]

[39] Tyrrell County Court of Pleas and Quarter Sessions, Minutes of the October Term, 1800. N C Archives. Joseph Oliver was appointed Constable and gave bond of £250; he was also appointed for two days' attendance on the Grand Jury.

[40] Tyrrell County Court of Pleas and Quarter Sessions, Trial and Appearance Docket, N C Archives. July Term, 1799, Oliver was found not guilty, with leave to Pettigrew to file a special plea. An arbitration bond dated September 1799 signed by Joseph Oliver is in the plantation accounts, Pettigrew Papers, N C Archives. October Term, 1799, a commission was named to take the deposition of Charles Spruill. January Term, 1800, Oliver was found not guilty, with leave to Pettigrew to file a special plea. April Term, 1800, an awards jury was named.

[41] Copy of Arbitration Decision, Case of Pettigrew vs. Oliver. Pettigrew Papers, N C Archives.

[42] Tyrrell County Court of Pleas and Quarter Sessions, Execution Docket,

Pettigrew cared well for his slaves, and seldom bought or sold one. In this respect he was like the Methodists, who while abhoring slavery thought the sale of slaves a greater sin. The problem, of course, as it was with all men of good will, was their disposition after freedom. Pettigrew set none of his free, but seems to have been just and understanding with them otherwise. At one time he expressed the wish that "there was not a slave in the world," although he also felt that "there is no such thing as having an obedient & useful Slave, without the painful exercise of undue & tyrannical authority."[43] He recognized that one of the greatest problems was the effect slavery had on the master. He advised his sons that:

> To manage *negroes* without the exercise of too much passion, is next to an impossibility, after our strongest endeavours to the contrary; I have found it so. I would therefore put you on your guard, lest their provocations should on some occasions transport you beyond the limits of decency and christian morality.[44]

Laziness in the absence of constant supervision was one of the problems which sorely tried Pettigrew. He exploded to his wife:

> The negroes had done just nothing from the time I had left them last. The fodder hangs all dead on the stalks except about a couple of cart loads of Blades. and they can offer very little in excuse.

Nor was it his problem alone; Allen and Dickinson had left some of their slaves on the lake under an overseer "which seems to be as much of a negro in principle as is a one of them; so that the chief they had done was to weed a broad road down to that delightful spot called the *Bee* Tree."[45] He understood fully why this should be so and attempted to explain it to his sons.

> Let this consideration plead in their favour, and at all times mitigate your resentments. They are slaves for life. They are not stimulated to care and industry as white people are, who labor for themselves. They do not feel themselves *interested* in what they do, for arbitrary masters and mistresses; and their education is not such as can be expected to inspire them with sentiments of honor and gratitude. We may justly expect rather that an oppressive sense of their condition would naturally have a tendency to blunt all the finer feelings of nature, and render them callous to the ideas of honor and even honesty.[46]

July Term, 1800 and October Term, 1800; also Minutes of the July Term, 1800. N C Archives.
[43] Charles Pettigrew to Ebenezer Pettigrew, May 19, 1802. Pettigrew Papers, UNC.
[44] "Last Advice to His Sons, 1797," p. 10. Pettigrew Papers, N C Archives.
[45] Charles Pettigrew to Mary Lockhart Pettigrew, Oct. 1, 1795. Pettigrew Papers, UNC.
[46] "Last Advice to His Sons, 1797," p. 10. Pettigrew Papers, N C Archives.

He rather expected the abolition of slavery within a few years; to this end, he advised his sons, "Endeavor to treat your negroes well, and to get your plantations in the best order possible, as a change may take place sooner than is generally expected in respect to slavery."[47]

As long as slavery existed, however, a firm hand should be used at all times to control and direct the Negroes. In 1802 there was an insurrection scare which spread over northeastern Carolina and across the the line into Virginia. Pettigrew mentioned it on May 19th: "We had heard of the *negro plot*. I wish it may be properly quelled—lenity will not do it—it will make them worse—"[48] A month later he reported:

> We have had a rumpus in the upper end of this County with the negroes —whether there are any of the conspirators among us I know not—no Discovery has been made nor any one implicated that we hear of. I wish that when the[y] enter upon the tryal of the Edenton boys, The examiners would be very particular in regard to the negroes at the Lake whether any of them have Joined for it is extraordinary if every other place abounds so with conspirators & there should be none there or among us.[49]

A letter was received from Washington, North Carolina informing Thomas Trotter that fifteen were found guilty there and six or seven shot "on their way to Williamston—I suppose for running," Pettigrew added.[50] Although there is no copy extant of an Edenton newspaper of this date, the *Raleigh Register* contained an article: "The fear of an insurrection amongst the negroes, has created the greatest alarm in the county of Bertie and the adjoining counties." The militia Major General had called on the officers and corps to hold themselves in readiness for duty. Continued the paper: "Upwards of one hundred negroes are said to be imprisoned in the jail of Martin county and many others in the neighborhood." Most of the rumors came by way of Norfolk, Virginia, thus sifting through several hands before reaching Raleigh. One D. Jones wrote to the *Norfolk Herald* that a Mr. Browning at Nixonton had said that Bertie County negroes near Windsor has risen "and committed great havock; from thence they marched to Chowan river, where they are embodied and armed at the ferry about seven miles from the river." Another gentleman had heard that "they have embodied in large companies, armed, in the Great Swamp; near the Virginia line."[51] The insubstantiality

[47] *Ibid.*, p. 11.
[48] Charles Pettigrew to Ebenezer Pettigrew, May 19, 1802. Pettigrew Papers, UNC.
[49] Charles Pettigrew to Ebenezer Pettigrew, June 21, 1802. Pettigrew Papers, UNC.
[50] *Ibid.*
[51] *The Raleigh* (North Carolina) *Register*, June 22, 1802. Microfilm, N C Archives.

of the reports was finally revealed when a man from Winton on his way to see if Windsor had been burned by the revolters met a man from Windsor coming to discover the same thing about Winton. Neither report was true, much to their individual relief. Said the *Raleigh Register* editorially, that while "vigilance on all occasions is truly laudable and praiseworthy, yet it would be highly commendable to trace the authors of such false reports. . . ."[52] As a result of the "rumpus," however, a new law was passed adding to the death sentence for conspiracy to make insurrection, passed in 1741, the additional penalty "without benefit of clergy," or transportation out of the United States with the death penalty upon return.[53] Ebenezer took note of a movement in 1806 to revive the night guard in Edenton as a good measure, since "the negroes are two [sic] numerous there to have uncurbed liberty at night, Night is their day, you may think my observations severe but I know them to be true."[54] The elder Pettigrew was quite ill at this time, however, and probably had no inkling of this recent problem.

Yet Charles Pettigrew had a touch of leniency which was needed with certain personalities. In 1803 his slave Pompey ran away, probably, so Pettigrew decided, to Edenton where his father lived, perhaps with the thought of "trying to get to a Brother whom Cambridge boasts of having a white wife somewhere northwards." Ebenezer was asked to make discreet inquiries in Edenton. "I am sorry," said Pettigrew, "I had occasion to take him to Town lately, as he had opportunity to hear of so many getting off so easily from there."[55] Pompey did not run very far, however. A week later he "came in on Sunday afternoon, expecting I suppose that as it was Sunday, he would escape with impunity." And so he did, until Monday, when "I made George give him a civil cheek for his impudence." He had left because he had to take the family to church on Sunday when he was supposed to be off; when he was chided on Monday for sulking, he ran away. For the rest of his punishment, he was sent to the lake to work, which sounded rather as if he were being sent to limbo.[56] On a different occasion, however, Pettigrew directed his wife, "Should

[52] *Ibid.*, July 6, 1802.
[53] Rosser H. Taylor, "Slave Conspiracies in North Carolina," *North Carolina Historical Review*, V (January, 1928), p. 22.
[54] Ebenezer Pettigrew to James Iredell, Jr., Dec. 31, 1806. Pettigrew Papers, N C Archives.
[55] Charles Pettigrew to Ebenezer Pettigrew, May 19, 1803. Pettigrew Papers, N C Archives.
[56] Charles Pettigrew to Ebenezer Pettigrew, May 22, 1803. Pettigrew Papers, UNC.

that fellow be caught pray have him put in the Stocks & kept securely—"[57]

His slaves were clothed, fed, and cared for medically. He purchased barrels of herring for their food each year; he had winter shoes made for them and gave them worsted stockings. When the work was especially heavy, he hired other labor on at least two occasions to assist in the tasks.[58] Constant advice was given Ebenezer about the tasks and the kind of work to give them, as well as the medications which they might require.

Pettigrew operated Belgrade and Bonarva as two plantations. The older of the two, Bonarva, he had lived on from 1789 to 1792, employing an overseer; an overseer supervised Bonarva until 1797; when he returned to Tyrrell County to live in 1797, he resided at Belgrade while Bonarva was still operated under an overseer. After Ebenezer came home from school in 1803, he was the master of Bonarva with almost complete charge, receiving only guidance from his father. With a distance of just nine miles between the two, it was easy to send laborers and messages back and forth, even for Pettigrew to ride over frequently to observe the situation.

Pettigrew did not have a very high opinion of overseers. He addressed his sons on the subject in 1797:

> It will be necessary that you keep an *overseer;* and this will be attended with so much *expense* that it will require you to be very cautious, that your expenditure may not in the run of the year, exceed the clear income of your respective farms; and to fall back but a little every year, will soon destroy your small capital. . . . pay a close attention to the man into whose hands you entrust the management of your plantation affairs. Overseers are too generally very unfaithful in the discharge of the trust reposed in them. This never fails to injure the indolent and careless employer.
>
> To make him attentive to your business be not too *familiar.* Familiarity will totally destroy your influence over him, and while you maintain a prudent reserve towards him, be not wanting in decent *respect* for him as a *man,* and a man whom you have honored with a trust. If he has any merit he will endeavor to deserve it—and if he has none, it may have a different effect; in this case it will be proper, if you can do better, to dismiss him.[59]

In 1791 he had one Lightfoot as overseer, to whom he "allowed a fifth, agreeable to our Articles, without putting in any Claim for what

[57] Charles Pettigrew to Mary Lockhart Pettigrew, Oct. 8, 1795. Pettigrew Papers, UNC.

[58] Plantation Accounts. Pettigrew Papers, N C Archives. March 1794, hired slave; January 1794, hired slave; 1796, shoes made by Jethro Coffield; 1788, five barrels of herring purchased; 1791, seven barrels of herring purchased; 1799, 18 dozen worsted hose, etc.

[59] "Last Advice to His Sons, 1797," pp. 10-11. Pettigrew Papers, N C Archives.

assistance I furnished in the Summer'' and then dismissed him.[60]
James Chew was the overseer in 1794, receiving £40 wages for one
year.[61] It is evident that Pettigrew was careful to have written con-
tracts with his overseers. The name of his 1796 overseer is not known
—it may still have been Chew—but the overseer carried a list of
goods to be purchased in Edenton at Littlejohn's store.[62] Since there
was no overseer in May, 1799, Pettigrew was unable to make a trip
to Nixonton because it was the busy season of the year.[63] He was
forced, in 1800, to pay ''an hundred a year'' to obtain an overseer.[64]
By 1802 he was quite fed up. To Nathaniel Blount he wrote:

I have taken to riding to a plantation which I have on a Lake about 9 miles
off once & sometimes twice a week, which I find greatly conducive to health.
This I am under the necessity of doing, from the fullest conviction that
overseers require little less oversight from their imployers than the negroes
require from *them,* & that in point of *fidelity,* there is not so much *Difference*
between *white* & *black* as our natural partiality for the former would persuade us.[65]

After 1803 he had no more overseers. Declining a visit to his wife's
niece, Mrs. Tunstall, he told her:

We have no Overseer, choosing rather to oversee the negroes, than an Overseer & them too, without which Employers generally go to leeward. The
negroes at the Lake plantation have commonly done better by themselves
with a little direction than with such overseers as we have had.[66]

Following this, he recalled Ebenezer from attending the academy in
Edenton and placed him in charge of Bonarva.
    The major crops were corn, wheat, and rice, which were his cash
crops. He planted two varieties of wheat: the white wheat ripened a
little earlier than the other. The rice birds and pigeons in 1803 had
''fallen very badly upon it, also upon M.ʳ Trotter's.''

The birds are as bad at the Lake as ever. I have almost all our force there
at present, to assist in replanting, keeping out the birds & going over the
corn with the Hoe.

    [60] Notation, March 2, 1791, on back of draft of letter to Nathaniel Allen.
Pettigrew Papers, N C Archives.
    [61] Receipt for wages, April 7, 1795. Plantation Accounts. Pettigrew Papers,
N C Archives.
    [62] Thomas B. Littlejohn to Charles Pettigrew, Dec. 18, 1796. Pettigrew
Papers, UNC.
    [63] Charles Pettigrew to John Pettigrew, May 18, 1799. Pettigrew Papers,
UNC.
    [64] Charles Pettigrew to Mary Verner, May 26, 1800. Pettigrew Papers, UNC.
    [65] Charles Pettigrew to Nathaniel Blount, May 1802. Pettigrew Papers,
N C Archives.
    [66] Charles Pettigrew to Mrs. — Tunstall, June 22, 1803. Pettigrew Papers, UNC.

Anthony was out in the field "keeping the birds off the rice. . . ."[67] Squirrels were another problem, solved by shooting them. Ebenezer was asked to bring "1 lb. of Gun powder and 4th of good squirrel shot"[68] from Edenton. A "terribly rainy time now six weeks, which has greatly injured our Corn & some of our wheat" occurred in 1803.[69] Wheat was generally harvested in June; the rice and corn in October. When Pettigrew went over to Tyrrell in 1795 for the rice harvest, he found that:

the negroes had been cutting Rice almost all the week—we finished reaping yesterday, & there is a good deal down which I must see put up in stacks before I leave them, which I expect we can have done by saturday evening. Indeed if I could I would have the corn got into the Crib before I quit—[70]

The rice was not threshed until the following April. John Pettigrew wished his father a good harvest in 1796, writing from the University:

I am in hopes you have been over [to Tyrrell County from Scotch Hall], got your rice beat out, and returned before now, although you have had very disagreeable weather, it has been so warm that the rice I suppose broke very much, & it was also very laborious for the beaters.[71]

Hogs were raised, although the number is not known; Cambridge fed the hogs, and Ebenezer brought two and a half bushels of salt from Edenton to cure the meat.[72] Clover was also planted.[73]

Other products of the plantation included raccoon skins[74] and shingles. The shingles were a very large item of trade, together with staves. Some staves and shingles were sold in Edenton, some in New York, and some in the West Indies; it depended chiefly on what shipping space was available at the time. In 1805, Ebenezer made a business trip to New York to sell the staves as well as to do some sight-seeing. The staves he sold to the coopers, but the price offered

[67] Charles Pettigrew to Ebenezer Pettigrew, May 19, 1803, Pettigrew Papers, N C Archives; May 22, 1803, Pettigrew Papers, UNC.

[68] Charles Pettigrew to Ebenezer Pettigrew, May 22, 1803. Pettigrew Papers, UNC.

[69] Charles Pettigrew to Mrs. — Tunstall, June 22, 1803. Pettigrew Papers, UNC.

[70] Charles Pettigrew to Mary Lockhart Pettigrew, Oct. 1, 1795. Pettigrew Papers, UNC.

[71] John Pettigrew to Charles Pettigrew, April 12, 1796. Pettigrew Papers, UNC.

[72] Charles Pettigrew to Ebenezer Pettigrew, May 22, 1803; and Dec. 21, 1802. Pettigrew Papers, UNC.

[73] "And pray don't forget the Cloverseed." Charles Pettigrew to Ebenezer Pettigrew, Dec. 21, 1802. Pettigrew Papers, UNC.

[74] "The negroes will carry over some Raccoon Skins, & I shall enclose you a 40/ Bill for which I wish you to get two good hatts from Mr. Wharf." Charles Pettigrew to Ebenezer Pettigrew, Dec. 21, 1802. Pettigrew Papers, UNC.

for shingles was so low that he had them brought back.[75] Six thousand shingles were sold in 1793, 3,200 of one kind and 800 of another in 1789, and "shingles" in 1803.[76] In 1802 Capt. Nickerson "seemed to have some notion to take our Shingles & corn for the west indies—but he seems to know so little of his own mind, he could not determine." A reference was made in the same letter to "half a Dozzen or more New england men at Edenton . . . to come into the River, to load with lumber for the W. Indies. . . ."[77]

Rice was the chief crop for cash sale and shipping. The earliest record of a sale of rice by Pettigrew is 1793, at which time he shipped thirteen tierces of rice to St. Bartholomew on the brig *Governor Johnson*, consigned to Thomas Andrews.[78] Two years later, 18 casks of rice were sold by Pettigrew to Dr. Samuel Dickinson, who then shipped it elsewhere. Pettigrew noted that he was "cheated" by Dickinson, for the latter paid only $3.50 for the rice whereas it was selling at $7 in New York.[79] The merchant Millen at Edenton also incurred Pettigrew's displeasure for charging $4 freight on a half tierce. This was "too much—I therefore want no more of Millens Calculations in favor of his friends among whom I am afraid I am not considered one."[80] The year 1799 was a good one, for Pettigrew sold 41 tierces of rice at Lisbon and "as many more on credit till Nov."[81] A portion of the remainder may have included the 12 casks sent to Jamaica by John Little, Edenton merchant.[82] Capt. Butler took his rice in 1802, paying $180 for it; Ebenezer was asked to check the weight in Edenton and to receive the remainder of the sale price. Capt Butler also took "1000 of the staves & says Mr. White is to pay you, & he expects a Lighter will call for the remainder, &

[75] Ebenezer Pettigrew to Charles Pettigrew, Aug. 17, 1805. Pettigrew Papers, UNC.
[76] Plantation Accounts. Pettigrew Papers, N C Archives.
[77] Charles Pettigrew to Ebenezer Pettigrew, Dec. 21, 1802. Pettigrew Papers, UNC.
[78] Bill of Lading for Charles Pettigrew's Rice, Aug. 6, 1793. Pettigrew Papers, UNC. A tierce weighed in the vicinity of 600 pounds.
[79] Invoice for 18 Casks of Rice, June 26, 1795. Pettigrew Papers, N C Archives. These casks ranged in weight from a low of 533 pounds to a high of 596.
[80] Account of Sales of Mr. Pettigrew's Rice, no date. Pettigrew Papers, UNC.
[81] Charles Pettigrew to Dr. Andrew Knox, Aug. 20, 1799. Pettigrew Papers, UNC.
[82] John Little to Charles Pettigrew, March 12, 1799. Pettigrew Papers, UNC. "Mr. Oliver handed me your letter of the 1st inst. & deld. me twelve casks of Rice, which I shall ship for Jamaica in the vesall mentioned to you at Tyrrel; observing your directions respecting the manner in which you wish the proceeds to be employed."

some more Mr. Cumstock has."[83] The rice crop of 1803 was handled by Ebenezer in Edenton, with directions from his father to send it to New York by "Mr. Martin, Mr. Poppleston, or some other good man who can be relied on to negotiate for us." He was warned to store the rice carefully, but not to "let it go into a cellar, for rice is but too apt to grow musty even in a dry place."[84]

Seldom was cash paid for these crops; instead, other produce was usually bought so that the transactions resembled barter more than sale. Pettigrew offered in 1799 to ship all his rice if the shipper would accept one half "for carrying the other & fetching the neat proceeds either in money, or the produce of the Island by the return of ye vessel."[85] Money or credit was deposited to the order of the planter with a merchant, to be drawn on as needed; an example of this occurred in 1801 when Walter Bell took Pettigrew's rice to load the *William Littlejohn*, and "lodged" the money with a merchant in Edenton.[86] Pettigrew sold his rice on one occasion to the merchant Bond of Edenton, accepting in return "a Barrel of good Brandy in part." He also "fetched home 140 Lb. of good Sugar, but for that paid the money." He obtained two scythe blades as well, "& shall have them Cradled tomorrow if possible." He sent Ebenezer a jug of the brandy to sample, "also some yeopon which is said to be very good."[87] One interesting item of trade accepted by Pettigrew in 1802 was $12.00 worth of "Lottery Tickets."[88] After 1802 he began to deal directly with the New York firm of Kelly & Mollan; he sold five tierces of rice for $149.19, less charges amounting to about $16.00 including the freight to New York.[89] Following his father's death, Ebenezer dealt almost entirely with Kelly & Mollan for years. If money was used in these transactions rather than credit, it was usually paid in the form of drafts on a bank. On one occasion, Pettigrew sent three bank notes to Samuel Tredwell in Edenton to change them into cash; he received "three hundred dolls." in return.[90] Such long distance trading placed the planter at the mercy of the merchant,

[83] Charles Pettigrew to Ebenezer Pettigrew, June 21, 1802. Pettigrew Papers, UNC.

[84] Charles Pettigrew to Ebenezer Pettigrew, May 22, 1803. Pettigrew Papers, UNC.

[85] Charles Pettigrew to John Pettigrew, May 18, 1799. Pettigrew Papers, UNC.

[86] Walter Bell to Charles Pettigrew, Jan. 30, 1801. Pettigrew Papers, UNC.

[87] Charles Pettigrew to Ebenezer Pettigrew, June 9, 1805. Pettigrew Papers, UNC.

[88] Account of Charles Pettigrew, Jan. 9, 1802. Pettigrew Papers, UNC.

[89] Kelly & Mollan to Charles Pettigrew, July 29, 1803. Pettigrew Papers, UNC.

[90] Samuel Tredwell to Charles Pettigrew, Feb. 19, 1801. Pettigrew Papers, UNC.

who could, if he chose, take little interest in selling the crop, or purchase indifferent supplies to send back to the grower. Pettigrew pointed this out in the case of "a certain Solomon Townsend" of New York, to whom he paid the full price for the best quality of iron, receiving in return "some of the *worst iron* I verily believe, ever before imported into the State. It drops in pieces in the hands of an excellent smith, who declares it to be good for nothing. a bar will break by throwing it off a man's shoulder."[91]

The European wars created great uncertainties in the markets. An upturn in trade occurred in early 1799; John Little wrote to apprise Pettigrew of the situation.

> I will inform you that Commerce is once more a float—vessels have risen very much in their value, & are in great demand—foreign markets are generally good—shipments are consequently encreased & fresh life given to trade, which seems to be much favord by the British; & more neglected by the French; which are certainly *favorable* auspices.[92]

Deploring his straitened circumstances in the summer of 1799, Pettigrew explained to Dr. Knox, under whom his son Jackie was studying medicine,

> If we could have a free & uninterrupted traid once more, money would grow plenty, & untill then, I am affraid little comparatively will fall to my share, as what is in circulation is all too little for the grab of the Speculator.[93]

For a few brief years at the turn of the century, England and France were at peace; then war resumed. In May 1803 Pettigrew wrote to his son that "should it be war in Europe, rice & wheat will bear a good price. . . ."[94]

Nor were farmers spared the lean years. Not only hurricanes and freshets, squirrels and pigeons, were the farmer's enemies, but dry weather and other natural causes. One such bad year was 1801. Certain petitioners applied to the Tyrrell County Court for relief from the requirement of working on the public roads, since they were "fealing the hardness of the year." It was their hope "that the honourable Court will take the Hardness of the times in Consideration" because if these men had to work two or three days a week on the roads, it "Will be fatal for we and our Wives and Small Children will come to a mo[r]sel of Bread."[95]

[91] Fragment by Charles Pettigrew, 1806. Pettigrew Papers, N C Archives.
[92] John Little to Charles Pettigrew, March 12, 1799. Pettigrew Papers, UNC.
[93] Charles Pettigrew to Dr. Andrew Knox, Aug. 20, 1799. Pettigrew Papers, UNC.
[94] Charles Pettigrew to Ebenezer Pettigrew, May 22, 1803. Pettigrew Papers, UNC.
[95] Road Papers, April 6, 1801. Tyrrell County Records, N C Archives.

Although cash might be scarce and although Pettigrew might not be able to afford to send Jackie to medical school in Philadelphia, he lived comfortably as did his family. Belgrade plantation house was relatively simple, yet the family was small and did not care for ostentation. Nor would ostentation have been appropriate for a clergyman. However, Pettigrew had a carriage, "a complete double riding Windsor Chair," for which he paid ten barrels of corn. He bought silk stockings for himself, lutestrings for Mrs. Pettigrew, three black barcelonas for her. In 1796 he ordered a coat and three pairs of breeches from the tailor; the fireplaces had andirons, shovel and tong sets in them. Black silk was undoubtedly to make a dress for Mrs. Pettigrew, as was "cassimere"; buttons and button molds, a vest pattern, a paper of pins, all show that someone looked after his habiliments. The items of powder and shot that were purchased are testimonials to the fact that hunting was still a way of life, as much probably for food as for warding off the depredations of birds and wild animals. The purchase of baize and a box of wafers shows that Pettigrew continued to write a great deal at his desk, as is only too evident from the volume of correspondence which has survived the years.[96]

His ownership of more than 600 acres of land, developed into two plantations, plus 800 acres in Tennessee; thirty-four slaves; adequate barns and other out houses; the employment of an overseer for many years; plus the fact that he had no income from his clerical duties but was able to live entirely on the plantation income, is a strong indication that he was a man of some wealth. He already possessed enough property in 1797 to be able to tell his two sons that "Care and industry, sobriety and economy, are all that are necessary to make you *wealthy* in a few years."[97] His friend Dr. John Leigh congratulated him as early as 1791:

Your Situation is different; possessed of an ample Fortune, Independent of the World, you can enjoy yourself in the Shades of retirement, free from all Worldly concern; your mind is perfectly at rest, quiet tranquility, like the Muses, dance around you, all things are pleasing.[98]

To his sister, Mary Verner, in South Carolina Pettigrew remarked that "God has favored us with more than a Competency & what is more I find to be a burden. . . . We have a valuable plantation in cultivation beside the one we live on . . . I have within this four years built & finished a good house."[99]

[96] Plantation Accounts. Pettigrew Papers, N C Archives.
[97] "Last Advice to His Sons, 1797," p. 8. Pettigrew Papers, N C Archives.
[98] John Leigh to Charles Pettigrew, March 29, 1791. Pettigrew Papers, N C Archives.
[99] Charles Pettigrew to Mary Verner, May 26, 1800. Pettigrew Papers, UNC.

Pettigrew should most certainly be classified among the larger planters of North Carolina and also designated as a successful one, measured by Southern standards. According to Guion Griffis Johnson's able analysis, only six per cent of the population in the state owned more than twenty slaves; she defined the gentry as ''composed of the planters, those engaged in the learned professions, and the holders of important state and federal offices.''[100] Pettigrew's forebears were at least of country squire status; he was well educated and an ordained Anglican clergyman; to this he had added enough economic substance to place himself in that upper six per cent of the North Carolina gentry.

[100] Guion Griffis Johnson, *Ante-Bellum North Carolina* (Chapel Hill: The University of North Carolina Press, 1937), pp. 55-60.

CHAPTER VI

THE INTELLECTUAL MAN

Pettigrew, although not possessing the brilliant mind of Thomas Jefferson or Benjamin Franklin, nevertheless displayed some of the same catholicity of intellectual interest and was typical of the 18th century educated man of many tastes. While one would anticipate that, as a clergyman, he would read and debate theological points, one might not expect that he also practiced medicine, discussed scientific causation of natural phenomena, was regarded by his contemporaries as an educator of merit, and was a dilettante in belles lettres.

He perhaps came by his medical interests naturally. His father, whether or not he studied medicine in Ireland before emigrating to Pennsylvania, practiced "physick" and undoubtedly shared his interest and knowledge with his intellectual son. It was no disgrace in the 18th century to be called a "quack"; it denoted only that one had not received formal training in medical arts, but this did not mean the services of a quack were not just as much in demand as those of the very few M. D.'s. Pettigrew referred to prescribing for his friends and relatives in terms indicating that this was acceptable practice. To Nathaniel Blount he wrote, "Permit me as a quack to prescribe for you what I think will probably keep it off, & perhaps eradicate it entirely from the system."[1] He also told his wife, concerning an illness of her niece, "I would recommend a little physic but I hate to make well-people sick, and particularly, my friends, —so that I will put it off untill I return, when I am in hopes to find her restored to a confirmed state of health—but should she seem to require something to cleanse her Stomach, I will (if she should be agreed) undertake to be her Doctor—"[2] Ebenezer Pettigrew told his friend James Iredell Jr. that during a recent illness, "My Father was my Doctor, and through concurrent blessing of providence succeeded[.] I once thought myself verging on eternity."[3] Pettigrew referred at least once to looking for remedies in a medical book,[4] so

[1] Charles Pettigrew to Nathaniel Blount, June 6, 1803. Pettigrew Papers, N C Archives.

[2] Charles Pettigrew to Mary Lockhart Pettigrew, July 8, 1795. Pettigrew Papers, UNC.

[3] Ebenezer Pettigrew to James Iredell, Jr., Dec. 13, 1804. Pettigrew Papers, N C Archives.

[4] Charles Pettigrew to Dr. Andrew Knox, Aug. 20, 1799. Pettigrew Papers, UNC.

that he must have possessed a small library. His decision to have his older son study under Dr. Knox was surely related to his early exposure to his father's interests and to his own practice of the healing science.

Discussions of diseases and remedies for them are scattered throughout the entire Pettigrew correspondence. John Pettigrew suffered from an enlarged spleen, which he discussed much with his father. "I am about to use a method which I am in hopes will be of some benefit," he wrote to his father in 1795, "which is starroot steept in spirits that I am to take twice or three times a day which is said to be very good."[5] Not deriving much benefit from this medication, he then tried swinging by his hands "every morning and knight," and also took "the Steel Dust steept in Brandy for better than a week but cannot perceive whither it has done me any good or not yet. . . ."[6] After another two months, he informed his father that he thought the "spleen seems softer than it did, and not so far round me."[7]

A discussion of rheumatism ensued between Nathaniel Blount, who suffered from it, and Pettigrew. The latter recommended the use of

Brimstone. . . . And I am of opinion were you to get of the Roll which is much the strongest & most effectual, & powder it fine—and take of the powder as much as will Heap in a Tea spoon night & morning for about a fortnight, & then let a week intervene, then begin again with the process & continue for another fortnight you would feel the most salutary effect.[8]

Blount, however, was unwilling to try the brimstone treatment.

Should be rather afraid to make so free a use of brimstone as you advised, tho' from what I have before understood, added to your knowledge and advice in the matter, I have no doubt but it may be helpful, if carefully taken; while confined mostly to my bed, I took very considerable of it made up in pills with Turpentine.

His preference was for cold baths.

I have formerly thought the cold bath serviceable to me,—and think if I should live till suitable weather at the Fall to try it again; the weather was so very cold after I was taken last winter, was afraid to make very free with it; took it once before I got confined and desisted; and after I got about in the spring of the year and wished to try it, —the weather was so

---

[5] John Pettigrew to Charles Pettigrew, April 5, 1795. Pettigrew Papers, UNC.
[6] John Pettigrew to Charles Pettigrew, May 4, 1795. Pettigrew Papers, UNC.
[7] John Pettigrew to Charles Pettigrew, July 7, 1795. Pettigrew Papers, UNC.
[8] Charles Pettigrew to Nathaniel Blount, June 6, 1803. Pettigrew Papers, N C Archives.

often unsettled when I cou'd be at home, did not take it, only sometimes pour'd water on my knees, and one or both of ancles and feet.[9]

As a scientist, as well as a quack, Pettigrew pressed his friend.

I am still of opinion, that the free use of Brimstone would entirely rid you of it. Some who were in the most deplorable situation are indebted to it for relief[.] Such was the Situation of a M.[r] [Benners] Vail who lived at Edenton, but removed to Newbern. He took a Table spoonful of the powdered Roll three times a Day, until entirely well. I am apt to think you are too apprehensive of Danger from the use of it. Such experiments, & such happy effects have sufficiently proved both the harmlessness, & great utility of the medicine, when taken with proper care, at the same time, not to expos[e] onesself to too much cold or wets. I should think however, that reasonable exercise, such as riding in good weather, would tend to promote the cure. The cold Bath I have a high opinion of, having myself about 12 years ago tryed & experienced its happy effets.[10]

Since there was no further discussion of the brimstone, it is likely that the firm-minded Blount stuck to his cold baths and never tried the Pettigrew remedy. However, Mrs. Pettigrew was dosed with a "pound of Brimstone" in 1803 as she "has the rheumatic almost constantly & sometimes very ill."[11]

In 1799 an epidemic of something which Pettigrew called a "mortal fever" but which Dr. John Beasley thought only "one grade removed from yellow fever" broke out in Edenton and its environs. In August Pettigrew wrote to Dr. Andrew Knox of Nixonton:

We have had on this side the most mortal *fever,* ever known since the settlement of the place. The family it first appeared in, lost four out of nine, not one of whome escaped it. And most of the surviving have been reduced to the lowest extremity to recover. About as many more of those who visitted the family have also been taken with it, viz, 9 or 10, of whom but one has yet died, & I trust in providence they may recover. It seems however to spread, for one of our Negroes has it. It is the slow nervous fever, & in the advanced stage, it has been highly putrid.

Pettigrew tried "almost all my little stock of physic on them, & did everything I could as a Quack," finally discovering that yeast was a good medication. He read about this cure, so he said, in a newspaper and not in a medical book.

It has a miraculous power to quiet, & allay the agitation of the nervous

[9] Nathaniel Blount to Charles Pettigrew, Aug. 16, 1803. Pettigrew Papers, N C Archives.

[10] Charles Pettigrew to Nathaniel Blount, Aug. 23, 1803. Pettigrew Papers, N C Archives.

[11] Charles Pettigrew to Ebenezer Pettigrew, May 22, 1803. Pettigrew Papers, UNC.

system & the *putrid* flies before it. A couple of spoonfuls every 2 or 3 hours, or as the stomach of the patient will easily bear it is the dose.

He obtained the yeast from fermenting cider; he also discovered that cider and water mixed was as good as wine or french brandy to "raise the pulse." He was "happy for the poor" to have discovered the use of cider and water, for they could afford it, even if not the french brandy.[12]

John Beasley, nephew of the first Mrs. Pettigrew, who had studied medicine in Philadelphia, wrote to his uncle concerning the extent of the fever in Edenton. He sent over some medicines requested by Pettigrew—a bottle of castor oil, 23 boxes of Andersons Pills, and an ounce of opium. He wrote in haste but quite fully of the fever. Three of his friends had died from it; "every symptom which Capt[.] Warren had during his illness were accurately discribed by [Dr. Benjamin] Rush in his treatise on yellow fever." Beasley treated his friend by bleeding him.

I bled him twice in about 6 hours, tho' from the feebleness of his pulse I could not venture farther; there appeared from the first of my seeing him to be every tendency to dissolution. —he complained of a pain in the head & back with a prostration of strength & continued to sink, notwithstanding every stimulating exertion, till he died, which was in two nights & three days from the time I first saw him.

A second patient, the barber, was taken "with every mark of the same disease." Beasley also bled him.

I bled him to about 90 Ounces in two days, this blood was very different from Warrens as it was highly inflamed, even the last bleeding, —he is now in a state of recovery & will be well in a few days —there has been no other case in town similar to Jims since his attack & I hope we shall have no more of it. . . .

Beasley's letter concluded with a regret that his cousin John was ill and expressed the wish that "I was so near him as render what assistance my inclination prompts me to."[13] It is evident that this is the disease from which John died only three days after Beasley's letter was written.

There are other references to bleeding. Mrs. Rebecca Barnes, a niece of the second Mrs. Pettigrew, wrote to her aunt concerning a "swim[m]ing and gidyniss in my head" for which she was bled. "M.r Barnes tryed twice an fetch no blud the D^{oct} fetch a plenty at

---

[12] Charles Pettigrew to Dr. Andrew Knox, Aug. 20, 1799. Pettigrew Papers, UNC.

[13] Dr. John Beasley to Charles Pettigrew, Sept. 21, 1799. Pettigrew Papers, UNC.

once tryin say.[d] the Blud look very well. . . ."[14] Pettigrew suggested to Ebenezer when the latter was at Bonarva that he bleed a slave named Harry. ". . . if his pulse is full, bleed him, & if the blood is buffy it will grow fuller, & as long as his pulse is full & pretty strong repeat it, till it loses the buff. . . ."[15]

Many references were made to malaria, or "ague and fever" as it was called. Pettigrew was prevented from attending one of the North Carolina Episcopal conventions held at Tarboro, as was noted, by a "tertian ague." Mrs. Rebecca Barnes had "a short visit & shake" from the hand of "Mr. Ague & fever—But, thank God, she is got pretty well again, & has a pretty good apetite," wrote Pettigrew to his wife.[16] John was "taken with the ague & fever" while at the University, which he had for two or three days; he then "took a vomit, which relieved me for a few days; I then took the ague again, had a few fits more & then set inn upon the bark, which entirely relieved me. . . ." His strength remained low, but his appetite was "very sharp."[17] On another occasion he wrote of the use of "the bark & snake-root"[18] which was one of the standard remedies and preventatives as well. His father had a good deal of common sense, for while he agreed with, and even recommended, the continued use of quinine, he also urged outdoor exercise. "But you may be assured, you would probably have rec.[d] much greater benefit, had you not been so confined to a sedentary Life." He also recognized that the climate of Chapel Hill was more conducive to good health than that of Edenton and Tyrrell County. He warned his sons not to sleep on the floor during the winter weather, as "it may fix very bad & dangerous *colds* upon you. . . ."[19]

A strange malady was reported by Pettigrew to his son Ebenezer in 1802. It began with an attack of malaria, for which he bled himself, only to find that the fever and sick stomach remained. He then tried a grain of Tartar with a little Ipecac:

by which an enormous quantity of the thickes & worst Bile has been discharged. The sickness & flatulency still continuing, I last night took a Dose of Castor oil—But my fever continues, together with a total disrellish of

[14] Rebecca Barnes to Mary Lockhart, Aug. 6, 1792. Pettigrew Papers, N C Archives.

[15] Charles Pettigrew to Ebenezer Pettigrew, March 21, 1805. Pettigrew Papers, UNC.

[16] Charles Pettigrew to Mary Lockhart Pettigrew, July 8, 1795. Pettigrew Papers, UNC.

[17] John Pettigrew to Charles Pettigrew, Aug. 23, 1796. Pettigrew Papers, UNC.

[18] John Pettigrew to Charles Pettigrew, July 7, 1795. Pettigrew Papers, UNC.

[19] Charles Pettigrew to John and Ebenezer Pettigrew, Sept. 19, 1795. Pettigrew Papers, UNC.

all food—I ought to have mentioned a great oppression from the sickness of the stomach, by which my breathing was not good, this however has been greatly relieved by the drawing a large Blister on my left breast, so that I flatter myself, I am on the recovery, & that there may not be any danger . . . .

He was worried enough, however, to ask Ebenezer to return from Edenton bringing a doctor with him: preferably one Dr. Macfarlin but otherwise, Dr. John Beasley.

. . . not that I have any objection to Dr. Beasley taken in an unconnected view, for I have a sincere & personal regard for him & his—You will please to fetch me a couple of gallons of the best wine you can procure, & present my compliments to Dr. Macfarlin & request him to accompany you. . . .[20]

Only two references have been found to small-pox. A rumor circulated in Chapel Hill to the effect that the ''flux & small-pox'' were present, but no further cases, if indeed there ever were any, were reported.[21] The other reference concerned inoculation for small-pox. Pettigrew reported, in 1802, that while at Mrs. Horniblow's tavern in Edenton, he learned that Dr. James A. Norcom[22] had inoculated the Horniblow children with kine pox, and ''that it had taken very well. I asked the D.ʳ what he had for a patient in that way, he said 2 or 3 Dollars. I asked if he had any good & genuine matter, he said he had, for he brought it from Norfolk I believe by an insertion into his own hand. . . .'' He thereupon urged Ebenezer to be inoculated, saying,

would it not be much better to get inoculated with it, than to risk the small pox of which you are still in danger, & which taken in the natural way at this season, or betwixt this & cool weather would be so extremely dangerous —I wish you would have it done—[23]

Pettigrew's knowledge of medical practices seems to have included the enlightened knowledge of the times, and to have been free of merely superstitious practices and certainly no worse than that which then passed for sound learning.

Interest in other scientific pursuits would be a natural adjunct to interest in medicine. Pettigrew and Nathaniel Allen, who apparently had an inquiring mind and was a well-read man, discussed at some length a great fire which burned much of the swamp land in Tyrrell

[20] Charles Pettigrew to Ebenezer Pettigrew, Oct. 17, 1802. Pettigrew Papers, UNC.
[21] John Pettigrew to Charles Pettigrew, July 7, 1795. Pettigrew Papers, UNC.
[22] James A. Norcom, of Edenton, was a well-known North Carolina physician. John H. Wheeler, *Historical Sketches of North Carolina, from 1584 to 1851* (Philadelphia: Lippincott, Grambo and Co., 1851, 2 vols.), II, 124. The Norcom Papers are deposited in the N C Archives.
[23] Charles Pettigrew to Ebenezer Pettigrew, June 30, 1802. Pettigrew Papers, N C Archives.

County in 1791 and was finally put out by a rainstorm. The description of the fire was quite terrifying. Pettigrew wrote:

We have for some time past seen firelights toward the New land, also the Little Lake, & to the southward:—That to the southward probably came from Pungo. It had, night before last, got round to the Eastward, as far as the burnt grounds & looked dreadful. It was met yesterday by a fire, which some body at the instigation of the Devil, had set out from Indian-Town.

I shall not attempt a full Description of the fire, & the Thunder & smoke that issued from it. It would seem to be borrowed from some of our travellers, who have undertaken to describe the Bursting of a Volcano from some of the burning mountains.

It appeared yesterday as if every thing but the Lake itself, would be drawn into the general Conflagration. We seemed to be the Centre where the fires were aiming to unite from every quarter.

The atmosphere you know was clear, & the wind from north west— But when the fire got into the Cypress Grounds, it announced its own approach by such cracking & Thundering & Columns of Smoke as were truly frightful. The Cloud grew very heavy. The air grew Dark. I can compare it to nothing but the total Eclypse of the Sun which we had a few years ago. The ashes & coals from the burning Reeds, & other combustable matter, were scattered everywhere. . . . The Cloud at last became so thick & ponderous to the eastward that its pressure on the Atmosphere gave us ye wind out from thence, which rendered it still more alarming, & redoubled our apprehensions. . . .

Suddenly, "divine providence" intervened and sent a "Shower of rain, just when it had got nearly thro' to my high grounds." He reported to Allen that the latter's land had been "swept fore & aft as with the Besom of Destruction," with his orchard and garden and both sides of the Collins Canal burned. His question to Allen was, that he give a "phylosophic reason for the water that went up from the fire so black & dirty coming down again in an hour or 2 as clear as crystal; also inform me what became [of] the Dirt if you please."[24]

Allen replied in due time with a "phylosophical explanation." He did not "see the necessity of the interference of the Supreme Being. . . . dont say again my dear Sir that, providence intervened and saved your fence, by sending a shower of rain; it is no such thing believe me; had the fire never taken place, or had you never been born, it would have rained that very day. . . ." He continued by pointing out that "It is the highest presumption to suppose, that the almighty Ruler will watch over our fences, if we will not do it ourselves; what was the reason pray, that you and [Thomas] Trotter did not let the water out of the Lake; and cover all the face of the Earth with it, to the Northward, Eastward, & westward; a temporary

[24] Charles Pettigrew to Nathaniel Allen, March 2 [or 15?], 1791. Pettigrew Papers, N C Archives.

dam thrown across the Canal, would have effected this in the twinkling of an eye. . . .'' To answer Pettigrew's question, however, he suggested that if he had examined the water as it ''went up,'' he would have found it pure, not muddy; for short of a waterspout, earth and mud could not have been drawn up into the air.[25]

Pettigrew, in replying, denied that he had called on a miracle as explanation of the rainfall that quenched the fire. Instead, so he said, he had ascribed it to natural causes, always maintaining that God Himself made the laws of nature. He would not agree that it would have rained on that day in spite of the fire, as the day was otherwise clear with the wind at the northwest and ''the air strong & bouyant.'' He retorted that dirt and mud had indeed gone up with the evaporated water, for Allen himself had spoken of particles of burnt matter floating into his garden as far away as Edenton. No satisfactory answer had been given for the blackness of the clouds if no mud and dirt had risen into the air; although the water appeared clear when it trickled from the eaves, Pettigrew was sure it would have shown sediment had it stood for an hour or two. ''However,'' he concluded, ''upon the whole my D.ʳ Sir I am sensibly pleased with your way of answering me. . . .''[26] Actually, no answer was given, the question was not settled, yet it reveals a typically inquiring turn of mind in Pettigrew.

The promotion of education, having been a motivating force throughout Pettigrew's life, both for himself and his sons, was also a concern of his for others, yet not as much so as might properly be anticipated. Following his return from England in 1775, he did not resume teaching school, although he taught his boys with the exception of one year until they were ready to be sent to the University in 1795. Yet his reputation was such that, after the resignation of James Iredell, Senior from the board of trustees of the newly chartered University in 1790, Pettigrew was nominated by Charles Johnson to replace Iredell, and was elected unanimously.[27] He was not officially notified, however, for more than a year, when at the regular meeting of the trustees in New bern in 1791, it was ordered that the secretary ''inform the Revd. Mr. Charles Pettigrew of his

[25] Nathaniel Allen to Charles Pettigrew, April 25, 1791. Pettigrew Papers, N C Archives.
[26] Charles Pettigrew to Nathaniel Allen, May 19, 1791[?]. Pettigrew Papers, UNC.
[27] Minutes of the Trustees of the University of North Carolina meeting at Fayetteville, Nov. 20, 1790; quoted in *A Documentary History of the University of North Carolina*, compiled by R. D. W. Connor (Chapel Hill: UNC Press, 1953, 2 vols), I, 72-73. Hereinafter cited as UNC Trustee Minutes, *Documentary History*.

being appointed a Trustee of the University of North Carolina."[28]
A notice was sent out dated January 2, 1792, advising all trustees of
a meeting to be held in Hillsborough on August 1, "in order to agree
on the place, at which the UNIVERSITY shall be fixed. . . ."[29]
Whether or not Pettigrew originally intended to attend this meeting
is not known, although he was certainly contemplating it in March;[30]
yet later it conflicted with another duty, that of attending the Triennial Convention of the Protestant Episcopal Church to be held in
New York. He was perturbed. To the presiding bishop, Dr. White,
he wrote:

I have a great desire to attend, but I am also importuned to be at Hil[l]s-
borough at y.[t] very Juncture, at the meeting of a Board of Trustees for a
University in this State. The Business that claims my presence there is
particularly *fixing on the place* where s.[d] University shall be situated; and
unless the eastern Members generally attend, it will probably be carried too
far westward. This is an object w.[ch] I feel myself also a goodeal interested.
So that I am at present in a kind of Dilemma.

It was not a question of expense, for as he pointed out to Dr. White,
it would cost about the same to travel to Hillsborough as to New
York, and the latter trip would assuredly be more comfortable.[31]
As it developed, he attended neither meeting, sending no excuses.
The minutes of the board of trustees list the names of those attending,
of whom Pettigrew is not one. At the same session of the board, a
resolution was adopted "that the Secretary write to the several Gentlemen who have been appointed or chosen members of this board
and who have not hitherto attended, requesting of them to signify
whether they accept of the trust."[32]
Two more annual meetings passed without the presence of the
new member from Edenton District. Finally, at the 1793-1794 meeting at Fayetteville, "Mr. [David R.] Stone moved that the vacancy's
[*sic*] in the District of Edenton might be filled occasioned by the resignation of Mr. Charles Johnson, and Mr. Charles Pettigrew refusing
to act, whereupon Mr. Thomas Wyn[n]s was nominated in the room
of Mr. Johnson, and Mr. Josiah Collins in the room of Mr. Pettigrew,
and were unanimously chosen."[33] Since there is no draft of a letter

[28] UNC Trustee Minutes, meeting at New Bern, Dec. 19, 1791-Jan. 2, 1792;
Documentary History, I, 128.

[29] *Ibid.*, I, 151.

[30] Henry Pattillo to Charles Pettigrew, April 6, 1792. Pettigrew Papers, UNC.

[31] Charles Pettigrew to Bishop William White, March 12, 1792. Pettigrew
Papers, UNC.

[32] UNC Trustee Minutes, meeting at Hillsborough, Aug. 1-4, 1792; *Documentary History*, I, 167-168.

[33] UNC Trustee Minutes, meeting at Fayetteville, Dec. 9, 1793-Jan. 10, 1794;
Documentary History, I, 255.

of resignation from Pettigrew, it may be assumed that the minutes meant exactly what they said in stating that Pettigrew was dropped because of "refusing to act."

That he was interested in higher education and in the University, however, is apparent from the fact that he sent his two sons there to enroll in the first class. That spring the boys begged him to attend the examinations, saying on several occasions that General William R. Davie had told them he was asking their father to come to the examinations with him. Pettigrew did so. Not only is his attendance referred to in letters from his sons, but he is also listed in the minutes of the meeting of the board of trustees for July 13-14, 1795, as being present.[34] Undoubtedly he was an invited guest at the meeting, and had come to see his sons and to listen to the performances at the first formal examinations held at the new university. Although letters from his sons request their father's presence at the examinations and comment on their father's presence at Chapel Hill in other years,[35] he is not listed as among those present at any other trustees' meetings.

Later he became antagonistic to the University. Davie, in a letter to James Hogg of Hillsborough, commented on the rumors against the school he had heard emanating from Edenton and the Cape Fear region. Friendly though he and Pettigrew were, he found that the clergyman was the source of the talk in Edenton. As he wrote from Halifax:

Upon inquiring into the business at Edenton, I found that Bishop Pettigrew had said "it was a very dissipated debauched place"; some priests have also been doing us the same good office to the westward; nothing it seems goes well that these *Men of God* have not some hand in.[36]

It was in that same year that Pettigrew withdrew John and Ebenezer from the college, first making a trip there to talk with Presiding Professor Joseph Caldwell concerning it, but finally concluding that there was too much swearing and too much Thomas Paine.

Surprisingly also his name was not on the list of those who proposed to establish an academy in Edenton in 1800. Although a circular was received by Pettigrew, and although he decided to let Ebenezer attend for two years, the twenty-one trustees included nearly all the prominent men of the area with the exception of Pettigrew.[37] Was he too much the planter to have time for educational

[34] UNC Trustee Minutes, July 13-14, 1795; *Documentary History*, I, 408.
[35] See, for example, John Pettigrew to Charles Pettigrew, Aug. 23, 1796. Pettigrew Papers, UNC.
[36] William R. Davie to James Hogg, Aug. 9, 1797; *Documentary History*, II, 196.
[37] A Circular Requesting Support for Edenton Academy. Pettigrew Papers, N C Archives. Among the trustees were Samuel Johnston, Josiah Collins, Jacob

services? Had he been rebuffed in Tyrrell County by a less educated community? Did his poor health limit the strength he could spare for such activities? It was probably all of these.

His reading preferences were chiefly for the classics and for theological literature. His friend Thomson sent to him copies of Dr. Blair's lectures on Rhetoric and the Belles Lettres for his reading pleasure.[38] His New York factor tried to subscribe to the *Life of General Washington* for him in 1804.[39] Pettigrew recommended to his nephew Frederic Beasley that he read Addison, Locke, Grotius, Newton, Boyle, and Littleton "besides those eminent writers of the Clergy who have set forth the divine evidence of Xtianity in the most convincing Light."[40] Among such books of theology with which he was acquainted were Jennyn's on the Internal Evidence and Leland's View, besides Paley's Evidence of Christianity. One of the best replies to such deism and atheism as argued in Paine's *Age of Reason* was made by a Bishop Watson, who is referred to several times.[41] Watson's book, advertised for sale in *The State Gazette* of February 23, 1797, was an "apology for the Bible, in a series of letters, addressed to Thomas Paine." For lighter reading, Pettigrew took the newspaper, presumably whatever Edenton one was being published that particular year, whose pages he read carefully enough to draft occasional letters to the editor in reply to some other letter with which he disagreed. John Little once sent him a packet of Philadelphia papers,[42] and the firm of Wills & Beasley referred to a list of papers which Pettigrew wished to receive regularly.[43] No references were found to periodicals. Pettigrew was exceptionally well read, however. The impression is strongly left that the decades immediately following the end of the Revolutionary generation were years of declining learning: gradually the handwriting of court minutes, for instance, grew worse until it was almost illegible by 1800; spelling became poorer until it was sometimes only semi-literate; the worldliness of taste expressed in James Iredell's diary of 1773 where ladies asked gentlemen to read aloud to them from *Clarissa Harlowe* and *Sir*

Blount, Samuel Tredwell, Nathaniel Allen, Samuel Dickinson, and David Stone.

[38] James H. Thomson to Charles Pettigrew, May 18, 1784. Pettigrew Papers, UNC.

[39] Samuel Jackson to Charles Pettigrew, Jan. 9, 1804. Pettigrew Papers, UNC.

[40] Charles Pettigrew to Frederic Beasley, March 1, 1796. Pettigrew Papers, N C Archives.

[41] Frederic Beasley to Charles Pettigrew, Dec. 12, 1796. Pettigrew Papers, N C Archives.

[42] John Little to Charles Pettigrew, March 12, 1799. Pettigrew Papers, UNC.

[43] Wills & Beasley to Charles Pettigrew, March 12, 1806. Pettigrew Papers, N C Archives.

Charles Grandison had vanished. It is quite possible that this was culturally the most starved period in American history. Pettigrew became almost an anachronism.

Pettigrew was extremely fond of poetry, although his own efforts to write it demonstrate an unwillingness to conform to, in spite of knowledge of, the accepted cannons of the time. He believed that poetry should consist of "spontaneous effusions" of genuine passion, "in whatever kind of poetry the thoughts most naturally flow." He objected to limiting his thoughts to the restrictions of "Just so many Lines, which always renders a *poem* to *me, heavy* & disagreeable."[44] He possessed enough talent to know that rhyme did not make poetry: "That is very often the least Poetical. And I very often find more real poetry in prose than in verse."[45] He frequently sent poems of his composition to his friends, among whom were Henry Pattillo, James L. Wilson, and John Leigh. On one occasion Wilson complimented him, saying that "The subject is moving, the mode & stile poetical."[46] Only Pattillo criticized him, as a former teacher might do, pointing out in the case of an elegy that "you have not observed the usual measure of elegy . . . you have not trammel'd yourself with uniformity, nor confined yourself to any particular measure . . . you have not mentioned to any of us the name of the family . . . nor . . . the happy effects that might be expected to follow so remarkable a dispensation."[47]

Pettigrew's subjects ranged from the light to the serious, from love and spring to death. He composed rapidly, writing his lines in small pocket-sized notebooks of the same type in which he wrote his sermons. Many are interlined with improved wording, and some copied over in their final form on later pages. Since he wrote, as he said, with "spontaneous effusions," much evidence of his beliefs and emotions are revealed by these lines. The only record of his stormy courtship of Mary Blount, for instance, is found in his poetry written during that time. While these poems are chiefly valuable for the glimpses they reveal of the man, nevertheless they are not altogether worthless as poetry. His vocabulary was excellent, his feeling for meter good, some of his phrasing felicitous. Delicate emotion is felt in these lines:

> The little Birds, now on the wing
> From spray to spray
> Preach all the day

[44] Charles Pettigrew to Henry Pattillo, May 12, 1792. Pettigrew Papers, UNC.
[45] Charles Pettigrew to John Leigh, April 5, 1792. Pettigrew Papers, UNC.
[46] James L. Wilson to Charles Pettigrew, March 10, 1792. Pettigrew Papers, N C Archives.
[47] Henry Pattillo to Charles Pettigrew, April 6, 1792. Pettigrew Papers, UNC.

While in sweet artless notes they sing
Their Maker's praise. . . .[48]

Congratulations to a recently wedded friend were extended in the
form of a poem, conceived in the English classical style:

Fond man seek happiness in wedded Life,
And to his Bosom clasps the lovely Wife:
Is she a tender, a prolific Vine?
And do her Virtues with a lustre shine? . . .
Do soft sensation glow in each the same,
And mingling burn in the Chaste nuptial flame,
Consuming harsher Tempers from each mind,
While all the passions are by Love refin'd? . . .
To please is Amoroso's steady Aim,
While fair Amanda's virtues fan the flame
The pleasure He derives from his success,
He recommunicates, in soft address,
And she, with fond endearment, all repays,
In cordial Love's insinuating ways,
So two Rattans with tender Spires ascend,
And close entwin'd, to perfect union bend,
To part no more, till vegetation end.[49]

While at one time he wrote in "Miltonic verse" a poem on the birth
of his first son, at another time he attempted a Pindaric ode.

While the revolving spheres
In soft & son'rous airs
    Chant natures praise
Let Love that pow'r benign
Where all perfections shine
Both moral & divine
    Inspire my lays!

Inferior all the nine
Altho' they're call'd divine,
    Compar'd with Love;
Love first taught Bards to sing,
Join'd music to the string,
Gave raptur'd thought the wing
    To soar above.

* * * * * * * *

Love makes the silken Chain
That binds the nymph & swain:
    Sweet bondage this!
The humble & the grand

---

[48] Charles Pettigrew to Francis Asbury, May 1, 1784. Pettigrew Papers, UNC.
[49] Charles Pettigrew to John Leigh, April 5, 1792. Pettigrew Papers, UNC.

Thus join'd both heart & hand,
In the soft social band,
Share mutual bliss.

He concluded his ode to Love by citing God's love to mankind in the Lamb.[50]

Although no dates were given for his poems, in two of them he noted that he had arrived at the age of sixty, which fact inspired him to express his emotions upon the occasion.

The blossoms of the almond Tree
Now deck my hoary Head,
And Death advances fast to me,
Great Monarch of the dead!

He revised this stanza to read, perhaps with less imagery,

The silver hairs of threescore years
Now deck my hoary Head
Lo! gloomy Death at last appears,
Grim monarch of the Dead!

In the final stanza he first altered "cherubim" to "seraphim" for a more euphonious sound, and then rewrote it entirely:

In concert with the raptur'd throng
Where seraphim adore
Loud praise should sound from ev'ry Tongue
Along the Heavenly shore.[51]

Death frequently occupied his thoughts, both in sermons and in poetry. A few brief lines scribbled on the fly-leaf of a little book illustrate the variance in verse form and rhyme which he used:

Great Herbert's dead!
His pious soul has wing'd its flight
To mansion of divine delight,
Where fear & dread
Cannot an[n]oy,
The perfect harmony & joy,
That ever reigns
Thro' all the plains
Where pleasures never cloy.
From troubling there the wicked cease,
And there the Pilgrim rests in peace.[52]

"For the funeral of a pious & exemplary Christian" he composed these lines:

[50] Poems. Pettigrew Papers, N C Archives.
[51] Ibid.
[52] Paper dated May 2, 1789. Pettigrew Papers, UNC.

Tho' Death's the gloomy king of Dread,
   Our friend had nought to fear,
For Jesus was her vital head,
   Nor need we drop a Tear.

But rather bless the father's Love,
   For calling an exile,
Up to those blissful seats above,
   Where nothing can defile.

* * * * * * * * * *

Prepare us also Lord that we,
   May spend our fleeting Days,
In living wholely unto thee,
   And dying shout thy praise. . . .[53]

Shifting to a five-line stanza, he reflected "on the last Judgment" in an appropriate heavy style.

Alarming sight! behold the signs
Which shew the Day is near,
When we before the Judgment seat
Of Jesus must appear
Though little now we fear.

The following signs have long been seen
   Which Jesus did repeat,
As setting forth his near approach
      When great & small must meet
      Before his Judgment seat.
All wickedness abounding much,

Tryumphing everywhere,
The Love of many very cold,
   True Love exceeding rare,—
Which plainly do appear.

We've heard of war, & earthquakes too,
   In Heaven have wonders seen,
And these are sent to warn the world
Of this most awful scene
To all ungodly men.

Deceivers & Blasphemers bold,
   With those who make a lie,
And several other signs were giv'n,
   Which I shall now pass by,
   For sake of brevity.

The final stanza is amusing in its indication that the inspiration had suddenly run out. This poem is no "Dies Irae!" Part II, however, is improved greatly.

[53] Poems. Pettigrew Papers, N C Archives.

While in a silent grove I sate,
My mind in pensive mood,
Reflecting on the signs I saw,
My guardian Angel stood
    And did these things intrude.

The awful Day seem'd to come on,
When all the Dead must rise,
In flames infold Earth sea & all
That is beneath the skies, —
    Nature dissolving lies!

* * * * * * * * * * *

With dreadful glare the lightnings flash
And frightful thunders roll,
Convulsions Dread, & horror fill'd
The Earth, from pole to pole,
    And flames possess'd the whole.[54]

Contemplation of such an awful sight, lacking only a mushroom cloud, proved too much for Pettigrew, for the poem here ended abruptly.

A number of hymns written by Pettigrew also fill the little poetry notebooks. While it is not easy to distinguish the poems from hymns, as often the sentiment is the same, some are clearly so labelled, and others obviously are set to a familiar hymn tune. One can sing these words to "Come Thou Almighty King":

Now to our god & king,
Our grateful thanks we bring,
    His name adore!
Our king is all glorious,
He makes us victorious,
And he shall reign over us,
    For ever more.

Let Joy & mirth abound,
Let Heaven reflect the sound,
    Of Lofty praise;
Let different nations join,
To own our King divine,
Who doth in glory shine,
    Antient of Days! . . .

Hence, let us not offend,
Our God, our King & friend;
    But still obey;
That he may ever bless,
Still give our arms success,

[54] *Ibid.*

And all our woes redress,
Amen! we pray.[55]

"A Funeral Thought" could be sung to any Common Meter tune,
such as "Jesus, the Very Thought of Thee":

Alas! how short our span of Life,
Tho' threescore years & ten—
How full of pain—of toil & strife,
To all the sons of men!

*   *   *   *   *   *   *   *   *   *   *

We know in whom we have believ'd,
And that our Souls he'll keep,
Nor shall we be at last deceiv'd,
But own'd amongst his Sheep.[56]

A little set of prayers was composed as a gift to one of the Harvey
children. Pettigrew, in his first draft of what must have been carefully copied over, wrote:

The above prayers are address'd to Master Tommy Harvey, —as a
present from his *God-father,* who requests him to learn, & use them evening
& morning; And at the same time, to remember the promises which he made
to his dear dying Father—That is,—To be dutiful to his Mother—Loving
to his brothers & sisters, & attentive to his Book—

In the morning, he urged him to pray thus, in the dignified manner
of the Book of Common Prayer:

O God! the Creator & preserver of all mankind! I return thee my humble
& hearty thanks, for thy Care of me the night past. Pardon all the Offences
of my Life, and assist me by thy Grace, that I may Love & serve thee ac-
ceptably all my days. Bless my dear parent! Bless my brother, & incline
us to love & Dutifulness; that as we grow in years, we may increase in fitness
for the Society of the blessed in Heaven, through Jesus Christ our Lord,
Who hath taught us to pray saying Our Father who art in Heaven etc.

The evening prayer was similar, beginning:

. . . I thank thee for the support of my Life, and particularly for the
enjoyments of the Day past. Protect me this night also from all harm—Re-
fresh & strengthen me by repose, for the Duties of tomorrow. . . .

For some unknown reason, Pettigrew originally asked Tommy to
pray for his "brothers," but struck out the plural, and also deleted
the word "sisters" from the original.[57] Perhaps some one else was
praying for the girls.

[55] *Ibid.*
[56] *Ibid.*
[57] Prayers. Pettigrew Papers, N C Archives.

Although no theologian, Charles Pettigrew was sufficiently intelligent, well-read, and educated to express clearly and forcefully his theological beliefs. Holding to the tradition of apostolic succession, he abandoned his Methodist leanings in 1784 when Francis Asbury approved ordination and consecration outside that tradition. He agreed with certain of the Quakers, with whose writings he was familiar, who pointed out "the *absolute necessity of religion* to the *well being & happiness* not only of *individuals,* but of *society in general.*"[58] To his sister Mary Verner he expressed the hope that his nephew and namesake Charles would grow up "in the path of Life, Virtue & happiness. . . . We can expect," he added, "no happiness in either Life or Death, in a State of Detachment & estrangement of mind from God & religion."[59] He disagreed with the doctrine of election, regretting that his former teacher Pattillo had published a sermon on the subject. "I wish'd never to have seen [it] revived," he deplored. Belief in predestination not only failed to produce good, but instead it actually resulted many times in evil. He cited the instance of a man who lived near Edenton, a thoughtful hearer at church "till Childs the Anabaptist Preacher, came athwart him" and frightened him with the doctrine of predestination. The man decided that he was one of the condemned, and might as well live as one; he "had a Child by his sister in law, & grew daily more *extravagantly wicked & profane*" until, being suddenly taken ill, "he made his Exit as he lived." This would not have happened had it not been for the doctrine of election. Pettigrew attempted to understand this doctrine by studying "Dr. Edwards & Elisha Cole" but found it too difficult of comprehension. In his opinion, it was not essential to salvation, and therefore he gave up his efforts to understand.[60]

He viewed the life hereafter as certain. Heaven was "the happfy'd spirits' Residence till the resurrection & its reunion with the Body, let it suffice to say it is with the omnipresent God." The "souls of our dear dec.ᵈ friends" might sometimes act as guardian angels, and "even supplicate the Throne of grace for us," he wrote concerning his deceased mother to his somewhat shocked Presbyterian brother. Hell was "the Hell of the conscious Sinner, immediate on his Dissolution, and that without the formallities of a Tryal." The horrors of the last judgment as depicted in the sermons and harangues of the Great Awakening and the camp meetings of his time were not accepted by him. Emotion had no real place in religion; instead, true

[58] Charles Pettigrew to Dr. Andrew Knox, Aug. 20, 1799. Pettigrew Papers, UNC.
[59] Charles Pettigrew to Mary Verner, May 26, 1800. Pettigrew Papers, UNC.
[60] Charles Pettigrew to Henry Pattillo, Jan. 9, 1789. Pettigrew Papers, UNC.

religion "consists in an humble walk with God, & a constant endeavor after higher degrees of personal holiness." A calm, serene, and constant faith was his ideal rather than an emotionally excitable "conversion" which lacked the depth of true understanding and thus faded following the cooling of the passions.[61]

Infant baptism was the subject of one of the major theological arguments of the time, with Episcopalians, Lutherans, Methodists, and Presbyterians lined up on one side against the Baptists on the other. Pettigrew was a strong defender of infant baptism, not only preaching on it to his own followers but writing letters on the subject to other clergy and publishing a series of ten letters signed "Philanthropos" in the *Edenton Gazette* in 1805. His arguments were basically, first, that since the Hebrews, from the time of Abraham, had accepted children into the body of the faithful, and since Jesus adhered to the Hebraic law, he could not and did not exclude infants. As Philanthropos demanded,

Do you not boldly deny, & also unjustly refuse & withold from Infants a divine & indefeasible right of membership in the Church of God? a right originally conferred on them by their heavenly Father, who is their God and our God, a right they were in possession of no less than 2000 years prior to the commencement of the Christian era . . . a right which neither Christ nor his apostles ever annulled, or any other man by their authority. No the Redeemer & his apostles rather sanctioned & confirmed their right, by a variety of expressions in their favor.[62]

Secondly, he analyzed the 18th chapter of the Gospel according to St. Matthew, with its many references to "little children" or "a little child." How, he asked, could the Baptists "*despise & reject* in a religious view, those whom [Christ] in his unerring wisdom thus proposed as a *standard* of *purity & Christian perfection* to his Disciples"? He who so rejects infants would be better off if "a millstone were hanged about his neck, & that he were drowned in the depth of the sea."[63] Third, in an analogy he pointed out the error of the Baptists who maintained that since no express command had been given, infant baptism was unbiblical. Pettigrew asked if there were an express command that women be admitted to the Lord's Supper? or that the Sabbath should be observed on the first instead of the seventh day of the week? Since the answer is obviously "No," why do Baptists insist on the necessity of an express command for infant baptism?[64] In the fourth place, Pettigrew quoted St. Paul who wrote, in the

[61] Charles Pettigrew to (brother) Ebenezer Pettigrew, May 25, 1789. Pettigrew Papers, UNC.
[62] Philanthropos, Letter I. Pettigrew Papers, N C Archives.
[63] Philanthropos, Letter III. Pettigrew Papers, N C Archives.
[64] Philanthropos, Letter VII. Pettigrew Papers, N C Archives.

Epistle to the Colossians, II: 11, that baptism was the Christian circumcision; infants are circumcised, therefore they should be baptized.[65] His fifth argument was the command given by Christ in the Gospel according to St. Matthew, XVIII: 19 to baptize "all nations" which assuredly included "all". He did not add, "except little children."[66] In the sixth place, he recalled the Acts of the Apostles, in which are named three complete households which were baptized—not just adults, but all members of the household.[67] Finally, he begged to differ with those who said infant baptism was not known until some 200 years after Christ, citing the writings of Justin Martyr, Irenaeus, Clement of Alexandria, Tertullian, and Origen as evidence that it was practiced widely during the first and second centuries.[68]

To Nathaniel Blount, as well as to the readers of "Philanthropos," he recommended a book by "the pastor of a Baptist Church in England," a Mr. Edwards, who gave therein his "candid reasons for renouncing the principles of Antipaedobaptism."[69] Blount was anxious to procure a copy, and hoped it would "open the eyes of many . . . if they could be prevailed upon to read it."[70] It is to be supposed that few of those who opposed infant baptism ever read it, however. It was this book, in fact, which led Pettigrew to write the "Philanthropos" letters, as he had intended sending a copy of it to one Mr. Ross whom he knew, but decided against it in favor of writing essays for the newspaper instead.[71]

Pettigrew also believed that all forms of baptism were valid, if performed in the right mode by "water and the spirit." It did not matter if it were by immersion, aspersion, or affusion. Circumstances would dictate, perhaps, one as being better suited to the time than another, as in the case of an ill person, or one on the point of death. All that was necessary was to have enough water to represent decently the blood of the Lamb; the "washing" could be of a part for the whole, or it could be all over. "Is it said Christ was baptized by immersion? I will not say that he was not—but I can safely say we have nothing that ascertains it from the Original," he wrote. Christ was never specific on the mode of baptism, any more than he specified the amount of bread and wine for the Lord's Supper; he left both

---

[65] *Ibid.*
[66] *Ibid.*
[67] Philanthropos, Letter I. Pettigrew Papers, N C Archives.
[68] Philanthropos, Letter VII. Pettigrew Papers, N C Archives.
[69] Philanthropos, Letter I. Pettigrew Papers, N C Archives.
[70] Nathaniel Blount to Charles Pettigrew, May 25, 1805. Pettigrew Papers, N C Archives.
[71] Charles Pettigrew to [Ross?], May 29, 1805. Pettigrew Papers, N C Archives.

discretionary. Therefore, felt Pettigrew, the Baptists were "selfish & illiberal" when they dictated that only those who had been immersed were true members of the Church of Christ.[72] This he bitterly resented.

In fact, his criticisms of the Baptists led Pettigrew into unchristian controversy. He called them conceited and petulant;[73] he accused them of using the tactics of the Jesuits in "sophistical arguments. . . . They had a remarkable knack of quoting a great many authors, as authorities," out of context. "This however," he charged, "is a fine expedient to blind & mislead the ignorant."[74] They practiced "Sophism," knowingly, he feared, "with design to deceive the ignorant."[75] It even upset him that they greeted their congregations at the door of the church with "such pretty little seductive arts, as that of . . . Shaking hands with the people after preaching with an Air of uncommon sanctity & the coaxing familiarity of an affected brotherly kindness."[76]

The greatest anathema to Pettigrew, however, was Thomas Paine, author of *The Age of Reason.* Because this book was popular among the students at the University, Pettigrew withdrew his sons; because Paine was a friend of the Republican President Thomas Jefferson, Pettigrew was a Federalist in politics. He congratulated Pattillo on publishing "a very happy conclusion to addresses to the Deist" in a small book.[77] He warned Frederic Beasley to read the antidotes before exposing himself to the devil, Paine. He agreed with Nathaniel Blount, his fellow-minister, who deplored Paine's influence on America; America had so many blessings, but was hard of heart and dominated by "satanical principles." Her citizens were depraved and full of vice and immorality; yet, unlike the prodigal son, they were unwilling to go by faith to the throne of grace and ask for forgiveness.[78] Possessing such a neutral attitude toward the Church, they would fall prey, so Blount believed, to the deistical teachings of the French Illuminati.[79]

Pettigrew's sermons reflect a mixture of his theology and his literary, poetical style. Several of his contemporaries held him in

[72] Philanthropos, Letters I, IV, IX, X. Pettigrew Papers, N C Archives.
[73] Charles Pettigrew to Thomas Harman, July 16, 1792. Pettigrew Papers, N C Archives.
[74] Philanthropos, Letter IX. Pettigrew Papers, N C Archives.
[75] Philanthropos, Letter X. Pettigrew Papers, N C Archives.
[76] Philanthropos, Letter I. Pettigrew Papers, N C Archives.
[77] Charles Pettigrew to Henry Pattillo, Jan. 9, 1789. Pettigrew Papers, UNC.
[78] Nathaniel Blount to Charles Pettigrew, May 9, 1803; and May 7, 1804. Pettigrew Papers, N C Archives.
[79] Nathaniel Blount to Charles Pettigrew, Jan. 23, 1802. Pettigrew Papers, N C Archives.

high esteem as a preacher because of his gentleness, sincerity, and use of noble language. A few of his notebooks containing sermons, some eight or ten, survived, and provide an excellent opportunity to consider at least some of the qualities which caused him to be thought worthy of election as a bishop in his church. Well-organized, clearly stated, pointedly illustrated, his sermons would have appealed to the person of some education and a reasonably good mind. He did not follow the extremely flowery Anglican perorations of the preceding century, nor did he adhere to the plainness of the Puritan divines; there was a moderate use of classical rhetoric at a not too difficult level of comprehension. Nor did his sermons continue for even as long as an hour, but would probably have lasted about thirty minutes.

One example of his style may be found in the sermon "On the Certainty of Death,"[80] in which he comments on the prevalence of enmity, discord, and misery. "These have ever since prevailed in our world, to the disgrace of humanity, & the frequent interruptions of both civil & religious order; & sometimes, to the effusion of much fraternal blood, & the subversion of States & Empires." In "On Self-Examination,"[81] he warned succinctly "That faith which consists in a bare assent, & the repentance that does not reform, are unavailing to Salvation." Or again, he admonished, "Let go your too eagre grasp of the world, for this is not your abiding place; you are but strangers & sojourners here." In more elaborate expressions, he proclaimed: "It is not ye shadow of Devotion; it is not the most eloquent service of the Lips; It is not empty parade, or splendid profession, that will pass for genuine piety & devotion with him, who is the searcher of Hearts. No; nothing can ever meet with his approbation, but internal truth & integrity." Describing the giving of the Ten Commandments, he pictured Jehovah: "For he bowed the Heavens, & descended with the clangor of the Arch-angels Trumpet. Thick clouds encompassed him round about, & shrouded from mortal Eyes the insufferable radience of his Glory. Even Sinai was moved at the presence of God. The Earth shook; The heavens droped; & inannimate Nature, trembling, confess'd its universal Lord, & Lawgiver." When we think of the gifts God has made to us, in comparison to the greatest gift of his Son, all others "shrink into nothing, or disappear like the retiring stars before the infinitely superior Lustre of the rising Sun."

Typical of Pettigrew's sermons was one preached at Edenton on December 11, 1783, by special request of the Congress of the United States, as thanksgiving for the treaty of peace with Great Britain

[80] Sermons. Pettigrew Papers, N C Archives.
[81] *Ibid.*

recognizing the independence of the new country.[82] His text came from I Samuel, 12:24, 25. "Only fear the Lord, and serve him in truth with all your heart: for consider how great things he hath done for you. But if ye shall still do wickedly, ye shall be consumed, both ye and your king." In his introduction, Pettigrew explained that the Jews at first lived under a theocracy, with Judges who governed. One such judge was Samuel. When Samuel was old and grey, the people revolted against their system of government, demanding a king in imitation of their neighbors. Obeying God's command, Samuel warned the people of the evils to follow, but nevertheless invested Saul with the powers of a king. This was the origin, so said Pettigrew, of the divine right of kings, which "has been so often & so absurdly pleaded, with a degree of enthusiastic veneration." Samuel concluded with a warning to the people, and here Pettigrew quoted the two verses of his text.

Proceeding then into the body of his address, Pettigrew examined one by one the phrases used by Samuel. First, what are we to understand by the fear of the Lord? The answer is, to hate evil; venerate the Deity; give Him filial love; thus you will pursue "the arduous ascent of piety & virtue, in opposition to the world, the flesh & the Devil." Fear brings about obedience to God's commands. Pettigrew condemned those who have ill manners, hold no regard for other men, or take the name of the Lord in vain. Second, what is the service required of us by God? Since God made us, we should "cordially . . . devote our lives to him" and imitate the Saviour. Truth, sincerity, and heartfelt service are God's due. Subdue one's passions; carry out the duties of one's station in life. Do good to those who are evil and unthankful, even as God sends his rain upon both the just and the unjust. Third, what are the great things which God has done for us? He gave us the continent formerly inhabited by dark heathen, brought it to opulence, interposed on our side for freedom, and "finally decided in our favour." America was David fighting Goliath: without God's help, we must have perished. Yet the greatest thing which God has done was to give us his Son. To show God your true gratitude, therefore, "fear the Lord, & serve him in truth with all your hearts." Finally, what is meant by the warning that if ye do wickedly, ye shall be consumed? Nations will be consumed, warned Pettigrew, if they allow infidelity and contempt of religion. Past states and empires have thus fallen. Fear the Lord, therefore, for this reason if for no other. Then, one can calmly "take a final leave of this passing world" and receive the perpetual enjoyment of such things as "Eye hath not seen, nor the Ear heard," nor the human heart conceived.

[82] *Ibid.*

CHAPTER VII

THE LAST YEARS

From 1797 until his death in 1807, Charles Pettigrew resided at Belgrade with his wife, Mary Lockhart Pettigrew, and much of the time with Mrs. Pambrun as a "permanent guest." Although the region was isolated to a greater degree than was Edenton or even Bertie County, nevertheless there was social life, visiting, and much correspondence to keep the family from being lonely. John Vail of New Bern, a Blount connection, invited both Mr. and Mrs. Pettigrew to stop there on a southern trip they had expressed intentions of making in 1801. Mrs. Pambrun was in New Bern to spend some time with the Vails. John Vail promised to visit the Pettigrews in June if he possibly could, "but its entirely uncertain." One of the vicissitudes of travel is pointed up by an incident which befell Mrs. Pambrun on her way from Belgrade to New Bern, as reported by Vail.

. . . seventeen or eighteen miles from [New Bern] Cousin Pambrun's Horse unfortunately stumbled and in the blunder the shafts of the Chair both snap[p]ed in too [sic], she fortunately fell out without sustaining any injury, and the Horse toar the Chair into pieces; I think if I had been in the place of the Horse I should have been very glad to have free'd myself of such a burthen as Cousin; I never in all my life saw any person fatten as she has, since she left us; I am apt to believe the Tyrrell air agreed with her, or the agreeableness of your & Mrs. Pettigrews good company was condusive to her health. . . .[1]

One of Mrs. Pettigrew's nieces, a Mrs. Tunstall, was invited for a lengthy visit in the fall of 1802, but was "balked" in her intention, for which the Pettigrews were sorry. Mrs. Pettigrew planned to visit the Tunstalls instead, but "An old gentle horse, to which she had a great partiallity as a chair horse, dropt dead the other day full fat, by the bursting of a blood vessel, & I do not know that we have another that she would drive." Another niece, a Mrs. Pugh, had been to stay with them but had "caught cold on her visit to us. . . ." The Pettigrews, in turn, hoped to visit the Tunstalls, but expected that only Mrs. Pettigrew would be able to go as Charles had no overseer and could not leave.[2] John Mare wrote to thank Pettigrew "for your very polite invitation to your house. Should I be able to undertake a

---

[1] John Vail to Charles Pettigrew, May 13, 1801. Pettigrew Papers, UNC.

[2] Charles Pettigrew to Mrs. — Tunstall, June 22, 1803. Pettigrew Papers, UNC.

jaunt to Scuppernong, I shall with pleasure, embrace it."[3] Another niece of Mrs. Pettigrew, Betsey Lockhart, spent three weeks at Belgrade in 1799.[4] Ebenezer and his stepmother, in 1805, made a fifteen day trip to some relatives on the Roanoke River, which was, so Ebenezer said, the longest he had been away in several years. He reported to his friend, James Iredell, Jr.:

> My stay up the country was agreeable, because I met with cumpany of that discription. It is a part of the country which I think not very desirable to live in, from the extreme uncertainty of croping which the freshes occasion. They have had one in January which far surpassed all others for a number of years back. It drowned vast quantities of hogs and cattle & drove many negroes from their houses, to take refuge under shelters on the hills to the injury of their feet by frost.[5]

Nathaniel Blount and Pettigrew frequently discussed the possibility of visiting each other. Blount wrote in 1801:

> I have not yet found it by any means convenient to take a ride to your house, which I much wished to do, & had hopes of doing, some time in the course of last winter. . . . Be assured D.r Sir it is my wish. . . . But I still hope shou'd my life & health Be Spared to find it convenient to Visit you, and also to make a satisfactory stay with you.[6]

In 1802 he was still planning to travel to Belgrade: "I still have hopes,—should my life & health Be Spared, of seeing a time (but cannot at present say when) that I may make it convenient to ride as far as your House. . . ."[7] In 1803 Blount wrote that "I still hope to see the time that it may be convenient for me to take a ride to your house. . . ."[8] Pettigrew replied, "You renew my hopes of seeing you at our Cottage. We shall be very happy whenever it shall be convenient, to see our hopes reallized."[9] Such additional courtesies are mentioned as an invitation to Ebenezer to attend a ship launching at Tarboro.[10] Pettigrew informed Ebenezer of a wedding which ended in "a complete Tuskarora frollick" to which he would have been in-

[3] John Mare to Charles Pettigrew, April 28, 1802. Pettigrew Papers, UNC.

[4] Charles Pettigrew to John Pettigrew, May 18, 1799. Pettigrew Papers, UNC.

[5] Ebenezer Pettigrew to James Iredell, Jr., March 20, 1805. Pettigrew Papers, N C Archives.

[6] Nathaniel Blount to Charles Pettigrew, May 21, 1801. Pettigrew Papers, N C Archives.

[7] Nathaniel Blount to Charles Pettigrew, Jan. 23, 1802. Pettigrew Papers, N C Archives.

[8] Nathaniel Blount to Charles Pettigrew, Aug. 16, 1803. Pettigrew Papers, N C Archives.

[9] Charles Pettigrew to Nathaniel Blount, Aug. 23, 1803. Pettigrew Papers, N C Archives.

[10] George L. Ryan to Ebenezer Pettigrew, May 18, 1805. Pettigrew Papers, UNC.

vited had he been at home; the elder Pettigrew did not attend.[11] Gifts passed back and forth between the Pettigrews and their numerous friends and relatives in the vicinity, of which two barrels of herring for Mrs. Pettigrew from her nephew George L. Ryan is an example.[12]

The longest trip taken by a member of the family during this period was that by Ebenezer to visit two of his friends who were attending Princeton College. A detailed description of his return trip was given by Ebenezer.

The stage which I took ran only in the day—I set out from Princeton at 11 A. M. & reached Philadelphia at sundown.—at sunrise I resumed my seat and arrived in Baltimore the succeeding day, at 1 P. M. the next day I took the packet, from calms & head winds we were four days on the passage; but as the north winds are apt to prevail about the first of October, it is probable you will not be more than two, I believe the stage runs every other day between Norfolk & Suffulk, and twice a week between Suffulk & Edenton, I, not meeting the stage, hired a horse & chair at Portsmouth, I set out from there about 10 A. M. and arrived in Edenton the third day to breakfast, the whole of which amounts to near 10 days. The expence is as follows.

Stage Fare from Princeton to Philadelphia	$ 5.00
Ditto from Philadelphia to Baltimore	8.00
Passage in the Packet from Baltimore to Norfolk	10.00
Horse and chair hire from Portsmouth to Edenton	15.00
Tavern expences 6 days (the 4 in the packet being deducted) at 2½ dollars per day	15.00
Total	53.00 [13]

Iredell, however, expressed his belief that "The route you took was certainly the most expeditious but I think the most agreeable would be thro' the Federal City, Richmond & Petersburgh, & I believe it is not much longer than the other."[14] The journey north, as made by Iredell in 1804, was similar to Ebenezer's return. His description in a letter to Ebenezer was a vivid one.

I left Edenton the 1st of May in a rain which continued till we reached Suffolk the next morning. The same evening (may 2nd) we got into Norfolk about Sunset. Our passage up the Chesapeak from Norfolk to Baltimore was short but extremely disagreeable. The packet was so crowded (mostly

[11] Charles Pettigrew to Ebenezer Pettigrew, Dec. 21, 1802. Pettigrew Papers, UNC.

[12] George L. Ryan to Charles Pettigrew, Aug. 13, 1806. Pettigrew Papers, UNC.

[13] Ebenezer Pettigrew to James Iredell, Jr., Aug. 6, 1806. Pettigrew Papers, N C Archives.

[14] James Iredell, Jr. to Ebenezer Pettigrew, Feb. 13, 1806. Pettigrew Papers, N C Archives.

with Frenchmen from St Domingo) as to render it impossible to be accommodated with any degree of comfort. Indeed the second night of my stay on board, I was obliged to sleep upon deck with no covering but an old sail. Had we been as long on our passage as packets sometimes are, I should not have been able to support it, but happily we reached Baltimore on the second day. Here we were detained a day & an half all the Stages being crouded, at which we were not very sorry as it gave us an opportunity of obtaining one night's sleep. We sat off the next day (Sunday My 7th) & travelled very expeditiously to Philadelphia (the stage running all night) where we arrived the monday following that on which we had set off from Edenton. . . . You may be sure my bones paid dearly for this hard riding in the stages. . . .[15]

Travelling was always fraught with difficulties. In 1806 Capt. Daniel Bateman was at the Ocracoke Bar during a storm; several vessels were wrecked, and Bateman lost his masts and rigging but was fortunate in saving both his life and the major portion of his cargo.[16] Voyages across Albemarle Sound often required five hours.[17] In 1806, the Sound was so rough that after being towed out of the harbor at the stern of a larger vessel, Pettigrew's boat ran aground several times "which was attended with much hard labour in heaving to get off, so that the bile appears to be much set afloat in my stomach, which will oblige me to take an Emettic in the morning."[18] Ebenezer had indeed a frightening experience in 1806.

. . . there was 6 men in the canoe with as much baggage as filled it there was not room for another person, however we made out tolerably well untill we got opposite Gen. Benbury's where we laid the course for our port of destination, we had not got above a mile out when the seas began to look dangerous. I was not fond of my situation, but I considered there was others on board whose lives were as dear to them as mine was to me & determined not to be the first to cry out, my expectation was soon verified one of the men (they were all white) at the oar swore he would not go & insisted on being put ashore; after some altercation his motion was agreed to. . . . by which time it was dark, having a side wind we hoisted sail & went over, from the hight of the seas when we crossed the ferreman said if we had persisted in crossing the first time we should certainly all have been lost.[19]

[15] James Iredell, Jr. to Ebenezer Pettigrew, June 4, 1804. Pettigrew Papers, UNC.
[16] Charles Pettigrew to Ebenezer Pettigrew, Sept. 2, 1806. Pettigrew Papers, UNC.
[17] Charles Pettigrew to Ebenezer Pettigrew, April 10, 1802. Pettigrew Papers, UNC. "Our passage was about 5 hours." Also, "I had an agreeable, and quick, passage down, of but five hours." Ebenezer Pettigrew to Thomas B. Haughton, Aug. 11, 1803. Pettigrew Papers, N C Archives.
[18] Charles Pettigrew to Ebenezer Pettigrew, June 9, 1805. Pettigrew Papers, UNC.
[19] Ebenezer Pettigrew to James Iredell, Jr., Dec. 31, 1806. Pettigrew Papers, N C Archives.

The amenities of life were not neglected at Belgrade in spite of the difficulties of conveying goods across the Sound. Ebenezer made trips to Edenton to bring back items for his father, and in return carried items across for sale or as gifts. Pettigrew sent Ebenezer, at Bonarva, a "Jugg filled with a sample of the brandy which I think to [be] very sweet, & of a good quality."[20] His accounts with Henry King, a merchant of Edenton, show the purchases of a fine hat, black silk, suspenders, Morocco shoes, Imperial tea, silk gloves, and loaf sugar, among other items.[21] The tastes early displayed when as a young man Pettigrew ordered goods from Bertie to be sent to Bute County were continued throughout life.

Pettigrew was also called upon to help others. He attempted to assist Mrs. Pambrun in collecting a debt owed to her by John Mare; in return, John Mare asked him to find a purchaser for his acreage in Tyrrell County.[22] He lent money to his wife's nephew, George L. Ryan.[23] From the number of original letters in the Pettigrew collection relating to affairs of the Beasley family, it is obvious that he also tried to assist the children of his sister-in-law to keep their financial affairs straight. He even received a request from a completely unknown man who was stranded in Boston asking him for financial assistance.[24]

Though never again as active in the church as he had been in the 1790's, Pettigrew continued his work as a parish priest. In October, 1803 and again in March, 1804, he is mentioned as having preached in Edenton.[25] When Jacob Blount died in Edenton in 1801, the family requested that Pettigrew hold the funeral service.[26] He preached the eulogy for James Iredell, Sr., who died in 1799 and was buried at St. Paul's Church, Edenton.[27] On March 27, 1804, he was summoned for the purpose of "solemnizing the nuptials" of Dr. Andrew Knox and Sally Dickinson.[28] In 1799 *The* [Edenton] *Herald*

[20] Charles Pettigrew to Ebenezer Pettigrew, June 9, 1805. Pettigrew Papers, UNC.

[21] The estate of the Rev.d Charles Pettigrew decs.d to Henry King, 1807. Pettigrew Papers, UNC.

[22] John Mare to Charles Pettigrew, April 28, 1802. Pettigrew Papers, UNC.

[23] George L. Ryan to Charles Pettigrew, Aug. 13, 1806. Pettigrew Papers, UNC. Ryan hoped to benefit from the settlement of an estate in St. Thomas.

[24] Robert L. Smithey to Charles Pettigrew, Nov. 1, 1794. Pettigrew Papers, N C Archives.

[25] James Iredell, Jr. to Ebenezer Pettigrew, Nov. 11, 1803 and March 28, 1804. Pettigrew Papers, N C Archives.

[26] Alexander Millen to Charles Pettigrew, Jan. 22, 1801. Pettigrew Papers, UNC.

[27] McRee, *Iredell*, II, 585. No copy of the eulogy has been found.

[28] Ebenezer Pettigrew to Thomas B. Haughton, March 18, 1804. Pettigrew Papers, N C Archives.

of Freedom published the cruel notice that the Rev. Charles Pettigrew performed the marriage service for "John Beasley, of mean parentage, but clear blood, by profession a quack Doctor, to Nancy Slade, of clear blood, and oldest daughter of Mr. William Slade, all of this town."[29] References to his duties were scattered through his correspondence with Nathaniel Blount. He mentioned that since he was to preach "at a Chapel up the County to morrow" he sat down to write, as he expected to find a conveyance for the letter from the chapel. In that same letter he stated that ". . . the people amongst whom I live are poor & I take nothing from them; I must therefore live from the *field,* while I perhaps render them a more imperfect service than it might otherwise be in my power to render."[30] In 1803, Pettigrew built two chapels to accommodate the congregations. One was twelve miles above "where I attend two Sundays in the month unless prevented by sickness or bad weather." Although that chapel was "open to all Societies who could hold mutual communion with the protestant episcopal Church," it was not open to "those of contrary principles, as two cannot walk together except they are agreed. By this means the anabaptist preachers, it is hoped, will be kept out."[31] The draft of a subscription list for this chapel began with a statement of purpose, in the handwriting of Pettigrew.

It being indispensibly the Duty of all men publickly to worship almighty God, in acknowledgement of their Dependence on his favor, & to contribute all in their power to the encouragement of true religion & sound morallity, as the surest means for securing Domestic tranquility & future happiness; We the Subscribers do contribute the Sums affixed to our respective names, for the purpose of erecting a Chapel somewhere within half a mile of Mr. Evin Skinner's of such Dimensions & at such place as the commissioners . . . may judge the most proper & convenient.[32]

The second chapel was on his own land close to his residence, built at his own expense. He reported to Blount in 1804:

Since I have got our new Chapels in such a State as to meet comfortably in them, I feel myself quite happy in the exercise of my ministerial function, from a variety of favorable circumstances, One of which is, the people attend

[29] *The Herald of Freedom,* May 1, 1799. N C Archives. Frederic Beasley wondered what enemy prompted the wording of this notice about his brother's marriage. Frederic Beasley to Elizabeth Beasley, May 28, 1799. Pettigrew Papers, N C Archives.

[30] Charles Pettigrew to Nathaniel Blount, May —, 1802. Pettigrew Papers, N C Archives.

[31] Charles Pettigrew to Nathaniel Blount, Aug. 23, 1803. Pettigrew Papers, N C Archives.

[32] Charles Pettigrew's draft of a subscription to build a chapel, no date. Pettigrew Papers, UNC.

much better. Indeed my own Chapel is generally crowded. while they hear with great seriousness & attention—And now I begin to hope that through the concurrent blessing of God my feeble Labours may be useful amongst this people. I am in hopes they now begin to think me in earnest, after having preached to them above seven years, & built them a Decent & commodious Chaple at my own expence, except a few days works, besides attending at their funerals to the neglect of my own business & taking nothing from them for any services I render them, in the united characters of their Clergyman & physician. This however, appears like boasting—Be that as it may, I must own that I derive a far greater pleasure from it, than ever I did while as a dependent I received an emolument for my services—Now I feel myself independent altogether, and am happy in the thought, that they cannot attribute my faithfulness in the Discharge of my Duty to an expectation of being paid for it, having long ago publickly relinquished all hope or expectation of any such thing during my Life, & indeed positivily declared I would receive nothing from them.

My reasons for this are, we (I thank God) can live without it, & the people are poor. But I have also discovered that such people when they are not under the influence of religious principles have little or no gratitude, & would consequently give or contribute grudgingly, which I could not bear to have wrung from their hands. Recieving would hurt me nearly or quite as much as giving would them. Before the Dissolution of the establishment, I absolutely forbid any thing to be collected from the Quakers for me, as I would not recieve it. Niether have I taken any thing for either visiting the sick, or baptising, during the cource of my ministry. But Alas! my Dear Sir, I am after all this vein of boasting but an unprofitable servant at best.[33]

In contrast to the formality of the Episcopal Church services as conducted by Pettigrew was a Methodist camp meeting held in Washington County in 1806, attended by Ebenezer. To James Iredell, Jr., he depicted it thus:

While preaching they are tolerable orderly but immediately after; they get together as they call it to pray & be prayed for; There will be half a dozen praying at a time some singing, some slap[p]ing hands, some laughing, some crying, some falling dead, with what they call the spirit of conviction. They lay in an entire state of insensibility, and some times with their limbs so stiff that it is believed they would break rather than bend, for 12, 24, & some 48 hours, —They will have no medical aid used to recover them. They say he that struck them down will raise them again—[34]

---

[33] Charles Pettigrew to Nathaniel Blount, Feb. 22, 1804. Pettigrew Papers, N C Archives. This chapel is now named St. David's Church; it is kept in repair but is used only on special occasions. It has been marked as an Historic Site. The chapel was under construction for more than a year, for on Aug. 13, 1802, Charles Pettigrew wrote to Ebenezer that he was sawing a frame for the Chapel. Pettigrew Papers, UNC.

[34] Ebenezer Pettigrew to James Iredell, Jr., Aug. 6, 1806. Pettigrew Papers, N C Archives. The Diary of William Ormond, Jr. contains similar information about meetings in eastern North Carolina.

This type of religion appealed to more of the Tyrrell County inhabitants than did the Episcopal Church; two chapels quite took care of Pettigrew's congregations.

In 1799 John, or Jackie as his family called him, died, bringing a great sadness to his father. After being unable to obtain a position studying law, John went to Dr. Andrew Knox at Nixonton, in Perquimans County, to study medicine. John found "physick" very difficult, because of his lack of scientific training earlier. He told his father:

> The study which I have commenced is truely an arduous undertaking & one that requires much time & application to books, which I should not regard had I a large fund of scientifical knowledge which I concieve to be the basis upon which all other studies of importance should be founded; as it is by a knowledge of these that the mind becomes supernaturally expatiated & the ideas grand & noble. I flatter myself it will not be too late to commence those studies after perfecting this which call fourth my present attention. . . .
>
> I am peculiarly ill situated here in being deprived of even an agreeable companion whose company would not only be instructive but relaxing to the mind after being much fatigued with intense application to study. . . .
>
> Doctor Knox requested me to inform you that he should be glad to take your Bees Wax & as much more as you can procure; as he has an intention of sending it to the Northard.[35]

Several months later Pettigrew invited the doctor, Mrs. Knox, and John, together with young Pattillo, another student, to come to Tyrrell County for a visit, although Mrs. Pettigrew "objects, that from the backwardness of the spring she has nothing good to entertain you with, by way of treats. . . ." He forwarded four shirts to his son by the bearer of the letter.[36] The Knoxes missed a pleasant visit, for there was an abundance of "excellent fruit, & have had also plenty of watermelons. But as you have now missed the *best Treat* we could have promised you, —we still beg leave to hope, that you will take a *run over* in *grape time*. This you may easily ascertain, from the time you were over last year.'"[37] Dr. Knox urged Pettigrew to send John to Philadelphia to complete his study of medicine, but Pettigrew did not do so.

In respect to Jackey's going to philadelphia I have no objection but *one,* & that I hope will be but temporary. It is the *gambler's* first good reason

---

[35] John Pettigrew to Charles Pettigrew, Sept. 4, 1798. Pettigrew Papers, UNC. Janson mentioned bees, honey, and wax in the vicinity of the Alligator River about 1798; *The Stranger in America,* p. 314.

[36] Charles Pettigrew to John Pettigrew, May 18, 1799. Pettigrew Papers, UNC.

[37] Charles Pettigrew to Dr. Andrew Knox, Aug. 20, 1799. Pettigrew Papers, UNC. Scuppernong grapes are native to North Carolina.

of *12* for not playing, for which the company *excused* him, without the trouble of giving him any more of them. I need not tell you it was that, *he had no money.*[38]

In the same letter by which he informed Dr. Knox of his temporary lack of ready cash, Pettigrew described "the most mortal *fever*, ever known since the settlement of the place."[39] The fever spread to one of Pettigrew's slaves. Shortly after this letter, John, "my Dear Jackey" was caught on the other side of the Sound, his crossing "was 3 or 4 times prevented by adverse winds, till he was taken sick—" He died on September 24, 1799.[40] John appears to have been his father's favorite. When he wrote the sad news to his sister in South Carolina, Pettigrew praised him lavishly.

He was a young man of the happiest tempers, the most regular life, & the most benevolent mind I ever knew. He never once murmured at any thing, nor Disobeyed my orders—I have never heard of his being in a passion, or using a bad word in his Life. I never knew him prevaricate, or be chargible with a misrepresentation, much less a falsehood in his Life; no not even when a Child. such was his uncommon Love of Truth. He was engaged in the study of physic. But it was the will of God to call him from me—He gave & he hath taken away, blessed be his name![41]

The shock of his brother's death caused Ebenezer to be so "melancholy" that his father feared "consumption" would result.[42] One among many condolences he must have received came from one H. Hooker:

I heard of your Distressing misfortune Wednesday morning. I can say I never was more [shocked?] the sound of the Blessed young man's Name was seldom out of the House since, and our minds are much Distrest on your & your Famileys account. . . . I condole with you, & would to God I could take part your Grief. I would Bear it, if it could Relieve you—a Distressing Loss it is. Such a one that few parrents can meet with a morrolised Obedient Dutifull youth: but, my Dear sir be Comforted, when you see the way you Raised and trained your Child, he did not Depart from it, and all who knew him may suppose that a well prepared, Soul has gone hence. . . . I sincearly wish that it was Convenient for you & your Distress.[d] Lady to come & pass away some of the Lonesome Hours with us. . . .[43]

[38] Charles Pettigrew to Dr. Andrew Knox, Aug. 20, 1799. Pettigrew Papers, UNC.
[39] *Ibid.*
[40] *Ibid.* The date of death is given in the Genealogy Section, Pettigrew Papers, UNC, as Sept. 23; a letter of condolence from H. Hooker is dated Sept. 7, but an illegible word before the date may have blurred what was intended to be Sept. 27.
[41] Charles Pettigrew to Mary Verner, May 26, 1800. Pettigrew Papers, UNC.
[42] *Ibid.*
[43] H. Hooker to Charles Pettigrew, Sept. 7 [27?], 1799. Pettigrew Papers, UNC.

On the back of this letter the bereaved recipient wrote:

This Letter speakes the goodness & benevolence of the Writers heart. It is so tender that it awakened all my sensibility of the inexpressible Loss which I have sustained in the death of one of the Best of Children, & made my sorrows bleed afresh; and yet, though my heart bled afresh, the tender sympathy which is express'd so much in the genuine symplicity of nature, was to me very soothing, & I give my D^r friend very great Credit. May he never want a friend to administer the Balm of consolation in any of the Distresses of Life!

William Albertson, a "very worthy and Good Quaker," of Nixonton, who likewise thought highly of John, wrote to Pettigrew.

. . . I had the pleasure to be intimatly acquainted with after his coming to this place, which I feignly would have Cherished & improved. —he being a young man of a steady mind & sweet disposition (in my op[in]ion) those internal principals that are worthy to be sought after by all mankind & such as would make respectable men & citizens, but as it has pleased the almighty in his infinite goodness to take him from works to rewards, we dare not say nay, as he who gives can take away when he sees meet, blessed be his holy name forever. —he being of an orderly life & conduct & religiously inclined, it is to be hoped he has gone to rest with Christ Jesus in the mansions of glory & ever blessfull & eternal peace. . . .[44]

The bereaved father tidied up his son's accounts with various merchants of Nixonton and paid his bills.[45] An odd outcome of the death of John was that its news travelled to the West Indies to a former slave of the family, who thought that it was the father who had died. She wrote a touching letter to comfort Mrs. Pettigrew, and asked to be remembered to Master Jackie.[46]

Meantime, Ebenezer was longing to return to the University. The evidence would indicate that while John was studying medicine, Ebenezer was at home helping with the farming. As was often the case, the education went chiefly to one son: in this case, the elder, Jackie. Ebenezer wrote to his friends who were still at Chapel Hill, after a year's silence, expressing his interest in all that they were doing, and hoping to be back with them soon. To Thomas Gale Amis,[47]

[44] William Albertson to Charles Pettigrew, Jan. 20, 1800. Pettigrew Papers, N C Archives.

[45] Samuel Whiting to Charles Pettigrew, April 22, 1800; and William Albertson to Charles Pettigrew, April 22, 1800. Pettigrew Papers, UNC.

[46] Phillis Jennings to Mary Lockhart Pettigrew, June 10, 1803. Pettigrew Papers, UNC. Phillis stated in this letter that she was Fortune's sister, and she addressed "Mrs. Pettygroe" as "My Dear Mother."

[47] Amis graduated in the class of 1801, and shortly after was lost at sea. Kemp Plummer Battle, *A History of the University of North Carolina* (Raleigh: Edwards and Broughton, 1907, 2 vols.), I, 165. Hereinafter cited as Battle, *History of UNC*.

of Northampton County, he said, "I wish I was one of your class again. . . . I dont know but I shall prevail on my father to send me back to finish my education where I begun it. I wish therefore you would write me whether I can board out in the village and on what terms. . . ."[48] To John London,[49] of Wilmington, he commented that "I expect I shall return next January and nothing will give me more pleasure than to be a student with you."[50] Ebenezer felt isolated in Tyrrell County, complaining that "I live in a remote not to say obscure part of the state"[51] and again, that opportunities to post and receive letters "are so seldom from where I live to Plimouth, it being 30 miles that I believe it [your letter] stayed there about 5 months, and was packed up to send to Philadelphia to be burnt."[52] He cherished the gossip from his old friends, such as the expulsion of Thomas Hart Benton for an undescribed cause: "I suppose however, it was not for building churches."[53] The insects continued to plague the students, as in the old days:

. . . they are too good republicans to be conquered or subdued. Should you think them unworthy of the name republican you may I hope call them carmagnoles without offence or sanscullottes or Citizen Chince; for as old veterans they certainly merit something out of the common stile.[54]

The president of the University, so London informed his friend,

has got a horsewiping [sic] from a boy which he and the Teachers had expelled unjustly and we have been in great confusion in taking his part for he was liked by all the boys but every thing is put to rights again only our president relished the wiping so badly as to retire. William Baker, Robert Alston, Samuel McCulloch are expelled for taking an active part in the business. . . .[55]

[48] Ebenezer Pettigrew to Thomas G. Amis, Aug. 6, 1798. Pettigrew Papers, UNC.

[49] London was probably the son of the president (1811) of the Bank of Cape Fear. Although Battle states that he was the president, he seems a little young. H. M. Wagstaff, ed., *The Papers of John Steele* (Raleigh: Edwards and Broughton, 1924, 2 vols.), II, 662, 828; Battle, *History of UNC*, I, 168.

[50] Ebenezer Pettigrew to John London, July 15, 1799. Pettigrew Papers, UNC.

[51] Ebenezer Pettigrew to Thomas G. Amis, Aug. 6, 1798. Pettigrew Papers, UNC.

[52] Ebenezer Pettigrew to John London, July 15, 1799. Pettigrew Papers, UNC.

[53] Ebenezer Pettigrew to Thomas G. Amis, Aug. 6, 1798. Pettigrew Papers, UNC. Benton who, according to the *D. A. B.*, took a "partial course" at UNC, was suspended for drawing a pistol on Archibald Lytle of Tennessee. Battle, *History of UNC*, I, 194.

[54] Ebenezer Pettigrew to Thomas G. Amis, Aug. 6, 1798. Pettigrew Papers, UNC.

[55] John London to Ebenezer Pettigrew, Sept. 29, 1799. Pettigrew Papers, UNC.

Ebenezer was not compelled to forego all his studies, however, for he mentioned that he had been "some employed in the study of Arethmetic,"[56] presumably under his father's tutelage.

Following the death of John, however, Pettigrew saw to it that Ebenezer resumed his education, not however at the University, but at Edenton Academy, apparently from the early spring of 1802 to the summer of 1803. Pettigrew admonished his son as he left home for the second time to display the good breeding which was expected of him.

. . . above all things don't be wanting in your polite attention to every branch of the family, & indeed every body with whom you may have occasion to be conversant. Your figure & time of Life require it. To be a gentleman does not, be assured, consist in formal Bows & scrapes, but in a discreet & manly deportment. This is very easy to a man, who cultivates in his mind the principles of true benevolence to all—This benevolence,—this generous *goodwill*, is diffusive through the man's whole Deportment, & gives an agreeable aire not only to his conversation, but to all he does.

I must therefore insist on the necessity of your acquiring happy tempers & Dispositions,—& entire self command. In order to do this, keep your passions alway down, & cool; this will give you time for thought & deliberation. An excellent help to this, is, an awful sense of the *Divine presence* impressed on your mind at all times. What will have a happy tendency to produce this, is secret prayer at your lying down & rising from your Bed, evening & morning. In *this* I recommend to you the practice of *my youth*. I am sensible I derived great advantage, in point of regularity, & a Demeanor which commanded respect, & procured me the friendship of the most worthy of my acquaintance.

He concluded with a fatherly blessing: "May God Almighty bless & preserve you, [and] make you a useful member of [Society] is the earnest prayer of your [affec.] father."[57] Pettigrew was glad to learn shortly thereafter that the Blount side of the family had "sent for" Ebenezer and some of his friends,[58] thus showing the wisdom of his advice to be polite to all branches of the family. Ebenezer seems to have lived with Dr. John Beasley and his wife,[59] who were family connections through Ebenezer's mother. Pettigrew invited the "Ladies" and Ebenezer to come over to Belgrade early one Sunday to have dinner. He wrote to his son:

[56] Ebenezer Pettigrew to Thomas G. Amis, Aug. 6, 1798. Pettigrew Papers, UNC.

[57] Charles Pettigrew to Ebenezer Pettigrew, April 10, 1802. Pettigrew Papers, UNC.

[58] Charles Pettigrew to Ebenezer Pettigrew, May 19, 1802. Pettigrew Papers, UNC.

[59] Charles Pettigrew to Ebenezer Pettigrew, addressed "at Dr. Beasley's, Edenton," May 22, 1803. Pettigrew Papers, UNC.

We are happy to find you are coming over, & will have the Double Chair at Mr. Lewises early in the Day, & an Horse for *you*—We wish you to be out with the Ladies by sunrise, that you may get down to Dinner, as I am to preach at Phelp's Chapel that Day.[60]

While he was at school in Edenton, Ebenezer was also an errand boy for the family at Belgrade. For his father, he delivered business papers. "I enclose you Mr. Bryan's Obligation which you will give to Mr. Slade, as he cannot levy attachment with out. In this you will not delay. . . ."[61] Again, he requested that Ebenezer "Write me respecting the criminal Tryals. . . ."[62] He was to watch his father's rice being weighed at Town and receive the money for it.[63] He had instructions to collect a debt from one White.

The longer some people can put one off, the more difficult it grows to get it at all. So that you had better push, & dun him, so as to give him no rest, for if you do not he may feel himself easy in putting you off, as some have served me.[64]

He even selected fabrics for his stepmother's dressmaking. Pettigrew reminded his son that Mrs. Pettigrew's was "the Old Taste, when the love of beauty in things of that kind prevailed," and he feared the merchants carried nothing that would please her. Nevertheless, "I believe you must venture to make a Choice for her also. And pray Try to get a handsome & as good patern, & if she should not like it, she may give it to M.rs Pambrun." At the same time that he made this request, Pettigrew regretted that he probably would not be able to attend Ebenezer's examination at school, while he also requested Ebenezer to send over a couple of bushels of salt by Capt. Starr.[65] For Mrs. Pettigrew, Ebenezer had to take some "cotton tied or sewed up in a little bundle to Miss Hunter, which she will know is to make into netting."[66] He also was asked to deliver some elder blossoms, probably for wine, to Mrs. Beasley from Mrs. Pambrun.[67]

[60] Charles Pettigrew to Ebenezer Pettigrew, May 19, 1802. Pettigrew Papers, UNC.
[61] Charles Pettigrew to Ebenezer Pettigrew, April 10, 1802. Pettigrew Papers, UNC.
[62] *Ibid.*
[63] Charles Pettigrew to Ebenezer Pettigrew, June 21, 1802. Pettigrew Papers, UNC.
[64] Charles Pettigrew to Ebenezer Pettigrew, Aug. 13, 1802. Pettigrew Papers, UNC.
[65] *Ibid.*
[66] Charles Pettigrew to Ebenezer Pettigrew, Aug. 13, 1802. Pettigrew Papers, UNC.
[67] Charles Pettigrew to Ebenezer Pettigrew, June 21, 1802. Pettigrew Papers, UNC.

Pettigrew was most careful about Ebenezer's health, undoubtedly doubly so after John's death. When he first left him in Edenton, he urged him to "Take great care of your health—I have always found sassafras tea, from the bark of the root good in a Cold—It ought not however, to be continued too long."[68] When the papers carried accounts of yellow fever at Norfolk and Philadelphia, Pettigrew was alarmed.

Pray attend to your health above all things, & beware of the small pox & yellow fever, the last of which I see by the papers are in both philadelphia & Norfolk. It is not improbably it may revisit Edenton. I have had some thoughts of sending up for you. . . .[69]

Ebenezer made lifelong friends during this brief stay in Edenton: Thomas B. Haughton and James Iredell, Jr., both later prominent in the affairs of the state. Both of these young men went from Edenton to Princeton to complete their educations, leaving Ebenezer behind, one supposes because his father could not bear to part with his remaining son. The correspondence among them gives an interesting picture of life at Edenton and at Princeton, as well as of the affairs of young men, especially courtship and marriage. Although a great deal of teasing passed among them, and much gossip about local affairs, none of the three married until later in life. To Ebenezer, it must have been the crowning blow to his young hopes, having already been recalled from the University by his father, to be called home from the Academy and his little "triumvirate" in June of 1803, ostensibly to help with the wheat harvest, but never to return to Edenton again except on business. Pettigrew wrote to his wife's niece, "Ebenezer has been over at Edenton some time, until the other day, he came over to take some of the burden of Harvest off my hand. He is now at the lake & well."[70]

Ebenezer longed for "a situation where life will be life," and his friend Haughton added, ". . . all that I can say is, may God grant your wish & prosper your designs."[71] To Iredell, Ebenezer begged that

you will excuse the barrinness of my letters as there can be very little either entertaining or agreeable in this lonesome but pleasant retirement believe me it is a sacrefice to spend so many of my days here but I console myself with

[68] Charles Pettigrew to Ebenezer Pettigrew, April 10, 1802. Pettigrew Papers, UNC.

[69] Charles Pettigrew to Ebenezer Pettigrew, Aug. 13, 1802. Pettigrew Papers, UNC.

[70] Charles Pettigrew to Mrs. — Tunstall, June 22, 1803. Pettigrew Papers, UNC.

[71] Thomas B. Haughton to Ebenezer Pettigrew, Aug. 15, 1803. Pettigrew Papers, N C Archives.

the great morril maxim 'that all is for the best' expecting it will not be many years before I shall be quite in a different situation.[72]

In October, 1803, Haughton visited at Belgrade for a few days before he set out for Princeton.[73] When Ebenezer went to Edenton on business, hoping while there to see his friend, the latter was gone. As Ebenezer said in a letter to him:

. . . what time I spent in Town was so lonesome, that I almost thought Scuppernong preferable, the principle one gone, the other gone, Iredell, Martin, Dickinson, gone, in a word all gone, no one at the Doctor's, but himself, and his Lady; it appeared to me that it would not have had a more solitary aspect if the Inhabitants had had the yellow fever for a month; Why Sir! I should have had the highstrikes if I had staid there but one fortnight.[74]

His sense of humor makes many of his letters enjoyable reading, even today. While commenting on the large number of weddings in the fall of 1803, he said:

If T. Jefferson's father and mother had never been married, it is probably we had never been so blessed in an immaculate republican president—And if T. Paine's father and mother had not happened to get into the nuptial noose, it is eqully probable he had not been produc'd nor ever honoured with presidential thanks for his useful labours of sedition infidelity and blaspheny, nor our Country poisoned with his principles—Neither would our most noble and virtuous president have had so famous a Bow-wow, to bark and insult our Countrymen from the new[s]-papers. These however are but small affairs, compared with many others,—Such as the birth of a Buonopart, the decapitation of Lewis the 16th, and the invasion of England & & &. I would not however be thought to insinuate a probability of such disasters happening from any of the late happy junctions you have mentioned. If I thought so, & that it was in the power of my father to disunite them, I would use all the influence I have to persuade him to go over and undertake the pious and Laudable business.[75]

On another occasion he commented satirically to Iredell:

The girls (would you think it) have found a way to propagate without husbands, & are as less fruitful than the Lake Lands of which you have heard so much. And what may appear still more wonderful two of father Bigs's spiritual children, whom he had washed from all their p[ollu]tions in

[72] Ebenezer Pettigrew to James Iredell, Jr., Aug. 17, 1803. Pettigrew Papers, N C Archives.
[73] Ebenezer Pettigrew to James Iredell, Jr., Oct. 15, 1803. Pettigrew Papers, N C Archives.
[74] Ebenezer Pettigrew to Thomas B. Haughton, Oct. 16, 1803. Pettigrew Papers, N C Archives.
[75] Ebenezer Pettigrew to James Iredell, Jr., Dec. 26, 1803. Pettigrew Papers, N C Archives.

Scuppernong River, made out some time ago to fabricate a natural produc-
tion. With such natural curioseities our Counties abound—And more is the
pity unless they were disposed to make more cord. We have however, sometimes mar[r]iages among us. . . .[76]

So remote was Ebenezer that he was obliged to ask Iredell to "tell
[all] that Read I live in washington county & not in the Town of
washington for I never get a letter but it either goes to W. or to
Plimouth."[77]

Unhappy and restless, Ebenezer thought of going west. To Iredell
he wrote: "I have it in contemplation to go to Tennessee and from
thence to Louisiana should I live till next spring. I therefore wish
above all things to see you before I set out, life is uncertain & I
should not die easy without having that pleasure again."[78] To which
Iredell replied:

You mention in your last letter something about going to Louisiana. I hope
you have relinquished all idea of it. I cant conceive what could put it in
your head to think of thus expatriating yourself & getting in a fair way of
being savagized. I should almost as soon think of living in Tartary or among
the Esquimaux as in that wild, uninhabited country.[79]

Yet none of this eventuated. More and more did Ebenezer take
over the responsibilities of his father's estates, finally being given
complete charge of the farm Bonarva at the lake. He declined an
invitation because "I shall be too much engaged at the Lake. . . ."[80]
He relieved his father by sowing "a pretty large crop of wheat and
gathering the corn," in addition to which he

had the lake to contend with, which from its extraordinary height has threatened a general inundation. I have been obliged, from its having swept away
such banks as had been raised, to make new ones, and to exert all my force,
and the small share of sagacity and contrivance I am master of, to prevent
the plantation from being swept fore and aft, as with the besom of destruction.[81]

He was remiss in answering Haughton's letter, because "I have

[76] Ebenezer Pettigrew to James Iredell, Jr., [received] Jan. 26, 1804. Pettigrew Papers, N C Archives.
[77] Ebenezer Pettigrew to James Iredell, Jr., March 15, 1804. Pettigrew Papers,
N C Archives.
[78] Ebenezer Pettigrew to James Iredell, Jr., March 20, 1805. Pettigrew Papers,
N C Archives.
[79] James Iredell, Jr. to Ebenezer Pettigrew, Feb. 13, 1806. Pettigrew Papers,
N C Archives.
[80] Ebenezer Pettigrew to Thomas B. Haughton, Oct. 16, 1803. Pettigrew Papers,
N C Archives.
[81] Ebenezer Pettigrew to James Iredell, Jr., Dec. 26, 1803. Pettigrew Papers,
N C Archives.

been so much engaged last winter & spring, that the time has passed
of[f] almost imperceptably.''[82] After a two weeks' trip ''up Roanoak''
in the spring of 1805, he was ''closely engaged in prepairing for
planting, which has not allowed me an hour to spare in the day, and
has consequently been attended with great sensibility of fatigue at
night.''[83] Haughton, following his return from Princeton and his
residence in New Bern, lost a bet with Ebenezer as to getting his rice
ground cleared, informing him that ''With pleasure I will pay the
punch at Mrs. Horniblow's the ensuing Superior Court—where the
interview & chat that we will have, will be worth more than 20 bowls
of punch[.]''[84]

The senior Pettigrew kept close watch on Ebenezer's work at
Bonarva, and constantly advised him with a succession of notes relative to repair and maintenance, care of the slaves, planting and
harvesting, and the like. He warned him that his wheat was

to[o] much exposed to the thevishness of the negroes. It is a very ready
article of trade, & Fortune has his mercantile correspondents, who are ready
at all times to receive him kindly. I observe the window at the back of the
machine is not safe—nor did I see any way to confine down the hatch, at
either of the ends. Pray my son be careful, & put no dependance in their
honesty, for be assured their condition scarce admits of honesty, & they will
improve opportunities of getting for themselves—[85]

He sent him an advertisement to post at his mill which ''may assist
the sale of your old wheat. . . .''[86] He warned him of rain and recommended shocking the wheat in time.

As there was no dew this morning with us, & things are in a withering state,
it is probable that rain is near, I would advise you therefore to shock what
you have cut in the evening, as it may rain in the night, & it would be attended
with great loss of time to have it to open & dry it, & bind it, & shock it
afterwards.[87]

He told Ebenezer to keep all his hands at Bonarva because of illness
at Belgrade.

[82] Ebenezer Pettigrew to Thomas B. Haughton, July 4, 1804. Pettigrew Papers,
N C Archives.
[83] Ebenezer Pettigrew to James Iredell, Jr., March 20, 1805. Pettigrew Papers,
N C Archives.
[84] Thomas B. Haughton to Ebenezer Pettigrew, June 7, 1806. Pettigrew Papers,
N C Archives.
[85] Charles Pettigrew to Ebenezer Pettigrew, Oct. 25, 1804. Pettigrew Papers,
UNC.
[86] Undated note, Charles Pettigrew to Ebenezer Pettigrew. Pettigrew Papers,
UNC.
[87] Charles Pettigrew to Ebenezer Pettigrew, June 13, 1805. Pettigrew Papers,
UNC.

If it is possible for us to make out with our harvest, I don't want your hands, for fear that they should also be taken with that dangerous & loathesome Disease—On this account I have ordered Fortune & Pompey back again, & sent Tom for the Craddle & sythe, as george says the one we have is too big & heavy, & I find he has either bent or broke it. . . .[88]

Ebenezer was also advised as to the care of his livestock. "Pray don't distress your Horses too much," his father wrote. "They have a great Deal to do."[89] He stressed the special care which should be given to oxen.

As you intend to plough the Oxen, be very cautious in respect to the heat of the Day, as they are easily killed, & now the sun shines intensely hot— You had better have them ploughed only Early in the morning & late in the afternoon, as you are sensible how careless the negroes are. . . .[90]

Ebenezer superintended the building of "a very large Barn and Threshing machine" at the Lake at the expense of "above 1000$ and hope to find my account in it though it has been attended with great fatigue, they are thought to be first rate by Mr Trotter. . . ."[91] John Colston, who was a mechanic of the county, billed Ebenezer for $228 in labor for the machine and barn, less $122 which he owed to Charles Pettigrew.[92] Some of the accounts and business correspondence with New York merchants were conducted with Charles Pettigrew & Son, or even with Ebenezer Pettigrew only.[93] Thus the son was gradually being trained to take charge of the plantations when it should become necessary for him to do so.

Although Pettigrew was a resident of Tyrrell County when he first moved across the Sound, in 1799 the county was divided and Washington County was created out of the western portion, with Lee's Mills as the seat of court until 1823. This division was awkward for Pettigrew because it placed his dwelling at Belgrade in the new county while leaving most of his land in Tyrrell. He was anxious for a redivision at the next session of the legislature, for which purpose he asked the delegate to the General Assembly, H. Hardy, to

[88] Charles Pettigrew to Ebenezer Pettigrew, June 15, 1806. Pettigrew Papers, UNC.

[89] Charles Pettigrew to Ebenezer Pettigrew, Oct. 25, 1804. Pettigrew Papers, UNC.

[90] Charles Pettigrew to Ebenezer Pettigrew, Aug. 7, 1804. Pettigrew Papers, UNC.

[91] Ebenezer Pettigrew to Thomas B. Haughton, Dec. 8, 1804. Pettigrew Papers, N C Archives.

[92] John Colston to Ebenezer Pettigrew, April 29, 1804. Pettigrew Papers, UNC; receipted Sept. 29, 1805.

[93] Samuel C. Patrick to Messrs. Charles Pettigrew & Son, Dec. 29, 1806. Pettigrew Papers, UNC. Also, Ebenezer Pettigrew to Stuart Mollan, May 7, 1806. Pettigrew Papers, N C Archives.

present a petition to do so. As this was not carried out at the 1800 session because of a technicality, Pettigrew tried again in 1801, this time with more success. A further part of Tyrrell was annexed to Washington, using the Collins Canal as the dividing line, which placed Belgrade Plantation, house and lands, in Washington County while leaving Bonarva in Tyrrell.[94]

At the same time that the two counties were being divided, trouble arose over the disposition of the glebe lands in Tyrrell County. As nearly as can be determined from the clouds surrounding the controversy, at a meeting of the vestry at a Mrs. Spruill's home on Easter Monday, 1800, Pettigrew stated that something should be done about the glebe lands, which he had attempted once before, in 1789. He maintained that his remark was to the effect that they should be sold and the money used to repair and build chapels; that he, as the clergyman in charge, did not want "a stiver" of the money for himself. To the truth of this statement four affidavits were later sworn by men present at the meeting.[95]

However, one man, Amariah Biggs, told a different tale. As Pettigrew heard the story,

M[r] Biggs told at Aligator, & I know not how many places besides, that I had said at the Table where the Vestry had been sitting on Easter monday before all present, I was determined that every stiver of the money arising from the sale of the Glebe should yet come into my pocket—And had even the assurance to assert it to my face the next time I saw him—Of this I am happy enough to have a Witness, who was along wth me or he might with an equally good face deny it—Now what must we think of such a man, who sets himself up as a public Teacher—I suppose I might find as many more, who were present, to prove the lie upon him.[96]

Accusations flew thick and fast for the next several weeks, more than one would think the matter worth. Pettigrew wrote a lengthy epistle

[94] H. Hardy to Charles Pettigrew, Oct. 25, 1800. Pettigrew Papers, UNC; William Slade to Charles Pettigrew, Jan. 2, 1801. Pettigrew Papers, N C Archives. *Laws of North Carolina*, 1799, Section IX of Chapter XXXVI; supplemented by Chapter XXXVII. At the 1801 session, an additional part of Tyrrell County was added to Washington: "all that part of Tyrrel[l] lying and being on the South and West side of Indian Swamp, and the [Collins] canal beginning at the present dividing line of said counties, in such place as shall make a straight course to the center of the Indian Swamp Bridge, thence in a straight line to the mouth of the canal, thence up said canal to Lake Phelps, thence a South course to Hyde county-line. . . ." *Laws of North Carolina*, 1801, Chapter LXX (p. 36).

[95] Depositions Concerning Glebe Lands, May 7, 1800. Pettigrew Papers, N C Archives. The signatories were Joseph Phelps, John Swain, Henry Norman, and (May 8) John Bateman.

[96] Appendix to Depositions above, no date. Pettigrew Papers, N C Archives.

to Biggs citing the 50th Psalm and applying it verse by verse; after quoting verse 18, he added:

When an attempt was made to rob a Church of its property, though small, you appeared publickly at the side of one of the gentlemen who made the attempt, & expressed your consent & approbation. And why? Because you had I believe apostalized from that Church—And although a Church of Christ, you wished her property taken from her. What for? To gratify your enmity to her,—and at the same time, if not to get a few pieces of Silver, *Judas Like,* yet to save as much of your *public Tax* as might perhaps amount to one of those tempting pieces.[97]

Biggs retorted that Pettigrew was "more Like a roaring Loian then a Lambe of god" and that he could not possibly be a Christian or "you never would Cold on me to acknoledge a posetive truth to be a Lye. . . ."[98] Scribbled on the outside of this letter is Pettigrew's remark, "a master piece of scholarship from Belshazzar Biggs—The stupidest puppy that ever disgraced a pen." The matter did not rest here; Pettigrew retorted that "all your *saintish, lamb-like looks* are nothing but *grimace*—a mere Disguise which you have artfully assumed, the more easily to impose upon the simple & credulous; for the Tree is known by its *fruit,* & the fountain by its *streames.*" With stern warning he continued, "*That Lyars shall have their part & portion in the Lake that burns with fire & brimstone.*"[99] In return, Biggs charged him with being the source of oppression against the people, and envisioned himself as a David. "May god bless the few smooth stones I have throne at the head of Joiant oppression for the sake [of] Christ our Lord."[100] Pettigrew had the last word, if that in any way represented victory, when he wrote to Biggs that "you have favored me with neither *sense, english, nor spelling. . . .*" He proceeded to point out historical events of the 16th century in Germany when the city of Munster was unhappily administered by a small group of Anabaptists.[101] Other copies exist of later letters to Biggs, but it is uncertain if the originals were ever sent. Three years later Biggs attended Pettigrew's church service, which led the clergyman to think he had perhaps repented, and to draft yet another letter to him. The final letter does not appear to indicate any softening on

[97] Charles Pettigrew to Amariah Biggs, May 11, 1800. Pettigrew Papers, N C Archives.
[98] Amariah Biggs to Charles Pettigrew, May 28, 1800. Pettigrew Papers, N C Archives.
[99] Charles Pettigrew to Amariah Biggs, June 7, 1800. Pettigrew Papers, N C Archives.
[100] Amariah Biggs to Charles Pettigrew, June 15, 1800. Pettigrew Papers, N C Archives.
[101] Charles Pettigrew to Amariah Biggs, July 3, 1800. Pettigrew Papers, N C Archives.

Pettigrew's part, for he said, "But Sir, how can you, after treating me as you have, with the Colour of reason expect to creep into my forfeited friendship." He further criticized him for receiving the sacrament of the Lord's Supper without having first been reconciled. "For when you took your gift to the Altar, you knew, & could not but remember what I had against you, & how culpable you had been." Pettigrew finished by saying, "And should you treat it, as you did my former Letters, I shall injoy the thought of having done my Duty in regard to you."[102] This was the end of the affair. It may indeed be that the "Father Bigs" whom Ebenezer satirized to his friend Iredell was this same Amariah Biggs. The entire affair delineates the gulf between Pettigrew and many of the inhabitants of Tyrrell County.

In politics, Pettigrew was a Federalist. During the ratification debates in both Virginia and North Carolina, he expressed a cautious hope that the constitution would be accepted, with a bill of rights. To Peter Singleton of Virginia he wrote in 1788:

In respect to the new federal Constitution, I have had the pleasure to see that your Convention have adopted & ratified it, but with a caution which does them honour, for I still think, though a friend to it upon the whole, that the rights of the people might have been better guarded from the future encroachments of *ambition,* when stimulated by the infatuating influence of power—

Our Convention has not yet met, but will it is expected in a few Days. The result of their deliberations will be, I expect, a concurrence with the other States who have adopted it; for although opposition is threatened, it will not be so powerful as that which it met with in Virginia—Besides they will not choose to risk the Consequences of rejecting it—[103]

In this he was, however, wrong; for it took a second convention in 1789 to bring North Carolina into the union. Although it was out of keeping with his Federalist leanings for Pettigrew to defend the unsatisfactory 1777 judicial law of the state, he apparently did so in a newspaper letter signed *Flagellator Scurvarum* because Samuel Johnston of Edenton was serving as governor and had been attacked by the antifederalists.[104] The defense was of a personal friend rather than of the law.

After the Republican victory of 1800, Pettigrew became even more strongly Federalist. Reviewing the situation in a letter to Nathaniel Blount in 1803, he remarked:

[102] Charles Pettigrew to Amariah Biggs, June 23, 1803. Pettigrew Papers, N C Archives.

[103] Charles Pettigrew to Peter Singleton, July 14, 1788. Pettigrew Papers, N C Archives.

[104] Charles Pettigrew to the Printers, July 16, 1789. Pettigrew Papers, UNC.

There appears at this time to be an infatuated majority, who first called themselves Antifederalists, that is, against, or enemies, to our Constitution, which is one of the best in the world, & truely framed on republican principles. They have now changed their name, and affect to be called Republicans. Yet are still opposed to the friends, and admirers of *Washington* under whose auspices it was framed, & by whose wisdom & integrity it was faithfully executed during the first 8 years.

He continued by pointing out the respectability which the United States earned during that time, and the wisdom in which it laid its taxes upon luxuries which the rich purchased, "to the easement of the poor." Now, however, the taxes were on the necessities of life, so he said, and in addition "We are attacked on the side of Religion, by those who despise & blaspheme it. Of these Tom Paine is a most inveterate Enemy." His greatest objection to Thomas Jefferson was the way in which he had honored Paine, "with open arms of cordial respect & affection, thanked for his useful Labours, And is now kept under his patronage, as his *Bow-wow* to bark at, & insult the friends of our Constitution, by his impudent Letters." The French he also criticized for becoming Deists under Paine's tutelage.[105] At the end of this strong letter, he made the notation that "This was not sent as directed on account of the political part of it—another was preferred." Yet his own views are truly shown here. One notes that the phrase "Bow-wow" was also used by Ebenezer to one of his friends about the same time; but whose was the original cannot be ascertained.

Ebenezer too was a Federalist, as he indicated to Iredell when he expressed the fear that Haughton would turn Republican without their stabilizing influence. He had found him "sadly warped towards antifederalism. And as the depravity of human nature inclines men to be more tenatious of the wrong than the right, I suppose he will be more firmly fixed in democratic than he was before in federal principles."[106]

Other than these comments, neither Pettigrew took active part in politics until after Pettigrew's death in 1807. Eventually Ebenezer served in both the state legislature and in Congress as a Whig.

Nathaniel Blount noted the death of Alexander Hamilton in the duel with Aaron Burr. Disapproving of dueling, he nevertheless felt that Hamilton must have repented before he expired.

How very remarkable it is that Gen.[l] Hamilton shou'd, and that in so short a time, come to the same kind of untimely end that his son did! But

[105] Charles Pettigrew to Nathaniel Blount, Aug. 23, 1803. Pettigrew Papers, N C Archives.

[106] Ebenezer Pettigrew to James Iredell, Jr., Oct. 15, 1803. Pettigrew Papers, N C Archives.

how great a consolation it must be to those of his surviving friends who truly consider the state of the Soul after Death,—that after entering into so desperate an affair, there is so much reason to hope that he made a happy end,—as I think they must have, by the account of Bishop Moore, who attended him in his distressing illness! It is the first time as far as I can recollect, of hearing, of a person's wishing to receive The Sacrament after receiving their Death wound in the manner that he did.[107]

It is scarcely to be expected that the affairs of the world would not receive some attention by the Pettigrews, especially since, as he wrote to his wife's niece, "We take the papers. . . ."[108] The Napoleonic Wars, the Santo Domingo revolt, the dangers to American trade, were of great importance to the planters and merchants of the seaboard. Since the Lockhart family were merchants, it is not surprising to find a letter from Capt. Joseph Bryan, Mrs. Pettigrew's nephew, from Brest, France, reporting on the French embargo. "We wait the return of the French Fleet that saild from this ye last day of Decembr 94 consisting of thirty seven sail of the Line & about twenty Frigats—the Armys Are in Winter quarters And doing little."[109] By 1799, following the cessation of the "undeclared war" with France, John Little informed Pettigrew that "Commerce is once more a float—vessels have risen very much in their value, & are in great demand—foreign markets are generally good—shipments are consequently encreased & fresh life given to trade, which seems to be much favord by the British; & more neglected by the French. . . . I cannot judge of the probability of Peace, not being in the secrets of the *Cabinet*, but as the President has appointed a new Mission to the French Republic . . . we may conclude that prospects are in favor of it." The wildness of rumors is also amusingly demonstrated by this same letter, in which Little reported that Napoleon "was assassinated by some African Chief whom he had admitted to his Confidence, & his whole army either slain or taken by the Arabs." Admiral Nelson's fleet had captured Malta, and a French fleet had attempted to seize Ireland from which to mount an attack against England. The French Directorate was referred to as the "five headed Monster."[110] John Little continued to keep Pettigrew posted on the progress of peace talks, sending him clippings from Norfolk that seem to relate to the "XYZ" affair. He also sent him news of a handbill which reported the French victory over the Austrians in

[107] Nathaniel Blount to Charles Pettigrew, Aug. 20, 1804. Pettigrew Papers, N C Archives.
[108] Charles Pettigrew to Mrs. — Tunstall, June 22, 1803. Pettigrew Papers, UNC.
[109] Joseph Bryan to Charles Pettigrew, Jan. 21, 1795. Pettigrew Papers, UNC.
[110] John Little to Charles Pettigrew, March 12, 1799. Pettigrew Papers, UNC.

1800.[111] Nathaniel Blount, in 1801, deplored the famine in England, Ireland and Scotland: "how lamentable a situation must the common people of that Country with Scotland & Ireland have been in, and especially Ireland, where there has been such great commotions, —so much confusion & loss of life,—so many widows & fatherless Children!"[112] Blount expressed great hope the following year with respect to the Peace of Amiens. Surely all true Christians would rejoice, he thought, although men who used war as a means of promotion and advancement would be sorry. If the United States would now adopt a "good policy" and "real and true Religion," it would surely become "the most agreable and flourishing Region in the World. . . ."[113]

Haiti and Santo Domingo also attracted the sad comments of Nathaniel Blount. "When will those one and indivissibles, those sticklers for liberty and equality . . . learn by the principles of humanity, to lay down the instruments of death, and cease from troubling!" He did not dread the Spanish as neighbors, but feared lest the French, "the most formidable nation in the world," cause trouble for America.[114] Just prior to the purchase of Louisiana by Jefferson's emissaries, he pointed out: "The consequence of the French Lousiana Scheme, I fear, may prove a serious matter to us;— if they do not look out, who have the Watch,—we may soon perhaps be involved in a most dangerous situation!" His fear lest the westerners join with the French "either through necessity or from choice"[115] indicates that he kept up with national affairs to a degree perhaps unusual in an eastern Carolina clergyman of the "Old Church." In 1803, when once again war broke out in Europe, Blount deplored the "poor unhappy creatures" who "must now loose their lives to gratify the thirst for power, of those rival rulers!"[116] In a prompt reply to this letter, Pettigrew again took the Federalist stand on foreign policy. "With England it is *now* or *never*," he said, "and as they are the nation from whence we claim our Origin, as they speake our own Language, & profess the same religion, I cannot but

[111] John Little to Charles Pettigrew, July 16, 1800. Pettigrew Papers, N C Archives.

[112] Nathaniel Blount to Charles Pettigrew, May 21, 1801. Pettigrew Papers, N C Archives.

[113] Nathaniel Blount to Charles Pettigrew, Jan. 23, 1802. Pettigrew Papers, N C Archives.

[114] Nathaniel Blount to Charles Pettigrew, May 4, 1802. Pettigrew Papers, N C Archives.

[115] Nathaniel Blount to Charles Pettigrew, May 9, 1803. Pettigrew Papers, N C Archives.

[116] Nathaniel Blount to Charles Pettigrew, Aug. 16, 1803. Pettigrew Papers, N C Archives.

cordially wish them success. . . . Should the first Consul succeed against England, his next Object would be America."[117]

Pettigrew's health, although it had been poor for many years, if not indeed for most of his adult life, began to fail in the fall of 1805. Ebenezer wrote to Iredell that "My Father has been in a very low state of health since october and at this time thinks himself bordering on a consumption, but I flatter myself as the spring opens he will regain his health."[118] Pettigrew felt sufficiently ill at this time to make his last will and testament. Although he evidently rallied during the summer, the following winter he was again unwell. Ebenezer reported that "My Father I am afraid is declining fast M[rs] Pambrun I think in a dangerous situation & my Mother very infirm, sometimes all are sick but myself. . . ."[119] On April 8, 1807, at the age of 63, Charles Pettigrew died.[120]

To his wife Pettigrew left the widow's rights to the manor house, all the cattle, two-thirds of the hogs, three horses, her choice of his riding chairs, two carts and a yoke of oxen, half of the sheep, half of all the furniture and plantation utensils, all the wheat and meat of that year, and thirteen of the slaves, including Pompey and Phillis. Everything else went to Ebenezer. To the Episcopalians and their heirs, he gave White Chapel [Pettigrew Chapel or St. David's], to be shared with all other denominations who accepted infant baptism. He especially pardoned Amariah Biggs. Finally, he named both his wife and his son as executors of the will.[121] One must conclude that he was indeed a prosperous planter.

Pettigrew's body was carried from Belgrade to Edenton where the funeral service was held in St. Paul's Church by the Rev. Dr. Freeman, a Presbyterian clergyman. Interred first at Mulberry Hill, where Mary Blount Pettigrew was buried, his remains were moved in 1831 by Ebenezer to the latter's new plantation Bonanza, on the shores of Lake Phelps.[122] For two years following his father's death, Ebenezer struggled with the New York merchants to obtain a grave

[117] Charles Pettigrew to Nathaniel Blount, Aug. 23, 1803. Pettigrew Papers, N C Archives.
[118] Ebenezer Pettigrew to James Iredell, Jr., Jan. 6, 1806. Pettigrew Papers, N C Archives.
[119] Ebenezer Pettigrew to James Iredell, Jr., Dec. 31, 1806. Pettigrew Papers, UNC.
[120] *The Raleigh Register*, April 30, 1807: "Died. In Washington county, on the 8[t]h inst. the Rev. Charles Pettigrew, in the 64th year of his age [.]" N C Archives. Also Genealogy Section of Pettigrew Papers, UNC.
[121] Will of Charles Pettigrew, Jan. 26, 1806. Pettigrew Papers, UNC.
[122] William S. Pettigrew's biography of his grandfather. Genealogy Section of Pettigrew Papers, UNC.

stone properly carved.[123] A memorial plaque in St. Paul's Church, Edenton, reads:

The Reverend
CHARLES PETTIGREW
Born in Pennsylvania

Master of Edenton Academy 1773-1775
Ordained by the Bishop of London 1775
Minister and Rector of St. Paul's Church Edenton
1775 many years
Trustee of the University of North Carolina
Chosen to be the first Bishop of North Carolina in 1794
but not consecrated.
Died in Tyrrell Co. 1807.
Educator, Patriot, Pastor

If Pettigrew did not achieve fame, either as a clergyman or as a great planter, he nevertheless lived a life which must have brought peace and comfort to many persons. With the exception of his petty anger at Biggs and his bitterness against the Baptists, he was usually a man of self control who accepted what came and tried to make the best of it. He sought to bring comfort to those who came to seek it, although he did not extend himself in the service of his church. As he wrote to his second wife, "Commit yourself to God, & aim at contentment."[124] This he seems to have done. He reared a fine son in Ebenezer; he stood *in loco parentis* to another fine young man, Frederic Beasley; he stressed usefulness to others, respectability in behavior and humility in demeanor, coupled with religious observance and faith in God. If the world to some extent moved too swiftly for him, yet he was not left completely behind, for the virtues he advocated and largely practiced were those still held in esteem by many. While deploring the trend toward secularization, he faced unafraid the problems of transition from the colony to the independent republic, although he never agreed with Jefferson that the common man could be trusted to govern. Having worked his way to the top in a colonial society, he became an aristocrat and a natural Federalist, a perfect example of social mobility.

Charles Pettigrew was a blend of many elements: Huguenot-Scottish-Irish, Presbyterian and Anglican, frontiersman and urbanite, schoolteacher and aristocrat, common man and Federalist—in other words, American.

[123] Stuart Mollan to Ebenezer Pettigrew, Aug. 11 and Nov. 28, 1808; Ebenezer Pettigrew to Stuart Mollan, May 29, 1809. Pettigrew Papers, N C Archives.

[124] Charles Pettigrew to Mary Lockhart Pettigrew, March 15, 1795. Pettigrew Papers, UNC.

BIBLIOGRAPHICAL ESSAY

Private Manuscripts

The papers of the Pettigrew family are deposited in two locations: the Southern Historical Collection of the library of the University of North Carolina at Chapel Hill, and the North Carolina State Department of Archives and History at Raleigh. Thousands of items are included in both groups, which extend from the time of Charles Pettigrew through the life of his grandson, William Shepard Pettigrew, also an Episcopal clergyman. Most of the Ebenezer Pettigrew letters, plus copies of the letters pertaining to the Episcopal Church, are at Chapel Hill. The originals of the latter, a large group of letters from Nathaniel Blount, and the business papers relating to the Tennessee lands, are at Raleigh. The copies must be used with care, if at all, in view of the accessibility of the originals, because corrections were made in punctuation and in spelling by William S. Pettigrew. There is a collection of sermons, hymns, and poems by Charles Pettigrew at Raleigh. The combined papers are now being edited and Volume I (1684-1818) will soon be released by the North Carolina Department of Archives and History, edited by Sarah McCulloh Lemmon.

The papers of James Iredell, Senior and the Charles E. Johnson Collection, both at Raleigh, provide much background for life in Edenton during the Revolutionary and post-Revolutionary period. More Iredell letters are in the Johnson than in the Iredell collection. The Josiah Collins Papers, recently accessioned at the State Archives at Raleigh, contain a wealth of material on shipping, land speculation and development near Edenton, especially in Tyrrell County, although there is no material relating directly to Charles Pettigrew. The unpublished diary of Jeremiah Norman (1793-1801) in the Stephen B. Weeks Collection at the University library at Chapel Hill sheds light on the itinerant Methodist clergy in eastern North Carolina. The diary of William Ormond, Jr., another such clergyman, in the William R. Perkins Library, Duke University, is not very rewarding, however. Other private collections containing one or more useful items are the Robert Johnston Miller Papers and the Samuel Johnston Papers, both at the State Archives at Raleigh; the Robert Drane Collection and the University of North Carolina Papers at Chapel Hill; and the James Iredell Papers at Duke University. Church records are disappointing because the earlier items are frequently missing. However, there are a few records of the vestry of St. Paul's Church, Edenton, with a gap during the critical years of 1779-1811; these are at the State Archives at Raleigh. The Edenton Methodist Church Record Book, on microfilm at Chapel Hill, begins in 1804 and has a little information. Some of the early Baptist records, such as those of the Holly Grove Baptist Church in the Manuscript Division of the William R. Perkins Library at Duke University refer to earlier events and controversies with the Episcopal Church but are not contemporary evidence.

Public Manuscripts

All the public records of the State of North Carolina which are extant for the period before 1900 are deposited in the original or on microfilm in the State Archives at Raleigh. Pettigrew lived at various times in the counties of Granville, Bute, Chowan, Perquimans, Bertie, Tyrrell, and Washington. Records for these counties have been thoroughly searched, including census (both State and national), Revolutionary land warrants, deeds, wills, county court records (dockets, minutes, and civil action papers), Edenton District Court records (dockets, minutes, civil and criminal action papers), road papers, tax lists, and marriage bonds. Unfortunately, many of the Washington County records prior to 1815 have been destroyed.

Newspapers

The newspapers are disappointing for the period, as so few have survived. Those which did, used most of their space in printing copies of news from the Congress, the State legislature, or the European wars. Very little was gleaned from them. Those searched are all at the State Archives at Raleigh, either on microfilm or photostated; a few are the originals but very fragile.

The State Gazette of North-Carolina (Edenton), 1788-1799
The Edenton Intelligencer, 1788
The Herald of Freedom (Edenton), 1799
The Edenton Gazette, 1800, 1806, 1807
The Raleigh (North Carolina), *Register,* 1802, 1807

Published Records, Public and Private

A full study of the Episcopal Church in North Carolina from 1776 to 1816 was made, in order to evaluate Pettigrew in the broader framework of his problems and achievements. This involved some study of other denominations as well, especially of the early Methodist movement. The physical scene, as well as brief comments on the personalities of that time, appear largely in travel accounts, diaries, and memoirs. Overlapping chronologically with the Pettigrew Papers are the Blount Papers, published by the Department of Archives and History, which reveal business methods of the day and illuminate land purchases in Tyrrell County and in Tennessee. References consulted include the following:

Asbury, Francis. *The Journal of the Rev. Francis Asbury, Bishop of the Methodist Episcopal Church, from August 7, 1771, to December 7, 1815.* 3 vols. New York: Bangs and Mason, 1821.
Attmore, William. *Journal of a Tour to North Carolina, 1787.* James Sprunt Historical Publications, Vol. 17, No. 2. Chapel Hill: University of North Carolina Press, 1922.
Blount, John Gray. *The John Gray Blount Papers,* Vol. I, 1764-1789, edited by Alice Barnwell Keith. Raleigh: State Department of Archives and History, 1952.
Cheshire, Joseph Blount, Jr., ed. *The Early Conventions: Held at Tawborough Anno Domini 1790, 1793, and 1794.* Raleigh: Spirit of the Age Press, 1882. This pamphlet is now a rare item; the recorded proceedings for 1790 and 1794 are in the Pettigrew Papers.
Connor, R. D. W., ed. *A Manual of North Carolina.* Raleigh: Uzzell Printers, 1913. This contains lists of all public office holders from colonial times to the year of publication.
Cumming, William P. *North Carolina in Maps.* With 15 plates taken from the originals. Raleigh: Department of Archives and History, 1966. The 1808 map drawn by Price and Strother has been the most valuable for this study.
Documentary History of the University of North Carolina. 2 vols. Compiled by R. D. W. Connor. Chapel Hill: University of North Carolina Press, 1953.
Hobart, John Henry. *The Correspondence of John Henry Hobart.* 5 vols. Edited by Arthur Lowndes. New York: Privately Printed, 1912. The title lists 6 volumes, but only 5 were actually printed.
Hunter, Robert Jr. *Quebec to Carolina in 1785-1786. Being the Travel Diary and Observations of Robert Hunter, Jr., a Young Merchant of London.* Edited by Louis B. Wright and Marion Tinling. San Marino, California: The Huntington Library, 1943.
Jarratt, Devereux. *The Life of the Reverend Devereux Jarratt, Rector of Bath Parish, Dinwiddie County, Virginia, Written by Himself, in a Series of Letters Addressed to the Rev. John Coleman, one of the Ministers of the Protestant Episcopal Church, in Maryland.* Baltimore: Warner and Hanna, 1806.

Janson, Charles William. *The Stranger in America, 1793-1806.* Reprinted from the London Edition of 1807 with an introduction and notes by Carl S. Driver. New York: The Press of the Pioneers, 1935.

North Carolina, State of. *Colonial and State Records of North Carolina,* 26 vols. Edited by William L. Saunders and Walter Clark. Raleigh: 1886-1890, and 1895-1914.

North Carolina, State of. *Laws of North Carolina,* 1790-1802.

Protestant Episcopal Church in the United States of America. *Journals of the General Conventions; from the year 1784, to the year 1814, inclusive.* Philadelphia: John Bioren, 1817.

Quincy, Josiah Jr. *Memoir of the Life of Josiah Quincy, Junior, of Massachusetts, 1744-1775.* Edited by his son, Josiah Quincy. Second edition, with notes by Eliza Susan Quincy. Boston: John Wilson and Son, 1874.

Ruffin, Edmund. *Sketches of Lower North Carolina and the Similar Adjacent Lands.* Raleigh: The Institution for the Deaf and Dumb and the Blind, 1861.

Steele, John. *The Papers of John Steele.* 2 vols. Edited by H. M. Wagstaff. Raleigh: Edwards and Broughton, 1924.

Tatum, Howell. *Major Howell Tatum's Journal While Acting Topographical Engineer to General Jackson.* Smith College Studies in History, Vol. VII, Nos. 1, 2, and 3. Northampton, Massachusetts: 1921-1922.

Washington, George. *The Diaries of George Washington, 1748-1799.* 4 vols. Edited by John C. Fitzpatrick. Boston and New York: Houghton Mifflin Co., 1925.

White, William. *Memoirs of the Protestant Episcopal Church in the United States of America.* 2nd edition. New York: Swords, Stanford, and Co., 1836. White was the first presiding bishop in the United States, and corresponded with Pettigrew.

Secondary Works

County, parish, and other local histories and biographies have their uses, although a keen eye must be kept for errors. Both the *Historical Magazine of the Protestant Episcopal Church,* and the *North Carolina Historical Review,* have been valuable, especially in suggesting some unusual primary sources. In spite of errors, the 19th century works have usually been more helpful than the 20th century ones because their authors were more interested in church matters and personalities. Works consulted include:

Ashe, Samuel A'Court. "Sketch of the Colonial Church in North

Carolina," reprinted from *The Carolina Churchman*, Vol. 20, December 1929.

Battle, Kemp Plummer. *History of the University of North Carolina.* 2 vols. Raleigh: Edwards and Broughton, 1907.

Biographical History of North Carolina, 8 vols. Edited by Samuel A'Court Ashe, Stephen B. Weeks, and Charles L. Van Noppen. Greensboro, N. C.: Charles L. Van Noppen Pub., 1908. Its articles must be used with caution. There are several errors, for instance, in the article on Charles Pettigrew.

Blackwelder, Ruth. *The Age of Orange.* Charlotte: William Loftin, 1961.

Buxton, Jarvis. "Early History of the Church in America, Particularly in North Carolina." Reprinted from *The American Church Review*, July, 1876.

Carraway, Gertrude. *Crown of Life.* New Bern, N. C., 1940.

Carson, James Petigru. *Life, Letters and Speeches of James Louis Petigru, the Union Man of South Carolina.* Washington: W. H. Lowdermilk and Co., 1920.

Cheshire, Joseph Blount, Jr., ed. *Sketches of Church History in North Carolina.* Wilmington: DeRosset Pub., 1892.

Coon, Charles L. *North Carolina Schools and Academies, 1790-1840.* Raleigh: Edwards and Broughton, 1915.

Crittenden, Charles Christopher. "Overland Travel and Transportation in North Carolina, 1763-1789." *North Carolina Historical Review*, VIII (July, 1931), 239-257.

Crouch, John. *Historical Sketches of Wilkes County.* Wilkesboro: Privately Printed, 1902.

Daughters of the American Revolution. *Patriot Index.* Washington: National Society of the Daughters of the American Revolution, 1966.

Devin, Robert I. *A History of Grassy Creek Baptist Church, from its Foundations to 1880, with Biographical Sketches of its Pastors and Ministers.* Raleigh: Edwards and Broughton, 1880.

Dillard, Richard. "St. Paul's Church, Edenton." *North Carolina Booklet*, V (1905-1906).

Dodd, William E. *The Life of Nathaniel Macon.* Raleigh: Edwards and Broughton, 1903.

Foote, William Henry. *Sketches of North Carolina, Historical and Biographical.* New York: Robert Carteret, 1846.

Foote, William Henry. *Sketches of Virginia, Historical and Biographical.* Philadelphia: William S. Martien, 1850.

Grissom, W. L. *A History of Methodism in North Carolina from 1772 to the Present Time.* 2 vols. Nashville: Methodist Publishing House, 1905.

Hawks, F. L. "Early Church in North Carolina." *American Church Review*, III (1850-1851).

Haywood, Marshall Delancey. *Lives of the Bishops of North Carolina from the Establishment of the Episcopate in that State down to the Division of the Diocese.* Raleigh: Alfred Williams & Co., 1910.

Historic Edenton and Countryside, Edenton, North Carolina, Incorporated 1722. Published by the Edenton Woman's Club. No date, no pages. Illustrated.

Johnson, Guion Griffis. *Ante-Bellum North Carolina.* Chapel Hill: University of North Carolina Press, 1937.

Lamb, George Woodward. "Clergymen Licensed to the American Colonies by the Bishops of London: 1745-1781." *Historical Magazine of the Protestant Episcopal Church*, XIII (June, 1944), 128-143.

Lefler, Hugh Talmage and Paul Wager, eds. *Orange County, 1752-1952.* Chapel Hill: University of North Carolina Press, 1953.

Lemmon, Sarah McCulloh. "The Genesis of the Protestant Episcopal Diocese of North Carolina, 1701-1823." *North Carolina Historical Review*, XXIX (1952), 426-462.

Masterson, William H. *William Blount.* Baton Rouge: Louisiana State University Press, 1954.

McRee, Griffith J. *Life and Correspondence of James Iredell.* 2 vols. New York: D. Appleton and Co., 1857. This has been cited only when the originals could not be found. An appendix contains a sketch of Charles Pettigrew written by one of his grandsons.

Montgomery, Lizzie Warren. *Sketches of Old Warrenton, North Carolina.* Raleigh: Edwards and Broughton, 1924.

Morgan, Jacob L., ed. *History of Lutheran Churches in North Carolina.* United Evangelical Lutheran Synod of North Carolina, 1953.

One Hundredth Anniversary Commemorating the Building of St. James Church, Wilmington, N. C. Historical Notices by Rev. Robert Brent Drane, 1843. Edited by William L. DeRosset. Wilmington: 1939.

Owens, Robert B. *Christ Church, Rowan County.* Charlotte: 1921.

Pascoe, Charles Frederick. *Two Hundred Years of the S. P. G.* London: 1901.

Patton, James F. "Glimpses of North Carolina in the Writings of Northern and Foreign Travelers, 1783-1860." *North Carolina Historical Review*, XLV (Summer, 1968), 298-323.

Perry, William Stevens. *The History of the American Episcopal Church.* 2 vols. Boston: James R. Osgood and Co., 1885.

Reed, C. Wingate. *Beaufort County: Two Centuries of Its History.* Raleigh: Edwards and Broughton, 1962.

Rumple, Jethro. *A History of Rowan County.* Salisbury, N. C.: J. J. Bruner, 1881.

Smith, Stuart Hall and Claiborne T. Smith, Jr. *The History of Trinity Parish Scotland Neck—Edgecombe Parish Halifax County.* Scotland Neck, N. C.: 1955. This is two small books bound as one, with the page numbers beginning over again with the second book.

Stokes, Durward T. "Henry Pattillo in North Carolina." *North Carolina Historical Review,* XLIV (Autumn, 1967), 372-391.

Stowe, Walter H. *et al.* "The Clergy of the Episcopal Church in 1785." *Historical Magazine of the Protestant Episcopal Church,* XX (September, 1951), 243-277.

Tarleton, William S. *Somerset Place and its Restoration.* Prepared for the Division of State Parks, North Carolina Department of Conservation and Development. Raleigh: Privately Printed, 1954. Somerset Plantation adjoined Bonarva at Lake Phelps.

Turner, J. Kelly and Jno. L. Bridgers, Jr. *History of Edgecombe County, North Carolina.* Raleigh: Edwards and Broughton, 1920.

Two Hundredth Anniversary of the Building of St. Paul's Episcopal Church, Edenton, North Carolina. The Chowan Herald Printers: 1936.

Tyler, John E. "The Church of England in Colonial Bertie County." Typed manuscript in the Department of Archives and History, Raleigh, North Carolina.

Wheeler, John H. *Historical Sketches of North Carolina, from 1584 to 1851.* 2 vols. Philadelphia: Lippincott, Grambo and Co., 1851.

INDEX

North Carolina Provincial Congress, 20
Northampton County, 133
Norwood, John, 67
Nut Bush Creek, 22

O

Occacock (Ocracoke), 29, 38, 126
Ohio River, 83
"Old Church," 13, 22, 146
Oliver, Joseph, 88, 95n
Orange County, 5, 51
Ormond, William Jr., 26n, 80n, 129n
Outer Banks, 9
Outlaw's Chapel, 22n
Overseers, 67, 89, 92, 93, 98, 123
Overseers of the Poor, 61n
Oxen, 140, 147

P

Paine, Thomas, 52, 109, 110, 120, 137, 144. See also *Age of Reason, The*
Pambrun, Elizabeth, 47, 55, 123, 127, 135, 147
Parsons. *See* Clergy
Parishes, 15, 28, 30, 31, 39, 60, 75; Barkley, 15; Lynnhaven, 29, 60
Pasquotank County, 18
Patrick, Samuel C., 140n
Patriots, 9, 16, 17, 18, 33, 41. *See also* Whigs
Pattillo, Henry, 5, 6, 7, 41, 46, 61, 79, 111, 117, 120, 130; identified, 6n; establishes school, 7; son of, 54; criticizes Pettigrew's poetry, 111; preaches sermon, 117
Peace, 121, 145, 146
Peddicord, Caleb B., 24, 25, 27
Pennsylvania, 4, 64, 100
Penrise, Thomas, 46
Periodicals, 12, 110
Perquimans County, 15, 39, 42n, 60, 64, 130
Perquimans River, 39
Person County, 75
Petersburg, 9, 10, 24n, 125
Petigru, James Louis, 4
Petitions, 33n, 43, 61, 97, 141
Pettigrew, "Big Jim," 19
Pettigrew, Charles, 5, 7, 8, 13, 17, 28, 29, 34, 41, 45, 50, 54, 55, 57, 58, 61, 69, 70, 98, 110, 111, 113, 115, 116, 117, 127-32 *passim*, 143, 148; birth

of, 4; education of, 4-6; poems by, 6, 33, 34-35, 35-36, 36-37, 37-38, 40, 111, 112, 113, 114; orders household supplies, 7, 98, 127; moves residence, 8, 39, 41-42, 46, 54-55; clerical duties of, 13, 16, 62, 75, 98; ordained, 14; called to St. Paul's, 15; salary of, 15, 16, 28, 34, 98, 129; preaches, 18, 21, 23, 30, 61, 62, 71, 127, 128-29; hymns by, 18-19, 115, 116; avoids military service, 19, 37; sermons by, 23, 111, 120-22; and Methodism, 24-28; health of, 27, 29, 30, 37, 41, 55, 56, 67, 69, 76, 91, 104-5, 110, 128, 147; contemplates moving to Virginia, 28-31; visits Haiti, 29-31; and first wife, 33-36, 86, 111; birth of children of, 36, 37, 38, 39, 112; and second wife, 46-48, 49, 80; as trustee of UNC, 50, 107-9; advises sons, 52-53, 89, 90, 134, 139-40; evaluated as preacher, 61, 121; opposes Baptists, 62, 70, 118-19, 120, 128; attends Tarboro conventions, 64-73; elected bishop, 71; not consecrated, 74-75; encourages North Carolina church, 75-78; criticisms of, 77-78; acquires land, 79, 80, 83, 84-85; views on slavery, 79, 89-92; involved in lawsuits, 82-83, 86-88; operates plantations, 92-95 *passim*, 139-40; wealth of, 98-99; practices medicine, 100-5, 129, 136; interested in science, 105-7; interested in education, 107-10; theological beliefs of, 117-20; political views of, 120, 143-44, 145-47; quarrels with Biggs, 141-43; death of, 147; last will and testament of, 147; memorial placque to, 148
Pettigrew, Ebenezer, 42, 53, 54, 83, 85, 91, 92, 94, 95, 96, 100, 104, 105, 124, 126, 127, 129, 135, 139, 140, 143, 147, 148; birth of, 38; moves to Tyrrell County, 44-45; education of, 50-54, 109, 133, 134-35; builds canal, 83; and Tennessee lands, 84, 86; travels of, 94, 125, 139; caught in storm, 126; attends camp meeting, 129; grieves for brother, 131; is lonely, 133, 137, 138; friends of, 136; health of, 136; sense of humor of, 137-38; considers moving west, 138; assumes plantation responsibilities,

Sprewel, Col., of Tyrrell County, 80n
Spruill, Mrs., of Tyrrell County, 141
Spruill, Benjamin, 44
Spruill, Charles, 88
Spruill, Evin, 80
Spruill, Samuel, 88
Squirrels, 94, 97. *See also* Animals,
wild
Stages, 43, 125, 126. *See also* Vehicles
Starr, Capt., shipping master, 135
State Gazette, The, 110
Staves, 9, 94
Stone, David R., 108, 110n
Storms, 9, 44, 45, 126. *See also* Weather
Suffolk, 125
Sugar, 8, 96, 127. *See also* Food
Sumner County, Tennessee, 83, 84
Surveyors, 42, 57, 80n, 84
Swain, John, 141n
Swamps, 3, 42, 43, 44, 55, 56, 81, 105;
fire in, 20; Great Dismal, 43; Great,
90; Indian, 141n

T

Tarboro, 10, 22n, 47, 48n, 65-69 *passim,*
104, 124
Tarboro Conventions, 104; first, 65-67;
second, 67; third, 68-69; fourth, 70-
73, 77
Tatum, Howell, 84, 85, 86
Taverns, 11, 23, 43, 53, 105, 125, 139
Tax lists, 50, 79
Taxes, 5, 15, 79, 84, 85, 87, 144
Taylor, Rev. Charles Edward, 17
Teachers, 4, 12, 58, 25, 141. *See also*
Schoolmasters, Teaching
Teaching, 6, 12, 23, 25, 33, 58. *See also*
Schoolmasters, Teachers
Templeman, Richard, 18
Teneriffe Island, 58
Tennessee, 41, 83-86 *passim,* 98, 133,
138
Theological studies, 57, 58, 77, 110, 120
Thomson, James A., 28, 110
Todd, John, 4
Tom, slave, 140
Tories, 20. *See also* Loyalists
Townsend, Solomon, 97
Trade and commerce, 20, 95; of Eden-
ton, 9; with Teneriffe, 58; in Tyrrell
County, 81; with Guinea, 81-82; with
West Indies, 94; effect of war on,
97, 145; with foreign markets, 145.

See also Merchants, Rice, Shingles,
Staves
Transportation, 43, 125. *See also* Vehi-
cles, Vessels
Travel, 48, 54, 108, 125; through
South, 9, 123; in Tyrrell County, 43;
by Asbury, 76; dangers of, 126. *See
also* Journeys, Voyages
Tredwell, Adam, 10
Tredwell, Samuel, 96, 110n
Trotter, Thomas, 82, 90, 93, 106, 140
Tunstall, Mrs., a relative, 93, 123, 145n
Tyrrell County, 3, 41, 44, 54, 55n, 60,
61, 63, 64, 76, 79, 80, 81, 84, 87, 88,
92, 94, 95n, 104, 110, 123, 127, 130,
133, 141, 143; described, 41-44;
travel in, 43; courts of, 43, 88, 97;
description of fire in, 105-6; divided,
140-41

U

United States, 146. *See also* America
United States Congress, 7, 9, 121
United States Constitution, 143, 144
University of Dublin, 3
University of North Carolina (UNC),
50, 54, 58, 68, 74, 94, 104, 107, 108,
120, 133, 136; student life at, 50-54;
Trustees of, 51, 68, 109; professors
at, 51n, 53, 54; student misbehavior
at, 52, 54, 133; examinations at, 58n,
109; opposition to, 109
University of Pennsylvania, 57

V

Vail, Benners, 102
Vail, John, 123
Vehicles. *See* Carriages, Carts, Chairs,
Stages
Verner, Mary Pettigrew, 48, 56, 93n,
98, 117
Vessels, 9, 44, 81, 95n, 96, 97, 126, 145;
packets, 74, 125, 126; brigs, 81, 95;
names of, 95, 96. *See also* Boats, Ships
Vestry, 29, 30, 31, 60, 70, 72, 75, 76,
141
Virginia, 4, 5, 14, 20, 24, 26n, 27, 29,
38, 39, 41, 60, 64, 67, 71, 90, 143
Visiting, 11, 93, 123, 124, 137
Voyages, to England, 13, 14, 27; to
West Indies, 29, 38, 79; to Haiti, 30,
38; to New York, 68; to Philadel-